THE
POPES

THE
POPES

50 EXTRAORDINARY OCCUPANTS
OF THE THRONE OF ST PETER

Michael J. Walsh

Quercus

CONTENTS

FOREWORD
A Word about Words

THIS IS A BOOK ABOUT THE LIVES OF THE POPES – not of all of them, but of the 50 who are possibly – 'possibly' because different authors might very well produce different lists – most significant. There is also a narrative linking one with another, so as to provide an outline history of the papacy, the oldest surviving European institution, and one of the oldest institutions in the world with a continuous existence. The word 'pope' comes from the Greek for 'father'. From the third century bishops were commonly called by that title (as priests in Greece still are), but as Greek was gradually replaced by Latin as the more common language within Christianity, it came to be used in the West only for the bishop of Rome. In the 11th century Pope Gregory VII decreed it should be used as a title for the bishop of Rome, and for no one else, though the head of the Coptic Church – of Egyptian Christians – is still also called pope.

The pope in Rome is the spiritual head of over a billion Roman Catholics. It is the fact that he lives in Rome, and Rome is regarded as the centre of the church (even though most Catholics live in Latin America), that gives rise to the name Roman Catholic. He not only lives in Rome, but is bishop of Rome. He is in charge of the diocese of Rome, it is his 'see'. The word 'see' comes from the Latin for seat, *sedes*, and it is the place where the bishop has his seat, or residence. The Greek for seat is *cathedra*, hence where the bishop actually has his seat, the centrepoint of the diocese, is known as a cathedral.

The cathedral church of Rome is called St John Lateran. It is so named because it was built next to the Lateran Palace which was bestowed on the bishop of Rome by the emperor Constantine after his conversion to Christianity. It remains the cathedral church even though the basilica of St Peter's is much better known. It was Constantine who built the original St Peter's on the Vatican Hill, across the River Tiber from the imperial capital. There was much that the church inherited from the Roman Empire, even including the term 'diocese', which was a Roman administrative region. And there was also the title 'pontiff'. The Roman emperor himself was the *pontifex maximus*, the chief priest of the pagan religion in the city. The title fell into abeyance towards the end of the fourth century, and pontiff came to be used eventually of the bishop of Rome. Though the adjective derived from pontiff, 'pontifical', is sometimes used of bishops, it is mainly applied to the pope – as is the noun 'pontificate', meaning a pope's period of office. The basilica of St Peter's is next door to the Vatican Palace, where the pope now lives. Both the basilica and the palace are located within the Vatican City, the world's smallest state. It was created only in 1929 by negotiation between the papacy and the (then) kingdom of Italy by a series of agreements called collectively the Lateran Pacts. Although the Vatican City is tiny, it has most, if not all, the institutions that one might expect in any properly-constituted state. It has citizens, though not many of them – around 550, and about half of these are papal diplomats. It has a bank, a newspaper, a publishing house, television and radio stations – and even a train station. It has extremely important museums and a world-famous observatory, though the latter is now located at the pope's summer residence at Castel Gandolfo, just outside Rome.

When people say 'the Vatican' they are, however, rarely referring to the Vatican City State. They usually mean the papal curia, or court, in other words the administration of the Catholic Church with the pope at its head. This is formally known as 'the Holy See' or sometimes as 'the Apostolic See'. The Holy See, which is recognized in international law as a sovereign entity, publishes a year book, the *Annuario Pontificio*, listing, among many other things, all the various offices of the papal curia, and the names of those who fill them. It names the dioceses throughout the world, and who is at the head of each. It lists colleges in Rome and elsewhere over which the Holy See has some kind of oversight. And it also includes a list of all the popes. This list is reproduced on pages 200 to 205, though some of the dates may differ from those that appear in the *Annuario*. At the head of the list is St Peter.

Michael J. Walsh

OPPOSITE *A 13th-century fresco showing the baptism of Constantine the Great, the Roman emperor who embraced Christianity and helped the early Church.*

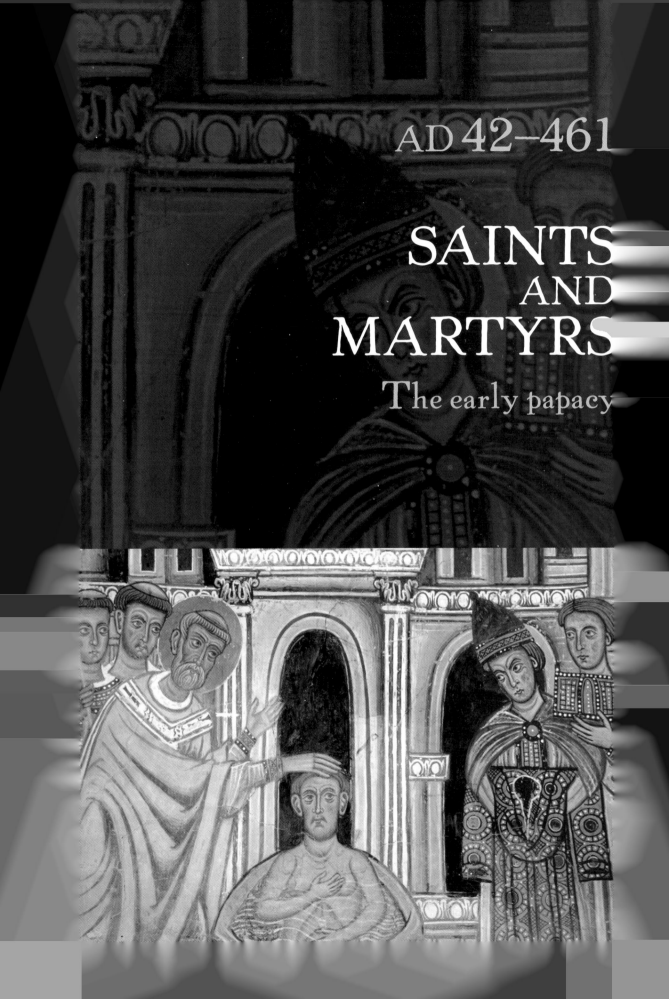

AD 42–461

SAINTS AND MARTYRS

The early papacy

St Peter

Peter is sometimes called 'the prince of the apostles'. Prince comes from the Latin word *princeps*, which simply means 'chief' or 'leader' – the first one, in other words. There is ample evidence that Peter was first among the apostles. There are four lists of apostles in the New Testament. The order of the names is different in each and even the names themselves vary slightly from list to list. But in each one Peter, or Simon Peter, comes first. Not only that, but in the gospels, and in the Acts of the Apostles, which tell the story of the earliest Christians, no one is mentioned more often. Peter disappears halfway through Acts, and the writer, Luke, then concentrates upon the missionary journeys of St Paul. But in the first part, Peter is the dominant figure.

We know a fair amount about him. He was a fisherman before Jesus called him, and he went back to being a fisherman on the Lake of Tiberias for a time after Jesus' crucifixion. We know Peter was married, because in the gospels Jesus is said to have healed his mother-in-law. He was, it seems, a natural leader, at times acting as spokesman for the other apostles. We also know something of his character. He was rash and he sometimes lacked courage. When Jesus was arrested he three times denied that he knew him. Yet despite this act of apparent betrayal, which Peter bitterly regretted, Jesus forgave him, telling him to feed his lambs and sheep.

'You are Peter'

Earlier, at Caesarea Philippi, Jesus had given him a new name. Up to that point he had been called Simon, but Jesus said to him, 'You are Peter and upon this rock I will build my church.' This simple sentence, which is inscribed around the cupola of St Peter's Basilica in Rome, over the papal altar, became very important in the history of the papacy. Jesus' statement to Peter contains a play on words: whether in the Greek of the New Testament, or in the Aramaic which Jesus would have been using, the word 'Peter' means 'rock'. Jesus appears to be saying that, in a particular way, Peter was to be the foundation of the church.

As one might expect, there are various interpretations of these words, but the academic debate is not relevant here. All that matters is that fairly early on in the story of the bishops of Rome, these words were used to demonstrate Peter's pre-eminence, and – since the bishops of Rome were his successors – the pre-eminence of that city among the other Christian churches.

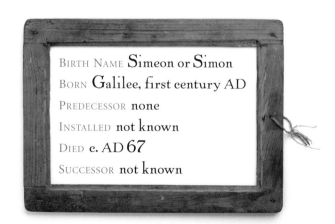

BIRTH NAME **Simeon or Simon**

BORN **Galilee, first century AD**

PREDECESSOR **none**

INSTALLED **not known**

DIED **c. AD 67**

SUCCESSOR **not known**

Peter, first among the apostles, was called by Christ 'the rock on which I will build my Church'. According to tradition he was crucified upside down on Rome's Appian Way between AD 65 and 67, during the reign of the Emperor Nero. He chose to die head down so as not to seem to emulate his master.

PETER IN ROME

There is no direct literary evidence that Peter spent time in Rome and died there. Certainly neither Peter nor Paul founded the church in the imperial capital. Paul wrote a letter to the Christians in Rome about the year AD 58. It is clear that there was already a community of believers in the city that had not been founded either by Paul or by Peter. It is certain that Paul went to Rome, where he met his death, and it is also now generally accepted that Peter likewise visited Rome, and was martyred there during the persecution of Christians by the emperor Nero between AD 65 and 67. As for evidence, there is a hint, at the end of the First Letter of St Peter, where he sends greetings from 'Babylon'. The Babylon he mentions is certainly not the ancient city in what is now Iraq, and it is quite possible that it is a disparaging name for Rome.

There is a book, written about the end of the second century, and probably composed somewhere in Asia Minor, which is known as the *Acts of Peter*. It has always been regarded as an 'apocryphal' book; that is, it is not listed among those writings that are believed to contain an authentic account of the doings and teachings of Jesus Christ and of his first disciples. However, the stories recounted in this particular book of *Acts* have entered the received life of Peter. This book definitely puts Peter in Rome. It describes a supposed contest between a magician, Simon Magus, and Peter, which Peter wins. It tells of Peter's decision to flee the city only to be met on the road by Jesus going in the opposite direction: 'Where are you going, Lord?' asks Peter: '*Quo vadis, Domine?*' There is a church on the old Via Appia, leading out of Rome, which is said to mark the spot of this encounter. The book also tells of Peter's martyrdom, dying on a cross, but upside down so as not to seem to be worthy of emulating his master.

There are quite a number of these pious 'novels' based on the lives of early Christians such as Peter. They are hardly evidence in themselves that Peter was ever in Rome, but they are evidence

> '*You are Peter, and upon this rock I will build my church.*'

that people *thought* he had been there. There are, however, firmer archaeological reasons for believing that Peter died in the imperial capital. Around the year 200 – roughly contemporary, therefore, with the *Acts of Peter* – a Christian named Gaius wrote that he could point to the places where Peter and Paul were laid after their deaths: the Via Ostia for Paul, and the Vatican Hill for Peter. Gaius says monuments, or *tropaia*, mark the spot. One of the monuments to which Gaius was referring has been found right beneath what is now the main, or papal, altar of St Peter's. The present altar was built at the end of the 16th century, but it was erected over earlier papal altars, probably going back to the first basilica built under the emperor Constantine. And beneath the *tropaion* there is a pauper's grave, which dates roughly from the date of the martyrdom of St Peter.

Although the presence of Peter in Rome is so important for the claims – often called 'the Petrine' claims – of the bishop of Rome, it is no longer much disputed even by those who do not accept them. It is a rather different matter, however, to claim that Peter, or those very early popes listed in the *Annuario pontificio* (the 'pontifical yearbook' of the holy see, listing all the popes to date), were bishops of Rome.

THE FIRST POPES

ometime around the year AD 180 Irenaeus, bishop of Lyons, wrote a book entitled *Against all Heretics*. Irenaeus had been born in Asia Minor, possibly in Smyrna, where he listened to the martyred bishop of Smyrna, St Polycarp, who in turn had been taught by St John the Evangelist. There was a direct link, in other words, from Irenaeus back to the preaching of the apostles. That was important to him. In his criticism of heretics he compares what they taught to the faith that had been handed down from the apostles. In order to exemplify the tradition he takes Rome as an example. He provides a list of the bishops of Rome from Linus, to whom, he says, the apostles Peter and Paul handed on their role, down to Eleutherius, who was bishop of Rome at the time at which he is writing – and whom he had met.

Between Linus and Eleutherius there are 12 bishops, the sixth of whom is – rather suspiciously – called Sixtus, or Xystus. It is suspicious for two reasons. One is that, according to Irenaeus, the faith of the 12 apostles had been preserved in Rome by another 12, a list ending conveniently with Eleutherius who was a contemporary. Secondly, there are other succession lists which do not exactly coincide with Irenaeus's, in particular one produced by Hegesippus who seems only to have known of three, rather than 12, successors to the apostles up to Eleutherius.

THE EARLY CHRISTIAN COMMUNITY IN ROME

So we know very little about who, if anyone, was in charge of the Christians in Rome after the death of Peter. It might be better to say that there was no single person in charge of them for a century or so after Peter's martyrdom. There are a number of reasons for this surmise. First of all, the notion of a 'bishop' who ruled over the local Christian community only emerged at the end of the first century. The first person to write about the office of bishop in this sense is Ignatius, bishop of Antioch. He was arrested in Antioch and taken to Rome under guard to be executed, dying about AD 107. On his way to Rome he visited a number of Christian communities – including the one presided over by Polycarp in Smyrna – and wrote letters to them in which his image of a bishop becomes clear. For Ignatius the bishop is the centre of unity of the church. Without the bishop's authority, no Christian can contract marriage, neither could the Eucharist (the religious service of Christians) be celebrated. It seems likely from the way he presents his case that this model of a bishop was not common throughout the Catholic (Ignatius is the first to use the term 'Catholic' to embrace all Christian communities) world of his day.

It certainly was not the case in Rome. The community there was small, for the most part poor, and it was scattered across the city. It seems at first to have been largely Jewish in origin, and quite possibly Christianity was not readily distinguishable from Judaism. The community was located in the poorer, immigrant areas of the city including the Trastevere quarter, technically outside the city because it was across the River Tiber, where there were three churches (or, at least, there were three houses where the Eucharist was celebrated). These became known as the *tituli*, because they took their names, their titles, from the person who owned the house where the community gathered for Sunday worship. In time these probably modest dwellings became built up into dedicated churches, and the ownership was forgotten – except that the original owner was given the title of 'saint'.

While it is very likely that the different groups of Christians knew of each other, it is highly unlikely that there was any single individual presiding over them until well into the second century. So it would be a mistake to talk of a 'bishop of Rome' for a good many years after the deaths of Peter and Paul. Take the case of Clement, who figures in the list of the bishops of Rome compiled by Irenaeus. Clement wrote a letter to the Christians in Corinth, where the community was in conflict, and urged on them repentance and obedience to their superiors. It is interesting that even at this early date, around AD 96, Christians in Rome were giving guidance to Christians of other churches. But more to the point here, it is clear from the letter that Clement was writing as the secretary of his community. He makes no claim whatsoever to be its bishop. Nor does he ever suggest that he is writing on behalf of a bishop: he is writing in the name of the community as a whole.

THE FIRST BISHOP OF ROME

The first person to whom the title 'bishop of Rome' can be applied with any conviction is Anicetus, who is supposed to have been in charge of the Christian community from 155 to 166 –

'supposed' because the dates of the pontificates of the bishops are disturbingly regular. What is important about Anicetus is that he received a visit from Polycarp of Smyrna. Anicetus himself had come to Rome from Asia Minor – from Emesa, now Homs (or Hims) in Syria, which may have encouraged Polycarp to make the journey to see him. Polycarp wanted to persuade the Christians in Rome to adopt the practice followed in the East of celebrating Christ's resurrection, the feast of Easter, on the 14th day of the Jewish month of Nisan, the day the Passover lamb was sacrificed. There was in Rome no fixed day for celebrating this festival. Anicetus replied that the community in Rome celebrated it every Sunday but he was quite happy for Polycarp, and seemingly for those in Rome who followed this practice (they were called Quartodecimans after the Latin for 14), to continue with their particular custom.

DIFFERENT CONVICTIONS, DIFFERENT CUSTOMS

The incident is significant because it demonstrates that there was in Rome a variety of different customs among the Christians. There were distinct communities, having ritual practices which were not yet entirely in line with one another, but living comfortably beside each other: despite their disagreement, Anicetus was happy to have Polycarp preside at the Eucharist. Not 40 years later, however, Pope Victor I took a tougher line, excommunicating Quartodecimans not just from the Roman Church, but from all Christian churches. There were protests from Irenaeus among others, but the Roman custom prevailed, and those who clung to the old way of celebrating Easter became a separate sect, which eventually died out.

The Quartodecimans were not the first to be excommunicated. Rome seemed to attract Christians with unorthodox belief. These were usually welcomed at first, but when their convictions became known they were cut off. There was Marcion, for example, the son of a bishop, who was excommunicated by his father for rejecting the Old Testament and much of the New. A successful businessman, a shop owner, he arrived in Rome about 140 and gave the church there a large amount of money. When, in 144, he set up his own church, he wanted the funds back. The Roman Church found the cash, which suggests that less than a century after its founding it was already flourishing, and seemingly beginning to attract not just the poorer classes but relatively well-off people as well.

VICTOR, ZEPHYRINUS AND CALLISTUS

By the end of the century Pope Victor, an African by birth, was apparently sufficiently well connected to have links to the imperial household. Marcia, the mistress of Emperor Commodus, was a Christian, and the pope supplied her with a list of names of Christians who had been sentenced to work in the mines of Sardinia during a persecution of the faith. There was one rather colourful character whom Victor had quite intentionally – or so it seems – left off the list. This was Callistus, a slave, who had been sent to the mines not because of his faith but because he had been involved in a fight in a synagogue. Not only that, but he had defrauded his master, also a Christian, and a freed slave, of considerable amounts of money.

Callistus somehow managed to get his name on the list, and returned to Rome. There was not much the pope could do about this except exile him from the Roman Christian community, but when Victor was succeeded by Zephyrinus as bishop, the new pope brought him back to the city, made him his deacon, or principal assistant, gave him responsibility for the lower clergy, and put him in charge of the Christian underground cemetery, or catacomb, which still bears his name – the catacomb of San Callisto. This is the first property which the church appears to have owned, but quite possibly it belonged legally to Zephyrinus himself, who was quite well off. After Zephyrinus's death in 217, Callistus was elected bishop, much to the disgust of another eminent Christian, Hippolytus.

HIPPOLYTUS: THE FIRST ANTIPOPE?

It is from Hippolytus that we learn about Zephyrinus and Callistus, and he was not a friendly reporter. He seems to have thought that he ought to have been elected pope rather than Callistus, and set himself up in opposition, the first of a large number of 'antipopes' down the ages. That at least was what used to be thought. It is possible that he was simply head of a dissident group, and did not declare himself to be a pope. But he was undoubtedly critical of Zephyrinus and particularly of Callistus. Hippolytus was from the East, and thought himself – and was – more theologically sophisticated than either of his opponents. He also objected to the way Callistus ran the church, making much of the fact that the pope apparently allowed Christian women to form liaisons with Christian slaves. This is an interesting detail. Marriage between a noblewoman and a slave was legally impossible. It looks very likely that there were far more women of the upper classes who were Christians than there were men. Callistus may simply have been countenancing these otherwise illicit unions because he was eager to prevent 'mixed marriages' between Christian women and pagan men.

There is much about the life of Hippolytus that is conjectural. In the Vatican Library there is a marble statue, found in 1551 and once thought to be a representation of him, which has a list of his writings inscribed upon its plinth, though it is now believed to represent a female figure. But the traditional story is that as a leading Christian he, together with Pope Pontian, was arrested during the persecution of the emperor Maximus Thrax, and transported to Sardinia, where the two became reconciled, and where they both died. Their bodies were brought back to Rome by Pope Fabian, and buried in the catacomb of San Callisto.

POPE FABIAN

Fabian himself (236–50) was a man of considerable stature. He was responsible for the division of Rome, which was broken up into 14 civil regions and 7 ecclesiastical regions, each with a deacon in charge, assisted by a subdeacon. This made abundant sense if, by then, the church had reached the stage of owning property corporately, though it is unclear what sort of legal corporation it constituted. The deacons were those who distributed alms to the poor and took care of widows and orphans on behalf of the community – there were said to be 1500 widows and others in distress of one kind or another. These works of charity certainly constituted an attraction for the needy to become members of the Christian community. But it also meant that the deacons, who performed these charitable activities, were well known to the community at large. They were, therefore, rather more likely to be elected by the community as the bishop of Rome than were the clergy who looked after the *tituli*. We know that, in Fabian's time, there were 18 *tituli*, or churches, each probably served by at least two priests.

PERSECUTIONS UNDER DECIUS AND VALERIAN

Pope Fabian died as a martyr in 250. A contemporary commented that the emperor Decius would rather cope with a claimant to the imperial title than deal with Fabian, bishop of Rome. When the emperor launched his persecution, then, it is understandable that Fabian was among the first to be martyred. Decius's persecution was followed by another under Emperor Valerian.

The emperor Constantine leads Pope Sylvester I's horse by the reins, in a symbolic gesture intended to demonstrate the subjection of emperor to pope. The image is one of a series of 13th-century frescoes in the chapel of San Silvestro attached to the basilica of the Santi Quattro Coronati in Rome.

This period of systematic oppression – for the most part earlier persecutions had been sporadic and localized – brought serious problems to all Christian communities. Some people left the faith, and then, when the troubles were over, wanted to return to it. The church in Rome was quite ready to receive them back, after a bout of penance, but there were some individuals, both in Rome and elsewhere, who wanted a more rigorous line to be taken. There was a schism, with another antipope, Novatian, being chosen as the head of the rigorists – quite possibly he had expected to be elected pope once the Decian persecution was over, but the community thought otherwise. A further problem arose when Pope Stephen told the bishop of Carthage, Cyprian, that it was the Roman custom to accept as valid the baptism carried out by heretics, and not to re-baptize those who wished to enter the Great Church, as was the practice in Africa. There was an acrimonious correspondence, in the course of which Stephen fell back, to bolster his authority, on the text quoted earlier: 'You are Peter, and upon this rock I will build my Church'.

CONSTANTINE AND THE FOURTH-CENTURY PAPACY

After the death of Valerian in 260 there was a period of peace for the church, but in 303 persecution broke out again, this time under the emperor Diocletian. Systematic, severe and empire-wide, Diocletian's persecution was the greatest threat to the continued existence of the Christian community in 250 years. It was so harsh that the history of the papacy in the early years of the fourth century is confused, even after the emperor Constantine succeeded to the throne, claiming to have won his victories 'in the sign of the cross'. Constantine did not convert to Christianity until his deathbed but by then he had become a 'catechumen', one being instructed in the belief of Christians. He heaped privileges upon the church, building St Peter's

Basilica (a basilica was originally a special form of hall, hitherto used for administrative offices) over the grave of the apostle, and the Lateran Basilica on the site of the barracks of a mutinous cavalry regiment (the name 'Lateran' comes from a Roman family which had a palace nearby).

Christianity, though flourishing, was not yet the dominant religion of the empire, and did not become so for at least a century. What lay behind Constantine's conversion is difficult to say, but it is certainly clear that he was eager to enforce upon his dominions one version of Christianity, that upheld by the bishop of Rome. There were two major problems. The first was in North Africa, where some Christians believed that the sacraments as administered by traitors were not valid. By 'traitors' they meant *traditores*, those who had handed over (which is what *traditor* means) the sacred scriptures to the imperial officials during the persecution. To try – vainly – to bring these back into the fold, Constantine held a church council at Arles in 314. In 325 he held another at Nicea (now Iznik, in Turkey) to try to reconcile the followers of Arius with the wider church (see box).

THE DONATION OF CONSTANTINE

Though Rome was its capital, the empire had for administrative purposes been divided in two for some time. In 330, on the site of the Greek city of Byzantium, Constantine inaugurated a new Eastern capital, a New Rome. He named it after himself: Constantinople, modern-day Istanbul. A legend arose that before he abandoned the old Rome he endowed Pope Sylvester (314–35) – who had, it was claimed, cured him of leprosy – with authority over the Western empire, both spiritual and temporal. The story was a complete myth, fabricated in the late eighth or early ninth centuries, but this 'Donation of Constantine', as it came to be called, played an important part in the later history of the church. It is illustrated in a remarkable series of 13th-century frescoes painted in a chapel dedicated to San Silvestro attached to the Roman church of the Four Crowned Martyrs (the Santi Quattro Coronati).

THE DEBT TO EUSEBIUS

It should not be surprising that the history of the early papacy is fragmentary and uncertain. Its events unfolded, after all, a very long time ago. It is perhaps more surprising that so much *is* known about it. For that we owe a particular debt to Eusebius, bishop of Caesarea, who died,

ARIANISM

ARIUS (d. 336) WAS A PRIEST FROM ALEXANDRIA, who appeared to hold that Jesus was not God by nature, but a creature, though a creature formed before time, and through whom the world was created. He was therefore not a human being similar to the rest of humanity, because he alone had been created directly by God.

The Arian debate dragged on for the remainder of the fourth century, with the bishops of Rome being frequently involved even though the controversy raged mainly in the East. Athanasius (d. 373), the bishop of Alexandria from 328, was the leading protagonist of the orthodox view. The creed, or statement of belief, which the Council of Nicea of 325 drew up against Arianism (the Nicene Creed) is still in use, though in a slightly expanded form, in the Eucharistic services of Christian churches.

quite possibly in his 80s, about the year 340. He wrote a history of the church which cited many documents no longer extant. It is clear that there was some effort put into maintaining such texts, a fact perhaps not to be wondered at in a religion which was based upon a collection of writings of the first century and, in the case of what has come to be called the Old Testament, even earlier. There was also the *Liber Pontificalis*, or *Book of the Popes*, which recorded the life of each pope in the first millennium and beyond. The later lives seem to be more or less contemporaneous with the events they narrate. The earlier ones are obviously added on for the sake of completeness, but they probably contain oral traditions which represent at least a version of the truth. Christians obviously kept libraries and archives, and in Rome the conservation of the community's history owes a great deal to one of the most controversial popes of the fourth century, Pope St Damasus.

DAMASUS I

ar more is known about Damasus than about any earlier pope, and even about a good many who came after him, but not always for creditable reasons. His father Antonius had served in several different offices in the church before becoming a bishop, though outside Rome itself. The family had lived in a house which Antonius turned into a church, San Lorenzo in Damaso, which still exists as part of the Palazzo della Cancelleria on Rome's Corso Vittorio Emanuele, although the original church was oriented rather differently. His mother was called Laurentia, and was a widow for 60 years, dying in her 90s. There was also a daughter, Damasus's sister Irene, who took a vow of virginity.

Damasus was a deacon under his predecessor Pope Liberius. When Liberius was banished from Rome in 355 by the emperor Constantius II because of his opposition to Arianism – which Constantius favoured – Damasus went into exile with him. Liberius was not allowed back until three years later, but Damasus, apparently missing city life, returned earlier. He began to work for the antipope Felix whom Constantius had imposed upon the church. Felix and the other clergy of Rome, including Damasus, had taken an oath of loyalty to Liberius, but this they both broke. When Liberius, who enjoyed popular support, returned, there were two bishops in Rome. Felix, however, thought it prudent to withdraw with his supporters to the suburbs. He died in November 365.

BIRTH NAME **Damasus**

BORN **Rome, fourth century AD**

PREDECESSOR **Liberius**

INSTALLED **1 October 366**

DIED **11 December 384**

SUCCESSOR **Siricius**

A CONTROVERSIAL ELECTION

Liberius himself died just under a year
later, in September 366. There had to be an
election to chose his successor. Those who
had remained loyal to Liberius, clergy and
people, met in the Basilica Julia (now Santa
Maria in Trastevere) where they chose
Liberius's deacon Ursinus. He was
promptly consecrated bishop of Rome by
the bishop of Tivoli. Those who had gone
over to Felix, however, stormed the Basilica
Julia, and left many of Ursinus's supporters
dead. They then elected Damasus as pope,
the election taking place in the Lateran
Basilica, and the consecration being
performed, as Roman custom demanded,
by the bishop of Ostia.

Ursinus's supporters fled from
Trastevere to the basilica built by Pope
Liberius, and took refuge there: the basilica
of Santa Maria Maggiore now stands on
the same site, or very close by. Damasus's
supporters again attacked them. One
(hostile) historian records that on this
occasion there were 137 dead.

This was not an auspicious beginning
to Damasus's pontificate, but he had a long
time in which to recover his authority. He
was consecrated on 1 October 366, and
died, in his 80s, on 11 December 384.

The battle of the Liberian Basilica was
not quite the end of the affair. Ursinus
made several efforts to return to Rome to
claim the papacy, but they were all rebuffed.

*Pope Damasus I promoted the cult of saints and martyrs
and tried to strengthen the claims of Rome over those of
Constantinople.*

The most troublesome episode was an accusation, apparently of immorality, made by Isaac, a
Jewish convert, against Damasus in 374. Ursinus attempted to exploit Damasus's embarrassment,
but when he was acquitted Ursinus was once again banished from Rome, this time to Cologne,
and Isaac was exiled to Spain. In all this Damasus had the backing of the emperor Valentinian I
(364–75), who – despite the fact that the emperor, even the emperor in the West, no longer lived
in Rome – was concerned for the well-being of the ancient capital of the empire.

ASSERTING THE LEADERSHIP OF ROME

It was the desire for peace and concord, above everything else, which motivated the emperor
in his dealings with the See of Rome, whatever the personal convictions of the ruler of the day.
Rome remained, despite some earlier aberrations, steadfastly anti-Arian – although the Latin

THE VULGATE

TO MAKE THE FAITH EVER MORE ACCESSIBLE TO HIS FLOCK, Damasus commissioned his secretary, Jerome (c. 345–420), himself now venerated as a saint, to translate the whole of the Bible into Latin from its original Hebrew and Greek . Jerome left Rome after Damasus's death, by which time he had already completed a translation of the gospels into Latin.

He continued after he settled as a monk in Bethlehem. What he produced is called 'the Vulgate', the *editio vulgata* – *vulgo* being the Latin name for 'ordinary people' – and Latin being the common, or vulgar, tongue. Jerome's version remained for more than a millennium the standard translation of the Bible and is still being reprinted in modern times.

West may not fully have understood the niceties of theological debate in the Greek East. The fourth century was a period of vigorous, and sometimes baffling, theological controversy, and Damasus's perhaps unsubtle approach did not always find favour even with otherwise – or would-be – sympathetic bishops in the East. In 377 he summoned a synod in Rome in an attempt to bring to an end the controversies raging in the East, and it produced a document which summarized and condemned a good number of them, including Arianism.

In doing this he was trying to assert the leadership of the See of Rome, which he increasingly called 'the Apostolic See', a term first used, it seems, by Liberius. The apostle of the Apostolic See was, of course, St Peter, and Damasus was falling back on the text from St Matthew, 'You are Peter, and upon this rock I will build my Church'. The claims he made for the authority of Rome seem to have been accepted, at least in the West. When the bishops of Gaul (modern France) had a problem they appealed to Rome for a solution, rather than trying to sort one out for themselves. Damasus gathered together decrees such as those he issued to the Gaulish bishops and kept them in the archives, along with other documentation, for future consultation.

Damasus's claims received remarkable endorsement in February 380, in an imperial decree addressed to the church of Constantinople which, as the new Rome, was vying with the old Rome for primacy in the Catholic, or worldwide, church (though 'world', in this context, it must be remembered, meant Europe, Asia Minor and North Africa only). The emperor told the people of new Rome that they had to accept the version of Christianity which was embraced by Pope Damasus, and that if they did not do so they would be punished by the state as heretics.

This edict of Emperor Theodosius did not prove to have quite as much impact as the pope might have wished. In 381 a council was

> The emperor told the people of new Rome that they had to accept the version of Christianity which was embraced by Pope Damasus.

called at Constantinople to which the bishop of Rome was not even invited. Canon 3 of the Council of Constantinople (a 'canon' is a norm, or ecclesiastical law) upset Damasus considerably. It declared, 'Because it is new Rome, the bishop of Constantinople is to enjoy the privileges of honour after the bishop of Rome.' This should, one might think, have pleased the bishop of Rome, putting him unequivocally in the first place. But the problem for Damasus was the form of the argument. Constantinople came after Rome because it was the new capital city. Damasus wanted Rome's authority to spring from its apostolic origins, to which – unlike the sees of Antioch or Alexandria – Constantinople, founded by the emperor Constantine, could lay no claim.

To bolster Rome's pretensions Damasus promoted the cult of the saints – the martyrs who had died for their faith. He built several new churches, and restored others. Most importantly, he renovated the martyrs' tombs, and provided inscriptions, composed by himself, for many of them. This was the material evidence of a faith stretching back to St Peter.

SIRICIUS

 fter all the problems which surrounded the election of Damasus, it came as a relief to the emperor Valentinian II that, despite a renewed attempt by Ursinus to claim the bishopric of Rome, in December 384 Siricius was elected unanimously to succeed Damasus.

Little is known about his origins except that he was Roman-born, the son of a certain Tiburcus. He had worked his way up through the ranks of the clergy under Liberius and Damasus, and had imbibed some of the high claims of the papacy from his predecessor. Not a great deal is known of his 15-year pontificate – he died on 26 November 399 – perhaps because the evolution of Christianity in the last quarter of the fourth century owed more to the powerful figure of Ambrose, bishop of Milan, a city which was by this time the residence of the emperor, than it did to Rome. Nonetheless, two events in Siricius's time as pope were of great significance for the future development of the papal office, and for the Catholic Church in general.

HIMERIUS'S 15 QUESTIONS

Soon after his election he was approached by the priest Bassian, who had been sent to Rome by his bishop, Himerius, who governed the See of Tarragona in Spain. Himerius wanted answers to a series of 15 questions on ecclesiastical discipline. Siricius gave his response, and added a rider requesting Himerius to make the papal decisions on these issues known not just in his own diocese, but to communicate them to the bishops elsewhere in Spain, in Gaul (France) and in North Africa. What Siricius said in

BIRTH NAME **Siricius**

BORN **unknown**

PREDECESSOR **Damasus** I

ELECTED **December 384**

DIED **26 November 399**

SUCCESSOR **Anastasius** I

Pope Siricius insisted that all bishops, priests and deacons should observe celibacy from their ordination onwards and that they should be worthy of their office.

these answers to Himerius's questions was not particularly new. Much of it was drawn from earlier councils and synods of the church. What *was* new, however, was the pope's manner of dealing with the request. He had issued a series of decrees to be followed not just in his own See of Rome, but around the Christian world. When he held a synod in Rome in 386 he again sent the decisions of the synod to other bishops.

THE QUESTION OF CELIBACY

The synod in Rome had dealt with important matters, important, that is, to the status of the clergy. Siricius was insisting that all those in major orders – bishops, priests and deacons – remain celibate from the time of their ordination onwards. He also laid down that no bishop should be consecrated without the bishop of Rome being told. He did not, of course, claim to have a say in the customary practice of the local election of bishops, but he wanted to make sure that they were worthy candidates for the office. He added that there were to be three bishops present to consecrate any newly appointed bishop: one would not be enough.

It was essential that the church should have worthy candidates for its ministers. Such had been the legal provisions of the emperors towards the church in the fourth century that a clerical career had come to look increasingly attractive, freeing the clergy from some of the heavy financial burdens entailed by public office. To become a priest was one way of escaping from the weight of such taxation. The Roman synod laid down that the previous life of a person presenting himself for ordination had to be subject to scrutiny to ensure that he was suitable. Those who had held public office, and those who had been in the army, were to be barred. It was not just a matter of money: those ruled out because of their past lives had been, or might have been, responsible for the shedding of blood, whether in battle or in authorizing executions.

THE CASE OF JOVINIAN

What was chiefly at issue, however, was the privileged status of the clergy themselves, as became clear in the case of Jovinian. Jovinian was a monk, which meant that, among other things, he had embraced chastity as a way of life. He did not think, however, that the clergy needed to be celibate. Or rather, he did not think that the clergy or the consecrated virgins – an increasingly large group – should enjoy special status within the church because they were celibate. There were some who suggested that those who had consecrated themselves to a celibate life would enjoy a higher status in heaven, a status above that of the ordinary Christians. Jovinian would have none of it, and was condemned in Rome, and then by

Ambrose in a synod held in Milan which Siricius endorsed in a letter to Ambrose.

There were all kinds of issues, not least the fact that Jovinian might have been thought to be muddying ecclesiastical waters. The growing number of consecrated virgins in Rome was becoming a matter of public concern, much of it relating to the inheritance of property and the survival of families. And there were worries, too, that an unsympathetic pagan prefect of the city –

Pagan Rome was used to a small number of consecrated virgins, but not to the number who were now offering themselves to the church.

the empire was still very far from being wholly Christian – might intervene. Pagan Rome was used to a small number of consecrated virgins, but not to the number who were now offering themselves to the church – and widows, likewise, were chosing to embrace chastity rather than marry again.

Rome was certainly not used to men consecrated to celibacy. But celibacy marked men apart. Those serving the altars were different from and, in Siricius's view if not in that of Jovinian's, higher than the ordinary Christian. So Jovinian, who held a contrary view – and he was not in favour of fasting either, as an ascetic discipline – was condemned.

THE EXECUTION OF PRISCILLIAN

Meanwhile, a severely ascetic group was flourishing in Spain. It began, it seems, with a layman, possibly of noble rank, called Priscillian, who in about 380 became bishop of Avila even though his teaching had been condemned by a synod at Saragossa. In 381 he was exiled to France. His followers looked to the bishops of Rome and Milan for support, but it was not forthcoming. Priscillian was again condemned in a synod, this time in Bordeaux. He appealed to the emperor Maximus, but the emperor's court in Trier found him guilty of sorcery, and he was put to death despite the pleas of churchmen that he should be spared. Siricius was incensed that an emperor should exercise jurisdiction in an ecclesiastical case, this being a function of the bishops. He wrote to Maximus, who humbly replied that in future such ecclesiastical matters would be left to the clergy.

INNOCENT I

ccording to his contempory St Jerome, Innocent I was the son of his predecessor Anastasius I. This is possible, as there were still married clergy in the church, and continued to be for centuries to come. But it seems improbable. For one thing, the *Book of the Popes* says that his father was also named Innocent, and that his family came from Alba, near Rome, rather than Rome itself, where Anastasius was born. St Jerome presumably means that Innocent was a spiritual son of Anastasius, whom Jerome had much admired, whereas he had not been at all well disposed towards Siricius.

Innocent, however, modelled himself upon Pope Siricius. He was as eager as Siricius had been to advance the claims of the bishopric of Rome to legislate for the church, at least for the church in the West. He no longer had to contend with charismatic bishops in Milan for the leadership. Ambrose had died in 397 and was succeeded by Simplicianus who, though scarcely less eminent, had died just before Innocent was elected in December 401. Milan, moreover, ceased to be the capital of the Western empire in 402, when the emperor moved to Ravenna, so the bishop of Rome's claim to be the leading bishop in the church was less open to challenge.

IMPOSING THE WILL OF ROME

The new pope exploited the opportunity he was offered. In a letter to the bishop of Rouen in February 404, for example, he reiterated the decisions of the synod of Rome which had been held under Siricius, and sharpened them. He was concerned about the rules governing admission to the higher ranks of the clergy – indeed, in writing to Rouen he spoke of 'the book of rules'. Rome had kept the rules, he claimed, whereas others had fallen away, and it was now up to Rome to bring the rest of the church back to the ideal. The discipline in Rome forbade anyone being ordained who had, since baptism (because baptism washed away all previous sins) served in the army, taken part in trials leading to execution, paid for public games (because these, too, involved violence) or had been in a pagan priesthood. And the same went for anyone who had married a widow, or who had married twice. In laying down these rules he claimed that he was speaking 'with the aid of the Holy Apostle Peter, through whom both the apostolate and the episcopate in Christ took their beginning'.

A dozen years later he was saying the same kind of thing to the bishop of Gubbio: 'what was transmitted to the Roman Church by Peter, the prince of the Apostles, and what has been guarded there

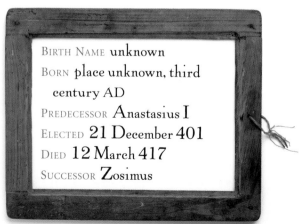

BIRTH NAME unknown

BORN place unknown, third century AD

PREDECESSOR Anastasius I

ELECTED 21 December 401

DIED 12 March 417

SUCCESSOR Zosimus

The sack of Rome by Alaric, king of the Goths, on 24 August 410, took place during the long pontificate of Innocent I. The first of many such attacks, Alaric's came to symbolize the fall of the Roman empire in the West.

until now, should be observed by all.' It was of particular significance that he was writing to Gubbio, because that diocese lay within Milan's sphere of influence, and in the past a bishop of Rome would have thought twice about interfering. But Innocent was perfectly ready to tell the bishop there that he ought to follow the customs and traditions of Rome. He claimed to be able to instruct bishops in this fashion because, he believed, all the churches in the West owed their origins to Peter or to his successors, his heirs, in Rome. The notion that the pope was the heir to Peter was an important one. In Roman law an heir became the person whom he had succeeded. All rights and duties passed on directly to the heir, so a pope could claim the authority of the prince of the apostles.

Rome was not always consulted by the other churches. In Africa, the bishops were struggling with a group of dissidents called Donatists (see box, page 27). To deal with them they called a major council in 411 which took place in Carthage, but did not involve the bishop of Rome. Possibly that was because Donatism was purely a local problem. The challenge of the teachings of the British monk Pelagius was spread far wider, however. He held that Christian teaching had been placing too much emphasis on God's intervention and not enough on an individual's free will in the struggle to achieve salvation. He also questioned the practice of baptizing infants. Augustine, the bishop of Hippo, was the main adversary of Pelagius and his supporters. Their teachings were condemned at Carthage in 411, then again in two further councils, both of them

In laying down these rules he claimed that he was speaking 'with the aid of the Holy Apostle Peter'.

in Africa, in 416. In between times Pelagius had found support in Palestine. When he was condemned in 416 Augustine put pressure on Pope Innocent to become involved.

Innocent's response was to thank the African bishops for referring the case to him – which was not exactly what they had done – and then, basing his arguments on the theology espoused by the Africans, simply to confirm their decision. Augustine commented that reports of the 'councils had been sent to the Apostolic See. Rescripts have come from there. The matter is finished.' *Roma locuta, causa finita est*: 'Rome has spoken, the matter is finished.' The phrase has come to be symbolic of the authority of the bishop of Rome – though in practice all Innocent had done was to have endorsed the thinking, and the decisions, of the bishops of North Africa.

RELATIONS WITH CONSTANTINOPLE

Relations with Constantinople, however, were not so satisfactory. The problem was John Chrysostom. John had been a monk in Syria and then a priest in Antioch, where he gained a well-deserved reputation as a preacher ('Chrysostom' means 'golden-mouth'). He was brought against his wishes to Constantinople as patriarch, or bishop, of the city in 398. John was a reformer: his sermons were sometimes expositions of the Bible, but often moral tracts on the sins of society. In his new post he immediately set to preaching about the sins of the inhabitants of the new Rome, not sparing the empress Eudoxia whom he rather undiplomatically compared to Jezebel and Herodias. Though he had many supporters in the Eastern capital, in 404 he was sent into exile. He appealed for support to Pope Innocent. Innocent was wary of entering into a dispute which by this time involved not only the emperor in the East but a number of other Eastern bishops. However, he eventually came down in favour of John. Naturally this did not please John's successor as patriarch. John himself, now a saint and doctor of the church, died in 407 – in effect, martyred – but relations between Rome and Constantinople did not improve until after Innocent's own death.

BARBARIANS AT THE GATES OF ROME

During Innocent's long pontificate of 16 years it might be said that the city of Rome was itself the chief actor. From the mid-fourth century nomadic hordes were pressing across the boundaries of the Roman empire. The Romans despised them, and called them, generically, 'barbarians', but they employed several of the tribes to serve as soldiers, often under their own kings as Roman generals. Such a general was Alaric, king of the Goths. In 403 Alaric led his troops into Italy. He was defeated by the emperor Honorius, and the Romans celebrated a triumph, the last to be held in the city. When Honorius came to Rome, remarked Augustine in a sermon, he did not go first to the pagan shrines, but to the shrine of the fisherman, the basilica built in honour of St Peter. But then he returned to Ravenna, and did not reappear when Alaric once again threatened the city of Rome.

There were still pagans, and perhaps not altogether convinced Christians, in Rome who wanted to offer sacrifices to the city's deities to ward off Alaric's attack. Such sacrifices were forbidden. They had therefore to get permission. They asked the approval of Innocent, who

DONATISM

DURING PERSECUTIONS OF CHRISTIANS, especially those under the Emperors Decius (d. 251) and Diocletian (abdicated 305) there was a problem not only about those who had lapsed from their faith and later wanted to return but, under Diocletian particularly, about those who had handed over the sacred books to be destroyed. They were the *traditores*, literally, 'the handers over'. Caecilian, bishop of Carthage *c.* 311, was accused of having been consecrated by a *traditor*, and this, said some in the North African church, meant that all Caecilian's acts, of baptism or ordination for instance, were invalid. This group elected Majorinus to replace Caecilian, and then Donatus, from whom this schism takes its name. Donatists were rigorists, believing that the church was only for the holy, not for those who had sinned.

naturally did not approve, though it is likely that at least some of the sacrifices went ahead anyway. But it was a sign of the bishop of Rome's standing that it was the pope they approached, and he was also included in the party of senators who travelled to Ravenna to seek, in vain, the emperor's assistance. Innocent was therefore out of Rome in 410 when Alaric captured the city and sacked it.

Rome was to suffer much worse sackings, but this first one was enormously symbolic. It marked the beginning of the end of the empire in the West. Not much more than half a century later there would be a Roman emperor in Constantinople only. It looked as though the Christian God had failed to defend the empire's ancient capital. Refugees fled to Africa, and in Hippo Bishop Augustine was inspired to begin writing *The City of God*, perhaps his greatest book, which explained that everything which happened, even the fall of Rome, was part of the Christian God's plan for humankind.

> During Innocent's long pontificate of 16 years it might be said that the city of Rome was itself the chief actor.

LEO I

ust over four decades later, Pope Leo, a deacon who was elected while on a diplomatic mission to Gaul, and consecrated bishop on 29 September 440, was facing a challenge similar to that of Pope Innocent I. In 452 Rome was again under threat, this time from an army of Huns, commanded by their king Attila. The Huns had already laid waste to northern Italy before the Western emperor, Valentinian III, sent Leo with a couple of Roman senators to negotiate with Attila. They met near Mantua, close to Lake Garda, and Attila agreed to withdraw.

It was an iconic moment – literally iconic, because the scene was depicted by Raphael in the Vatican palace's Stanza d'Eliodoro a millennium later to celebrate the military prowess of Pope Julius II (see page 156). The event gave the bishop of Rome enormous prestige as saviour of the city – though the money which changed hands may have helped to persuade Attila, as well as an offensive launched by the emperor in the East.

PLUNDER AND PILLAGE BY THE VANDALS

Three years later Rome was again attacked, this time by the Vandals, who had already devastated Africa under their king Genseric. Once again the bishop of Rome was spokesman for his city, but this time he was not quite so successful. The Vandals pillaged the city, though after a plea from the pope they did not ransack the larger churches, and spared the lives of Rome's inhabitants. One of the trophies that the Vandals carried away, never to be seen again, was the seven-branched candlestick which the Roman emperor Titus had brought back after looting the temple in Jerusalem nearly four centuries earlier.

These acts, in which the bishop of Rome defended the city from invaders, were highly symbolic. On the feast of Saints Peter and Paul – in papal perspective the apostolic founders of the Church of Rome – which fell soon after the fortnight of pillaging which the Vandals had enjoyed, Pope Leo made an astonishing claim. 'Through the see of Peter [Rome is] ruling more widely now through divine religion than it ever did by worldly dominion . . . What you achieved by war is less than what has been brought to Rome by Christian peace.'

BIRTH NAME **Leo**

BORN **Tuscany, 400**

PREDECESSOR **Sixtus III**

INSTALLED **29 September 440**

DIED **10 November 461**

SUCCESSOR **Hilarus**

No doubt the population of the city – by now almost wholly Christian – did not question their bishop, but Leo had to work hard to substantiate the claim. Not everyone in the Christian world was prepared to accept the governance of Rome. Leo faced greater problems in this respect in the East than in the West, but even in the West he had difficulties.

His major problem was with (St) Hilary, bishop of Arles. Hilary was a relatively young man, possibly only about

Pope Leo I was seen as Rome's saviour in 452 when he negotiated successfully with Attila the Hun, who agreed not to attack the city.

30 years old when he was chosen to lead the church in Arles, a position which he treated as if it were a patriarchate with jurisdiction over all the bishoprics of Gaul. When Hilary deposed the bishop of Besançon, an act which, in Leo's view, was beyond his authority, Leo was swift to respond. He confined Hilary to his diocese and persuaded Emperor Valentinian to issue a rescript, or decree, proclaiming that the writ of the See of Peter was to run throughout the Western empire, that bishops must act only within the established tradition, and that, if summoned to Rome, they must go of their own free will, or be forced to make the journey. The bishops of Gaul were unhappy, arguing that the See of Arles had great antiquity, and that with antiquity came authority. Leo's diplomatic solution, in 450, was to cut back the ambitions of Arles – Hilary himself had died in May 449 – but to recognize its prominence by creating two overarching jurisdictions in Gaul, one based on Arles, the other on Vienne.

Elsewhere in the West, however, the pope's problems were made easier by the barbarian invasions which had weakened the status of the bishop of Milan and of the bishops of North Africa, who were ready and willing to accept papal authority in matters of the liturgy, of the calendar, of the reconciling of heretics and of illegal ordinations.

THE MANICHEES

The Vandal invasions had another effect. In the reign of Innocent I, refugees had fled to Africa, now they fled back to the relative security of Rome. A good many of Leo's surviving sermons are addressed to the obligation upon Christians of almsgiving. But one group of refugees was not welcome. Manichees – among whom Augustine of Hippo had once been numbered – believed in the existence of two equally powerful gods locked in perpetual struggle, one of them good, the other the origin of evil. There were already plenty of Manichees in Rome, which is one of the things that had attracted Augustine to come there in the 380s, but now, as the Vandals flooded into Africa, their numbers began to increase. But Rome, to Leo, was by now a Christian city that he was rebuilding, putting up new churches and embellishing the old ones. Manichees were proscribed under existing imperial legislation, so Leo, rather than civil officials, set up tribunals and put them on trial. They might repent of their ways, but otherwise they were to be exiled, and in any case their holy books were to be destroyed. This he proclaimed not just for Rome, but for the whole of Italy. Valentinian backed him up: the persecution of Manichees was extended by the emperor throughout his empire.

PROBLEMS IN THE EAST

In the East the situation was much more complicated. The crisis in relations between Rome and Constantinople which had arisen over John Chrysostom durng the pontificate of Innocent I, had been resolved under his successor Pope Zosimus (417–18) – a process that may have been helped by the fact that Zosimus was Greek. But Zosimus's failure fully to understand the situation in the West led to other problems – for example, it was he who encouraged the patriarchal ambitions of the bishopric of Arles. Moreover, his rule in Rome had been heavy-handed, which led to a disturbed election for his successor, and an attempt by the emperor Honorius to lay down rules for papal elections. The result was that Boniface I, the man considered to be the rightful bishop, backed by Honorius, had to face an antipope throughout his pontificate (418–22). 'It has never been lawful,' Boniface once stated, 'to reconsider what has once been decided by the apostolic see.'

Celestine I (422–32), who followed Boniface, had to face a major problem in the East, a dispute about the figure of Christ. It was started by Patriarch Nestorius of Constantinople, who claimed that it was wrong to say of Christ's mother, Mary, that she was the mother of God – the disputed term was *Theotokos* (see box, page 31). Nestorius was bitterly opposed by Cyril, patriarch of Alexandria. The emperor Theodosius II decided to settle the matter by a general council of the church, which was held at Ephesus in June 431. The council was effectively manipulated by Cyril, who opened it without waiting for the arrival either of his opponents, or of the pope's representatives. Celestine nonetheless expressed overall satisfaction at the outcome of the council, and his successor, Sixtus III (432–40), built an enormous church in Rome to celebrate Mary as *Theotokos*. It still stands today. as Santa Maria Maggiore.

'THE ROBBER COUNCIL'

During Leo's pontificate the whole controversy, or rather a variant of it, flared up again, this time around the figure of the monk Eutyches. The patriarch of Constantinople, Flavian, accused Eutyches of denying that there were two natures in Christ, the divine and the human. He was said to espouse the view – known as Monophysitism – that Christ had only one nature, a divine one which had, as it were, overtaken his human side. Eutyches was powerful at the court of Emperor Theodosius, and Flavian appealed to Rome for support. But Theodosius himself took a hand, calling another council, again at Ephesus, in 449. Pope Leo sent a message to Flavian, known as *The Tome of Leo*, in which he set out Rome's position, which was identical to the patriarch's. At Ephesus, however, it was the party of Eutyches which won out, and Flavian was deposed. Leo called it 'the robber council', and refused to accept its decisions.

The situation was changed by the death of Theodosius and the succession to the imperial throne in Constantinople of Marcian. Just as the pope wanted to exert his influence in the East, so Marcian wanted to lay a claim to the Western part of the empire, and the support of the pope was central to his ambitions. He therefore called a new council, which met in June 451 at Chalcedon, presided over by a representative of Leo. Leo's *Tome* was accepted as the standard of orthodoxy on the two natures divine and human, in the one person of Christ. This was a triumph for the old Rome. But in the 28th canon of the council, new Rome, Constantinople, was recognized as having primacy over the churches of the East, equivalent to that of Rome in the West. The primacy was based upon the political significance of the city, rather than on, as the pope wished, the apostolic foundation to which Constantinople, of course, could not lay claim.

Leo refused to accept canon 28, and worked tirelessly for the rest of his pontificate to win over bishops in the East to his point of view. But he was also troubled by the continuing threat to orthodoxy of those who espoused the Monophysite cause. A Monophysite was installed as patriarch of Alexandria after the patriarch who supported the decision of Chalcedon was murdered. The new patriarch, Timothy, was eventually driven out. But it was an omen of struggles to come. Leo died on 10 November 461. He is one of only two popes to whom history has attached the epithet 'the Great'.

THE CHRISTOLOGICAL CONTROVERSIES

ARGUMENTS OVER THE PERSON OF CHRIST dominated the church for several centuries. Though the Council of Chalcedon had been called in 451 to resolve the debate, its conclusion, that Christ was one person having two natures, the one human, the other divine, did not satisfy large parts of the church in the East. The opposing sides, both denying the Chalcedonian formula, were known as Nestorians and Monophysites. The former were named after Nestorius, who became patriarch of Constantinople in 428. Nestorians believed – though whether Nestorius himself ever taught this is arguable – that there were two separate persons in Christ. This gave rise to the belief that the title *Theotokos*, or 'God-bearer', could not be applied to Mary, because she was the mother only of the human, not the divine, Christ.

The term 'Monophysite', meaning having only one nature, came into use after the Council of Chalcedon, though in an extreme form it was preached before the council by Eutyches, the archimandrite, or superior, of a monastery in Constantinople. He believed that there was only one nature in Christ, and denied that Christ was human in the sense that people in general are human. Post-Chalcedon Monophysites did not typically hold the same view as Eutyches, but argued that while there was indeed only one nature in Christ, it was nevertheless composed of both the divine and the human natures. As will be seen, several different formulas were developed in an attempt to reconcile Monophysites to the orthodox position as defined at the council. Part of the ongoing problem was that the Western Church was, for the most part, much less concerned with theological niceties than the Eastern, and often did not entirely understand what was at issue, particularly as these theological debates were conducted in Greek.

Hilarus 461–68	John V 685–86	Benedict IV 900–03
Simplicius 468–83	Conon 686–87	Leo V 903
Felix III 483–92	Sergius I 687–701	Sergius III 904–11
*Gelasius I 492–96	John VI 701–05	Anastasius III 911?–13
Anastasius II 496–98	John VII 705–07	Lando 913–14
*Symmachus 498–514	Sisinnius 708	John X 914–28
Hormisdas 514–23	Constantine 708–15	Leo VI 928
John I 523–26	Gregory II 715–31	Stephen VII (VIII) 929–31
Felix IV 526–30	Gregory III 731–41	John XI 931–36
Boniface II 530–32	*Zacharias 741–52	Leo VII 936–39
John II 533–35	Stephen II 752	Stephen VIII (IX) 939–42
Agapitus I 535–36	*Stephen II (III) 752–57	Marinus II 942–46
Silverius 536–37	Paul I 757–67	Agapitus II 946–55
*Vigilius 537–55	Stephen III (IV) 768–72	John XII 955–63
Pelagius I 556–61	Hadrian I 772–95	Leo VIII 963–64
John III 561–74	*Leo III 795–816	AND 964–65
Benedict I 575–79	Stephen IV (V) 816–17	Benedict V 964
Pelagius II 579–90	Paschal I 817–24	John XIII 965–72
*Gregory I 590–604	Eugenius II 824–27	Benedict VI 973–74
Sabinian 604–06	Valentine 827	Benedict VII 974–83
Boniface III 607	Gregory IV 827–44	John XIV 983–84
Boniface IV 608–15	Sergius II 844–47	John XV 985–96
Adeodatus I 615–18	*Leo IV 847–55	*Gregory V 996–99
Boniface V 619–25	Benedict III 855–58	*Sylvester II 999–1003
*Honorius I 625–38	*Nicholas I 858–67	John XVII 1003
Severinus 640	Hadrian II 867–72	John XVIII 1003–09
John IV 640–42	John VIII 872–82	Sergius IV 1009–12
Theodore I 642–49	Marinus I 882–c. 84	Benedict VIII 1012–24
*Martin I 649–53	Hadrian III 884–85	John XIX 1024–32
Eugenius I 654–57	Stephen V (VI) 885–91	Benedict IX 1032–48
Vitalian 657–72	*Formosus 891–96	Sylvester III 1045–46
Adeodatus II 672–76	Boniface VI 896	Gregory VI 1045–46
Donus 676–78	Stephen VI (VII) 896–97	Clement II 1046–47
Agatho 678–81	Romanus 897	Damasus II 1048
Leo II 682–83	Theodore II 897	*Leo IX 1049–54
Benedict II 684–85	John IX 898–900	*Denotes popes featured within this section

OPPOSITE *A Russian icon pictures the Council of Nicea (325),
and the Second (553) and Third (680) Councils of Constantinople.*

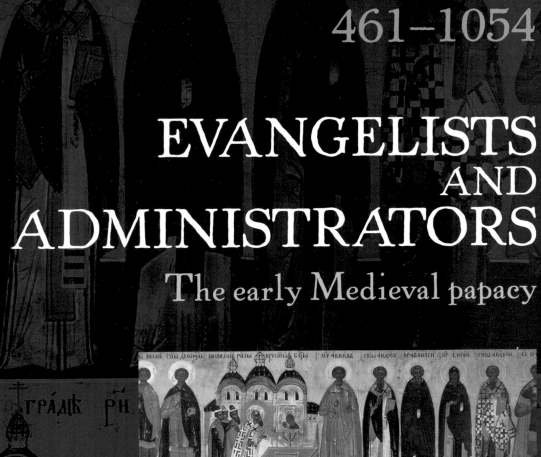

461–1054

EVANGELISTS
AND
ADMINISTRATORS

The early Medieval papacy

GELASIUS I

ope Leo I might have hoped that the Council of Chalcedon had resolved the dispute over the nature of Christ, but in the 30 years or so between his death and the election of Gelasius it became clear that the issue was not going to disappear. The Monophysites constituted a powerful and influential group, especially in Egypt. The Eastern emperors (the last Western one, Romulus Augustulus, was deposed in 476) were eager to re-establish some kind of doctrinal unity throughout the empire to bring an end to the conflict. A formula had to be found.

Apparently prepared by Acacius, the patriarch of Constantinople, with the aid of the unambiguously Monophysite patriarch of Alexandria, Peter Mongos, and backed by the emperor Zeno, such a formula was published in 482. Called the *Henoticon*, it seemed to reassert the church's traditional teaching about the person of Christ, but said nothing about the two natures, nor did it mention the *Tome of Leo*.

In Rome, Pope Felix III reacted vigorously to the news. He wrote to Acacius upbraiding him for his support both of the *Henoticon* and of Peter Mongos – who had been advanced to the See of Alexandria by deposing the existing bishop. He then sent a delegation, but when he learned that its members had been forced to receive communion from Acacius he excommunicated them, along with Acacius himself, at a synod held in Rome in 484, thereby beginning what came to be known as the Acacian schism. Felix also reprimanded Zeno for having interfered in the affairs of the church, something which was common enough in the East, and expected, but which was firmly resisted in the West.

AN AFRICAN POPE

If it is true, as is sometimes claimed, that Gelasius was Felix's deacon, he would have been closely involved in all this. He certainly continued the same policies as Felix, whom he succeeded on the very day of the latter's death. Gelasius seems to have been born into an African family resident in Rome. Other than that, little or nothing is known of his background, though he may have

BIRTH NAME **Gelasius**

BORN **Rome**

PREDECESSOR **Felix III**

ELECTED **1 March 492**

DIED **21 November 496**

SUCCESSOR **Anastasius II**

written one of his treatises on the Christological controversy (see page 31) before he became pope. He was much concerned with the controversy, not only as bishop of Rome trying to assert his authority over the whole church, but also as a theologian, discussing the matters at issue and extracting from the writings of other theologians' texts to demonstrate the correctness of the doctrine espoused by Rome, and encapsulated in the Council of Chalcedon.

Since there was no longer an emperor in the West, on his election Gelasius wrote announcing his appointment, as was the custom, to the emperor in the East. Zeno had been succeeded by Anastasius, but the new ruler in Constantinople was just as wedded to the *Henoticon* as his predecessor had been. What Gelasius did *not* do, however, was to announce his election in a letter to the patriarch of Constantinople, as custom also required. The patriarch was now Euphemius, a man of a conciliatory nature, who took the initiative in writing to the pope, re-establishing communion. But Gelasius was having none of it. He wanted a complete acceptance of Roman terms for communion, or the two churches were to remain at odds. In Constantinople Faustus, a senator who represented Theodoric, the Ostrogoth king of Italy, could not receive communion.

A LETTER TO THE EMPEROR

It was a dire situation, but Gelasius, determined to maintain the authority of Rome, was unyielding. The *Henoticon* had to be rejected in its entirety – and so had the memory of Peter Mongos. In 497 Gelasius wrote a letter to Emperor Anastasius, roundly putting him in his place. This letter does not seem to have created much of a stir at the time, but centuries later it came to be seen as an authoritative description of the relations that, in the view of the pope, ought to exist between the emperor, or by extension all rulers, and the church:

> *There are two powers, August Emperor, by which the world is governed, the consecrated authority of bishops, and the regal power. Of these two, the responsibility of bishops is the more significant, for they will have to give an account even for the rulers of men when they appear before the judgement seat of God.*

The emperor, Gelasius went on, was a son, and not a leader, of the church: the function of leadership fell to the bishops, and in particular to the bishop of Rome, who was heir to St Peter.

THE FIRST 'VICAR OF CHRIST'

Traditionally, emperors had been deemed to hold quasi-priestly powers. In pagan times they had been treated as priests, and that had carried over to the Christian emperors who had from the time of Constantine onwards involved themselves in the affairs of the church – most dramatically by calling councils. Perhaps emboldened by the fact that there was now in the West a barbarian king of Italy who did not lay claim to imperial authority, and who in any case was an Arian (see page 17), Pope Gelasius stated as clearly as possible the place of the church in the divine scheme of things. The emperor was subordinate to the church, and most definitely not vice versa. Papal claims

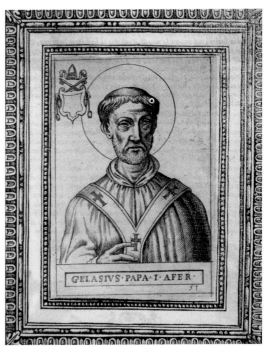

Pope Gelasius I was one of the first popes to put in writing to the emperor that an emperor was a son, and not the leader, of the church: this function fell to the bishop of Rome who was heir to St Peter.

were high: for what seems to have been the first time, Gelasius was addressed, at the Roman synod of May 495, as 'vicar of Christ'.

Though he was ready enough to subordinate emperor to church, Gelasius was not unaware of the lawful authority of princes. Theodoric's battle against the previous king of Italy, Odoacer, had devastated northern Italy. There were refugees to be taken care of, and he asked Theodoric for aid to help them, as well as finding money from his own patrimony: other bishops were likewise urged to intercede with rulers for the good of their people. Gelasius built churches, but he was also concerned with the shortage of clergy to staff those already existing, and was prepared to modify the rules governing the recruitment of clergy to increase their numbers.

Though he died after a relatively short, but eventful, pontificate, future generations have venerated Gelasius as a saint.

SYMMACHUS

Gelasius had bequeathed to the Roman Church the unsolved problem of the schism with Constantinople over the *Henoticon* (see page 34). The clergy and people of Rome therefore chose to succeed him someone who might be considered a conciliator. On his election, Anastasius II (496–8) sent the customary letter to the emperor (also named Anastasius), announcing that he had been selected, and making it clear that he wanted reconciliation. He sent two bishops with this letter as ambassadors to Constantinople. Also included in the deputation was the Roman senator Festus, who was seeking for Theodoric the Ostrogoth the title of king of Italy.

Emperor Anastasius granted him the title, apparently on the condition that Pope Anastasius II would accept the *Henoticon*. The notion that the pope might well do so was reinforced when Photinus, deacon of the bishop of Thessalonika, arrived in the imperial capital, sent by the pope to take part in the negotiations. The see of Thessalonika was theoretically under the jurisdiction of Rome, but in practice leant towards Constantinople and supported the *Henoticon*. When Photinus had come to Rome as an emissary of his bishop, the pope received him into communion without consulting his clergy, before sending him off to join his other ambassadors.

It seemed to many of the Roman clergy that Anastasius was about to capitulate to the emperor, and accept the *Henoticon*. They therefore withdrew from communion with the

BIRTH NAME **Symmachus**

BORN **Fifth century AD, Sardinia**

PREDECESSOR **Anastasius II**

ELECTED **22 November 498**

DIED **19 July 514**

SUCCESSOR **Hormisdas**

pope, so that there was now a schism within the Roman Church itself. At this point, however, Pope Anastasius died unexpectedly: a divine punishment, his detractors concluded.

A SPLIT ELECTION

The schism manifested itself in the election of Anastasius's successor. The majority of the clergy, meeting in the Lateran Basilica, elected the deacon Symmachus, a convert from paganism who had been baptized in Rome, although he was possibly born in Sardinia. A breakaway group, however, consisting of a minority of the clergy and some of Rome's nobles, met in Santa Maria Maggiore, and chose a priest named Lawrence. One of the leading figures who chose Lawrence was Festus, who had returned home after serving as Theodoric's ambassador to the emperor. Festus and perhaps the majority of the aristocracy wanted an accommodation with Constantinople, which, presumably, they expected Lawrence to deliver.

A seventh-century mosaic showing Pope Symmachus with St Agnes – during his pontificate the pope rebuilt the apse of St Agnes's church in Rome, which was close to collapse.

It was not to happen. Symmachus and Lawrence both turned to Theodoric. Theodoric may have been an Arian, but an appeal to the emperor was impossible: as an upholder of the *Henoticon* he was a schismatic. Theodoric declared himself in favour of the candidate with the most support, which was Symmachus. The pope then called a synod in Rome at which he made his rival bishop of Nuceria in southern Italy. When Theodoric paid a visit to Rome in 500, it seemed that Symmachus was secure in his office.

THE POPE ON TRIAL

But then Symmachus blundered. He set the feast of Easter on 25 March, when the custom of past years would have been to set it on 22 April, according to the Alexandrian custom. Theodoric, approached by Symmachus's enemies, summoned him to Ravenna, but when the pope reached Rimini he discovered that he was accused not simply of breaking the customs of the See of Rome, but of the far worse charges of simony and unchastity. He promptly returned to Rome, but this precipitous flight proved to be a mistake. Not only had Lawrence and his supporters occupied many of the churches of the city – including the Lateran Basilica, forcing Symmachus to make do with St Peter's, on the Vatican Hill and outside the city walls – but the fact that Symmachus had not appeared before King Theodoric was taken by his opponents as an admission of guilt. They therefore asked for Symmachus to be tried in Rome itself. Theodoric agreed, and a synod of bishops from all over Italy met in Rome at the church of Santa Croce in Gerusalemme shortly after

Easter 502. Symmachus agreed to attend, but two priests in his entourage, one of them the father of the future pope Agapitus, were killed on the way to the gathering by Lawrence's partisans.

In the end the synod for the most part vindicated Symmachus, on the grounds that, as pope, no human tribunal could sit in judgement on him. It did not, on the other hand, attempt to drive Lawrence and his supporters from Rome, so Symmachus had to remain at St Peter's, where he built the first papal palace. Still, it was a victory of sorts. Building on his success, Symmachus called another council for November that same year. It was less well attended, but was nonetheless important because it attempted to lessen the Roman aristocracy's influence on papal affairs, and insisted that no church property could ever be alienated, except by the pope himself.

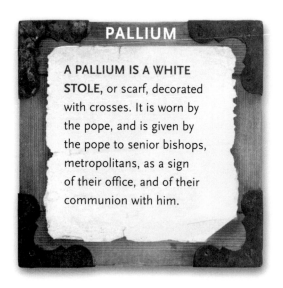

PALLIUM

A PALLIUM IS A WHITE STOLE, or scarf, decorated with crosses. It is worn by the pope, and is given by the pope to senior bishops, metropolitans, as a sign of their office, and of their communion with him.

So matters dragged on, with Symmachus virtually confined to St Peter's, while Lawrence's party held most of the city. Symmachus enjoyed the support of neither the emperor Anastasius nor, more importantly, that of King Theodoric. The latter's stance, however, gradually began to change as the king in Ravenna grew disen-chanted with the emperor in Constantinople. The pope's case was energetically put to Theodoric by the deacon Dioscorus, and Theodoric eventually asked Festus, whose embassy to Constantinople on behalf of Theodoric had been part of the original problem, to withdraw his support from the antipope Lawrence. This took place in 506, and the following year Lawrence disappeared from the scene. He appears to have spent his few remaining years at a farm owned by Festus outside the city.

SYMMACHUS IMPROVES ST PETER'S

Little is known about Symmachus's pontificate apart from the battle with Lawrence over the succession. He sent the pallium (see box) to Bishop Caesarius of Arles, giving him authority over the bishops of Gaul, and apparently including in his remit responsibility for Spain as well. This was the first time the pallium had been bestowed on a bishop outside Italy. As well as building a palace on the Vatican Hill, Symmachus also improved St Peter's itself, adding a baptistery and establishing a hostel for pilgrims to the shrine of Peter. He improved other churches in the city, and erected two more, one dedicated to St Agnes, the other to St Pancras. He is also reported to have banished the remaining Manichees from the city of Rome.

This last act may have been a response to the jibe of Emperor Anastasius, who accused Symmachus of himself being a Manichee. Anastasius remained hostile until, threatened by riots in Constantinople and Thrace, he decided to call a council of the church to address once more the problem of the schism. As a gesture of reconciliation he asked Symmachus to preside over it, but by the time the invitation arrived the pope had died.

VIGILIUS

here were seven popes between Symmachus and Vigilius – eight if Dioscorus, the deacon who had been so influential during the pontificate of Symmachus, and who was in exile from Alexandria because of his acceptance of the Chalcedonian formula (see box, page 31), is included. Dioscorus, however, survived for only three weeks after his election (in 530) and has, quite incorrectly, been treated as an antipope. The years that followed the death of Symmachus saw the passing of both the emperor Anastasius and the Gothic king Theodoric, and by the time Vigilius became pope in 537, Justinian was emperor. Justinian held sturdily to the decisions of the Council of Chalcedon, even though that still left him with the problem of unifying the faith of the empire.

There were still many opponents of Chalcedon, even within the imperial capital – even, indeed, within the imperial household itself, for Theodora, Justinian's wife, was a Monophysite. But Justinian was concerned to unify the empire in more than faith: he wanted to regain control both of North Africa and of Italy from their barbarian overlords. In Rome the church was split between those who favoured an alliance with the Goths, and those who wished for a restoration of imperial rule in Italy. Vigilius, an aristocrat whose father had been praetorian prefect, fell firmly into the latter camp, which is why he was chosen.

A CONTROVERSIAL ELECTION

But who was he chosen by? A great deal of controversy surrounds his election. He was certainly a likely candidate and already in 530 Pope Boniface II had attempted to name him as his successor. This procedure would obviously have deprived the senate of Rome and the city's clergy of any say in the appointment, and together they forced Boniface to retract his decision. Instead he despatched Vigilius, who was his deacon, as papal ambassador, or apocrisarius, to the imperial court at Constantinople. The story then becomes murky. According to sources hostile to Vigilius, he was a favourite of Justinian's Monophysite wife, Theodora. The situation was further

complicated because the king of Italy, Theodahad, alarmed at Justinian's designs upon his territory, had asked Pope Agapitus I (535–6) to go to Constantinople to plead with the emperor not to launch an attack. This Agapitus did, but he died suddenly in Constantinople, and, it was claimed, Theodora now entered into an agreement with Vigilius that he would be made pope. There were, however, conditions: he would be expected to reverse Rome's stance on the Council of Chalcedon, and to reinstate the

BIRTH NAME Vigilius
BORN Date unknown, Rome
PREDECESSOR Silverius
ELECTED 29 March 537
DIED 7 June 555
SUCCESSOR Pelagius I

Vigilius had a turbulent relationship with the emperor Justinian, who vied with him over theological matters. Pope Vigilius was finally imprisoned by the emperor and refused burial in St Peter's by his successor as pope.

patriarch Anthimus, who had been excommunicated as a Monophysite by Agapitus and therefore deposed from the See of Constantinople. It was also alleged that large sums of money changed hands.

Unhappily for Vigilius, by the time he reached Rome with Justinian's army, a new and pro-Gothic pope – Silverius – had been installed to replace Agapitus in June 536. Despite his sympathies for Theodahad, Silverius had persuaded the Roman senate to open the gates of the city to the imperial army so as to avoid bloodshed, but when the Goths renewed their attack, Justinian's general, Belisarius, accused the pope of betraying Rome to Theodahad, and declared him deposed, sending him into exile in Anatolia. There were protests at this summary treatment and the emperor ordered him to be returned to Rome to stand trial. By this time Vigilius was pope, foisted on the city by Belisarius, and he had his predecessor again despatched into exile, this time to an island just off the coast of Italy, where he was required to sign a document agreeing to abdicate. Within a month of doing so he was dead – of starvation, according to those hostile to the new pope.

This was hardly an auspicious beginning to Vigilius's pontificate, but for a time all seemed to go well, perhaps because Justinian's army was in control of the city. The pope got on with standard papal tasks – confirming the bishop of Arles as papal vicar in Gaul, promoting the bishop of Braga to a similar position in Spain, and repairing churches in Rome damaged by the siege. He was interested, too, in liturgical matters, and his letter to Bishop Profuturus in Braga contained the text of several masses. In addition, his brother Reparatus was promoted to the rank of prefect of the city.

VIGILIUS, JUSTINIAN AND THE THREE CHAPTERS

Towards the end of 544, however, things began to go wrong, and once again it was the Byzantine emperor's search for unity of faith within his dominions that precipitated the problem. As has been several times remarked, there were many Monophysites in the empire who were hostile to the Chalcedonian formula. Justinian could not go back on the Council of Chalcedon, so instead he decided to publish an edict condemning three theologians – the so-called 'Three Chapters' – whose writings were supportive of the idea that there are two natures in Christ. He wanted all patriarchs, Vigilius included, to sign the edict to show that they agreed with it. These theologians had, however, not been regarded as heretical by the Council of Chalcedon, so an attack on them looked to many like an attack on the council itself. Some of the Eastern bishops were prepared to sign, but only if the pope did so. The pope resisted. To ensure his adherence, on 25 November 545 Justinian had him arrested while he was at Mass in the church of St Cecilia in Trastevere. He was taken first to Sicily, where he spent a year, then to Constantinople.

Vigilius arrived in the imperial capital in January 547. The pope had two problems. First, whether Justinian's edict condemning the Three Chapters was contrary to the Council of Chalcedon, and second, how was he going to restrain the emperor from interfering in theological matters which were the province of churchmen. On the first, Vigilius gave his decision in April 548, though what he said is known only through the passages which Justinian chose later to quote. He accepted that the Three Chapters were to be condemned. On the second, he apparently won Justinian's agreement not to interfere again in theological issues.

Unfortunately for Vigilius, events refused to go his way. There was widespread shock in the West at the news that the pope was backing Justinian's edict and, at a synod in 550, the pope was excommunicated by the North African bishops. Even in Rome there was unease, and Vigilius had to excommunicate two of his deacons. Then Justinian again interfered, despite earlier undertakings, and in July 551 issued a new edict condemning the Three Chapters. This time Vigilius drew up a decree of excommunication against all those who signed up to Justinian's latest proclamation. He then abandoned the palace where he had been housed, and sought refuge in a church. The emperor sent troops after him, but in the fracas an altar collapsed, and the crowd turned on the soldiers, who fled. The pope went back to his palace, but after a short time escaped again, this time through a window, and in a symbolic gesture crossed over the Bosphorus and sought sanctuary in the church where the Council of Chalcedon had met. There he formally issued a decree of excommunication in which particular mention was made of Askidas, bishop of Caesarea, who was Justinian's closest theological advisor. He also produced an encyclical letter, in which he recounted all that had happened to him.

> The pope ... escaped again, this time through a window, and in a symbolic gesture crossed over the Bosphorus ...

By the summer of 552 Vigilius had reached some sort of accommodation with the emperor. In effect, Justinian gave way. The pope did not rescind the excommunications, and won an annulment of the emperor's 551 edict on the Three Chapters. Vigilius also got an apology of sorts for the attacks on his person, and felt it safe to return to the capital. At the beginning of the following year the new patriarch of Constantinople, Eustachius, proposed a council. Vigilius at first was wholly in favour, but when it opened in the city on 4 May 553 he refused to attend, saying he had not had time enough to prepare, and that there was an inadequate representation of Western bishops: only a handful of North Africans were there, hand-picked by Justinian because they, unlike the majority of their colleagues, supported the condemnation of the Three Chapters.

POPE VIGILIUS IS HUMILIATED

When Vigilius eventually issued his statement it was a carefully worked document. It condemned the Three Chapters for their content, but refused to condemn the authors because, when they had written what was now to be rejected, they would not have known of the conclusions of the Council of Chalcedon. This proved insufficient for Justinian who had Vigilius's document brusquely dismissed by the council, and the pope effectively excommunicated. He was placed once more under house arrest while his entourage was gaoled or exiled. By the end of the year the lonely 70-year-old pontiff capitulated. In February 554 he accepted Justinian's edict, and was received back into communion with the new patriarch Eutychius.

Despite all the humiliation he had undergone at the hands of the emperor, Vigilius chose to stay on in the imperial capital. He remained there a year more, negotiating with Justinian for privileges for the church in Italy, and for orderly government of the country, which was once more under imperial control. He set out to return, but never arrived. He died in Syracuse on his way back. His body was placed in a lead coffin and transported to Rome where Pelagius, who had been the late pope's chief advisor in Constantinople and succeeded him as bishop of Rome, refused him burial in St Peter's.

GREGORY I

 etween the death of Vigilius in exile in 555, and the election of Gregory, one of the greatest of all popes (he is one of only two called 'the Great', the other being Leo I) in 590, the political situation in Italy had undergone another dramatic shift. Lack of adequate leadership in the imperial administration had so weakened Constantinople's hold on the peninsula that it had fallen under the control of a new barbarian force, the Lombards.

During the sixth century, imperial and barbarian armies were constantly at war. The city of Rome was captured five times, and when the Ostrogoth king Totila captured it in 546 it was said that only 500 inhabitants remained within its walls – and even these Totila drove out, leaving it entirely empty for 40 days. When Totila was defeated and killed at the Battle of Taginae in July 552, allied with the imperial forces which overcame him and slaughtered the Gothic army were Lombard mercenaries.

THE LOMBARD INVASION OF ITALY

In 568 the Lombards were back, crossing the Alps under their king Alboin, and conquering all before them. They were a Germanic tribe, originally from the region which is now Denmark. They were still largely pagan, and remained so until the eighth century. If some of them were Christian at all, their version of the faith was Arian rather than Catholic. Paul the Deacon, a monk of the monastery of Monte Cassino south of Rome, who died, aged 80 or thereabouts, at the very end of the eighth century and was himself of Lombard descent, wrote a history of the tribe. He called them – as they were known in Latin and indeed in early English – the 'Langobards', and left a vivid description of the appearance of their warriors:

They shaved the neck, and left it bare up to the back of the head, having their

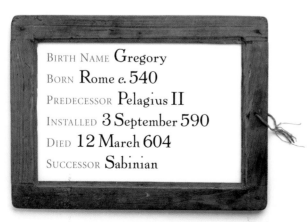

BIRTH NAME **Gregory**
BORN **Rome** *c.* **540**
PREDECESSOR **Pelagius II**
INSTALLED **3 September 590**
DIED **12 March 604**
SUCCESSOR **Sabinian**

hair hanging down on the face as far as the mouth and parting it on either side by a part in the forehead. Their garments were loose and mostly linen, such as the Anglo-Saxons are wont to wear, ornamented with broad borders woven in various colours. Their shoes, indeed, were open almost up to the tip of the great toe, and were held on by shoe latchets interlacing alternately.

After driving out the Byzantines, save for an enclave at Ravenna, in the northeast, where the exarch, or imperial governor, had his residence, they settled in Italy with their capital at Pavia.

GREGORY'S EARLY CAREER

It was in this world that Gregory grew up. His family was extremely wealthy and he was well educated with the legal training that was customary for his class in Roman society. The family was devout: it had already produced two popes, Felix III (483–92) and Agapitus I (535–6), and two of his father's sisters were nuns. After serving as prefect of the city of Rome between 572 and 574, Gregory himself decided to enter the religious life. The family home was on the Caelian Hill, and he turned it into a monastery dedicated to St Andrew. In addition he founded six further monasteries on the family's estates in Sicily.

Gregory the Great depicted on an ivory plate with his scribes. An enormously influential pope, Gregory wrote a treatise called 'Pastoral Care', an English version of which was produced by King Alfred of Wessex.

Gregory said afterwards that his years as a monk were the happiest of his life, which may be true, but it was something that holy men commonly claimed. But they did not last long. Around 578 he was summoned from his monastery to be ordained deacon by Pope Benedict I. He was too significant a person in Roman society to be allowed to spend his years in retirement. Late in 579 he was sent to Constantinople as apocrisarius. He carried a letter from Pope Pelagius II to the emperor, begging him to send troops to defend Italy: 'May God bid the Emperor to come to our aid with all speed before the army of that impious nation the Lombards shall have seized the lands that still form part of the Empire.'

For six years Gregory lived in the imperial capital without, it seems, learning the language: it was a period when knowledge of Greek was in decline in the West in general, and as pope Gregory complained that he could not find Greek translators. It seems difficult to imagine he learned nothing of the language, because he engaged in theological dispute with the patriarch, a debate so intense that both the patriarch and Gregory fell ill – and when the

'May God bid the Emperor to come to our aid with all speed'

emperor declared himself in favour of Gregory's view, the patriarch died. But if he learned little or no Greek, he learned a great deal about the Eastern Church.

This was important. One of the questions which still divided the church in Italy was the old issue of the Three Chapters, the northern Italian bishops having broken off from the papacy after Vigilius approved the emperor Justinian's decree (see page 41). The northerners were still in schism, and Pope Pelagius turned to Gregory to ask for his advice. Their combined efforts were, however, fruitless. Istria, as the region was called, remained divided from Rome.

Gregory's ordination as bishop of Rome

In November 589 the River Tiber burst its banks and flooded the city, giving rise to an outbreak of plague. Pope Pelagius was one of its early victims and Gregory was immediately elected in his place. He resisted the office and wrote to the emperor Maurice asking him to reject the appointment. Meanwhile he took charge of the plague-ridden city, providing food and organizing penitential processions to pray for an end to the pestilence. Maurice did not, as Gregory wished, declare Gregory unsuitable, and he was duly ordained bishop of Rome, becoming one of the most significant popes of the Middle Ages.

Not that one would guess that from the account of his life as it is written in *The Book of the Popes*. The first full life of Gregory was written not in Rome but by a monk living at Whitby in northeast England. In England he was revered as the man who in 596 sent the monk Augustine, albeit a reluctant missionary, from his monastery of St Andrew to convert the English (see box, page 45). Augustine's mission was aided by the fact that the king of Kent, Ethelbert, had married the daughter of the king of Paris, and she was a Christian. Ethelbert was baptized at Canterbury at Pentecost 597. In 601, when Mellitus and Paulinus, who became respectively the bishops of London and of York, were sent to assist Augustine, the monk received the pallium as archbishop of the English, with his seat at Canterbury.

In Rome itself Gregory's reputation suffered because he was a monk, indeed he was the very first monk to become bishop of the city. He lived in the Lateran with a community of monks who had fled from their monastery at Monte Cassino after it had been besieged and captured by the Lombards. He used monks in his administration, and put them in charge of the *tituli*, the parish churches of the city. This policy was bitterly resented by the ordinary clergy of Rome, and the conflict between monks and diocesan priests regularly re-emerged in papal elections.

The saviour of Rome and its citizens

But Rome owed him a great deal. He was the effective governor of the city in the absence of the imperial exarch. He readily accepted that he was subject to the emperor, and did not excommunicate the bishops of Istria over the ongoing problem of the Three Chapters because, had he done so, Emperor Maurice believed, they might have been driven into the arms of the Lombards. But as soon as Gregory learned of Maurice's death, murdered by a usurper in 602, he wrote to the exarch in Ravenna asking him to force the Istrian bishops into obedience to Rome.

The new emperor, the usurper Phocas, and his representative in Ravenna could not, however, either feed or defend the city of Rome. Pope Gregory did both. He brought in corn supplies, and improved the running of the estates where the food was grown. At his accession, he complained, he was faced with Lombards outside the city and rebellious troops within its walls. He paid the soldiers out of the papal treasury, and improved the structure of military command so efficiently that the Lombard armies were forced to retreat. There was, inevitably, a Lombard counter-attack. When King Aigulf marched on Rome in 595, Gregory negotiated a truce – or rather, bought him off, which upset the emperor. Relations between the pope and the imperial authorities deteriorated, but Gregory did all that he could to bring peace to Italy and to reinforce the Catholic version of Christianity: he plotted for the conversion of the Lombards from their Arian faith.

In all this Gregory was stepping into the vacuum left by the Byzantines. But he was also very much a bishop. He wrote a treatise on the topic, *Pastoral Care*, which was translated into Greek in his own lifetime, and an English version was later produced by King Alfred the Great. Gregory was as anxious as his predecessors had been to maintain the rights of the papal office, and insisted that papal jurisdiction extended to the Eastern Church as well as to the Western – hence he objected to the title of ecumenical patriarch assumed by the bishop of Constantinople, which seemed to Western eyes to undermine the papacy, though in the East it did not have the same connotations. But when Gregory himself assumed a new title, it was 'Servant of the servants of God', an expression of unfeigned humility. This humility extended to the emperor. When Maurice issued a decree limiting the right to enter a monastery or take up an office in the church, Gregory said he would disseminate the ordinance because it was the emperor's will that he do so – but added that he had also made it clear to those to whom he sent it that the emperor's decree was not in accordance with the will of God.

A TRADITIONAL POPE

In the more usual papal tasks Gregory did not depart from tradition. He had a great interest in liturgy, and especially in singing, and although 'Gregorian chant' appears not to have developed until after the sixth century, he seems to have established at least one singing school. He asserted papal authority over those lands that had traditionally fallen within Rome's jurisdiction. He again bolstered the See of Arles as the metropolitan see for Gaul; he tried to exercise influence in North Africa; he was in regular correspondence with Brunhild, the formidable queen of the Franks, and with many of the Frankish bishops; he welcomed the conversion from Arianism of

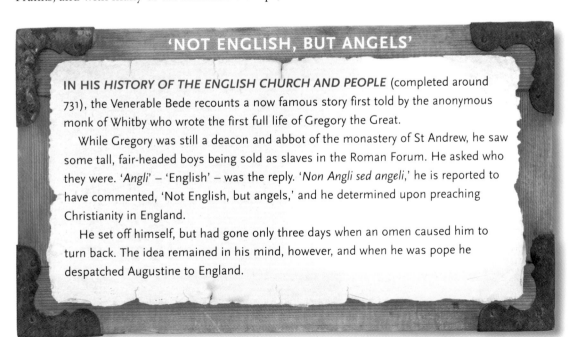

'NOT ENGLISH, BUT ANGELS'

IN HIS *HISTORY OF THE ENGLISH CHURCH AND PEOPLE* (completed around 731), the Venerable Bede recounts a now famous story first told by the anonymous monk of Whitby who wrote the first full life of Gregory the Great.

While Gregory was still a deacon and abbot of the monastery of St Andrew, he saw some tall, fair-headed boys being sold as slaves in the Roman Forum. He asked who they were. '*Angli*' – 'English' – was the reply. '*Non Angli sed angeli*,' he is reported to have commented, 'Not English, but angels,' and he determined upon preaching Christianity in England.

He set off himself, but had gone only three days when an omen caused him to turn back. The idea remained in his mind, however, and when he was pope he despatched Augustine to England.

the Visigoth king Reccared in Spain, where Leander, who had been a friend during his time in Constantinople, was bishop of Sevilla. He did not, however, congratulate Reccared until 599, more than a decade after his conversion, when Reccared and Maurice were reconciled – further evidence of his acceptance of the sovereignty of the emperor. Indeed, whenever he was dealing with bishops he was always careful to maintain good relations with the local monarch.

And in all this Gregory still found time to write. His *Pastoral Care* has already been mentioned, but there were further scriptural commentaries, books of homilies and the *Dialogues*, where he recounts the life of one of the founders of Christian monasticism, the great St Benedict of Nursia – Gregory's account is the only source – and the deeds of other Italian saints. These works are not greatly original – Gregory was not at all a speculative theologian – but they remained enormously influential throughout the Middle Ages. His undoubted genius was not as a thinker, but as an administrator of outstanding ability. He was, at the end of the sixth and the beginning of the seventh century, just what the church needed. When he was finally laid to rest in St Peter's his tomb proclaimed him 'Consul of God'.

HONORIUS I

regory the Great's immediate successors were troubled by famine, plague, rebellion, the Lombards, the emperor and such like in much the same way as Gregory himself – though Boniface IV (608–15) faced the additional hazard of an earthquake. They were concerned, too, with the progress of Gregory's mission to England, and they inherited the internal strife which he had unwittingly created between monks and diocesan clergy. They were, in a very real sense, Gregory's heirs. The last of their line was Pope Honorius, who was installed in 625, and whose epitaph – 'he followed in the footsteps of Gregory' – records his debt to his illustrious predecessor.

The similarities between Honorius and Gregory are striking. Like Gregory, Honorius turned his family home near the Lateran into a monastery – and he dedicated it, as had Gregory, to St Andrew, though he added St Bartholomew as well. His family, from the Campania, was extremely wealthy, and his father, Petronius, had been consul, though exactly what that meant by this time is unclear. As pope he employed monks in the more important offices, his closest collaborator being Abbot John Symponus.

One of the first tasks for a newly elected

BIRTH NAME Honorius
BORN Campania, date unknown
PREDECESSOR Boniface V
INSTALLED 27 October 625
DIED 12 October 638
SUCCESSOR Severinus

CONDEMNATION OF MONOTHELITISM

AT THE THIRD COUNCIL OF CONSTANTINOPLE IN SEPTEMBER 681, the council fathers confirmed the decision of the 680 Roman synod:

'This same holy and universal synod, here present, faithfully accepts and welcomes with open hand the report of Agatho, most holy and most blessed pope of elder Rome, that came to our most reverend and most faithful Emperor Constantine [IV], which rejected by name those who proclaimed and taught, as has been already explained, one will and one principle of action in the incarnate Christ our true God; and likewise it approves as well the synodal report to his God-taught serenity [i.e. Constantine], from the synod of 125 bishops dear to God meeting under the same most holy Pope, as according with the holy synod at Chalcedon and with the Tome of the all-holy and most blessed Leo, pope of the same elder Rome.'

bishop of Rome was to solicit confirmation of his election from the emperor. In Honorius's case it was granted immediately because the exarch, the imperial representative, happened to be in Rome at the time. It fell to the exarch to confirm Honorius's election because the emperor Heraclius himself was regularly away battling the Persians in an effort to recover former Byzantine-held territory. In this Heraclius had been fairly successful, but his success brought about yet another major theological crisis between East and West, one that led to Pope Honorius being accused of heresy.

THE COMPROMISE OF MONOENERGISM

As Heraclius's armies penetrated Persia and Armenia they discovered the undisguised hostility, already obvious in Egypt, to the formula devised in 451 at the Council of Chalcedon (namely that Christ was one person with two natures – one human, the other divine). As a result of a conference held in 624, there emerged a compromise position which came to be known as Monoenergism, or 'one energy'. According to this proposal, intended to reconcile the Monophysites, Christ would be understood to have two natures, as the Chalcedonian definition required, but only one 'energy', or mode of activity. This was readily accepted by Patriarch Sergius of Constantinople, and especially by Cyrus, patriarch of Alexandria. An Armenian church synod embraced the teaching in 633. But then it was rejected by Sophronius of Jerusalem. Sergius therefore wrote to the pope to solicit his views.

Honorius was not, however, theologian enough to cope with the subtleties. He had in any case little time for theologians whom, he said, 'croak like frogs'. He wanted a simple explanation for the simple faithful. In his response to the patriarch Honorius declared that Christ had one will. Monothelitism ('one will') then came to replace Monoenergism as the preferred doctrine of the imperial court in its eagerness to reconcile the anti-Chalcedonian factions, and Heraclius in 638, after Honorius's death, incorporated it in a decree called the 'Ecthesis' which forbade further debate about there being one or two energies in Christ, insisting that there was only one will. But the notion that there was only one will clearly

A mosaic portrait of Pope Honorius I. He was an active builder of churches as is shown here.

subordinated the human to the divine nature in Christ – which is why some in the East greeted the doctrine enthusiastically. It was rejected as heretical in the West, and by many others. This made Pope Honorius a heresiarch – the inventor of a heresy. He was condemned as such at a synod of Rome in 680, whose decisions were confirmed at the Council of Constantinople the following year (see box, page 47).

A PRACTICAL POPE

As pope, Honorius – a practical man – had got on with the business of governing the Church of Rome in the manner of Gregory the Great. Like Gregory, he was respectful of kingly authority. He came to power during a period of civil war among the Lombards. He backed the pro-imperial King Adoald, a Catholic, but when the ineffectual Adoald was overthrown, he established friendly relations with his successor Arioald, an Arian with a Catholic wife (whom the king locked up in a monastery). As his predecessors had been, Honorius was concerned to end the schism among the northern Italian bishops which had arisen out of the Three Chapters controversy. The See of Grado had been occupied by a schismatic bishop, Fortunatus, but to win favour Honorius took an unusual step. He not only sent one of his own Roman sub-deacons there, but also provided it with treasure to make up what Fortunatus had taken with him on his departure.

As pope, Honorius was an active builder of churches and a renovator of others, including St Peter's, whose doors he had covered with silver, and of the Lateran Basilica, whose roof he repaired with tiles taken from the Pantheon – though only after getting Heraclius's permission to do so. To symbolize the ties with the emperor, Honorius had a church built in Rome in honour of St Apollinaris, the patron saint of Ravenna, where the imperial exarch in Italy had his residence. In a further gesture of concord, he decreed that a weekly litany in honour of Saints Peter and Apollinaris was to be sung there. Just as Gregory had done, Honorius took care of the payment of imperial troops, and managed the finances of the city. He repaired the aqueducts, saw that the supply of corn to feed the city was kept up and gave advice to other government officials.

HELP FOR ENGLAND'S CHRISTIANS

Honorius also continued Gregory the Great's interest in England. When King Edwin of Northumbria converted to Christianity, he wrote him a letter of congratulations. He despatched Birinus from Rome to preach to the West Saxons and sent the pallium to the two archbishops of Canterbury and York, instructing that, when one of them should die, the other would have the right to nominate his successor. And he did something which was to have long-lasting consequences: he granted to the monastery of Bobbio, northeast of Genoa and founded in 612 by the Irish monk Columbanus, the right to be exempt from the jurisdiction of every bishop except the pope.

After all the travails that the city of Rome had undergone, Honorius wanted to bring back hope for the future. When he died, and was buried in St Peter's, his epitaph described him as '*Dux plebis*' – 'Leader of the ordinary people'.

> When he died, and was buried in St Peter's, his epitaph said '*Dux plebis*' – 'Leader of the ordinary people'.

MARTIN I

 he end of the Monothelite controversy has been recounted in the life of Pope Honorius, but before it could be settled to the satisfaction of Rome, despite Honorius's own dubious orthodoxy, it claimed the life of Martin, the last Roman pontiff to be hailed as a martyr.

The emperor Heraclius died on 11 February 641. Before his death he repudiated the Ecthesis (see page 47), which had caused so many problems. He had also lost all the territory he had won back from the Persians to a new enemy, who were adherents to a new faith – Islam. Islamic warriors had first ridden out of Arabia in 630 and at the Battle of Yarmuk in 636 the Arabs had inflicted a crushing defeat on a much larger Byzantine army. Syria and Palestine fell to the invaders, and, by the time of Heraclius's death, the army of Islam had almost conquered Egypt as well. Rome was flooded with refugees from the Christian East, one of whom, Theodore, who came from Jerusalem and whose father had been a bishop, was elected pope in 642.

It is highly likely that Theodore I had been chosen because he was Greek-speaking, and fully aware of the issues surrounding the Monothelite debate. Immediately after his election he wrote to the 12-year-old Emperor Constans II demanding to know why the Ecthesis had not been formally repudiated, and he sent Martin, then his deacon, to Constantinople as his apocrisarius.

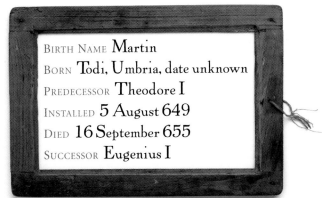

BIRTH NAME **Martin**
BORN **Todi, Umbria, date unknown**
PREDECESSOR **Theodore I**
INSTALLED **5 August 649**
DIED **16 September 655**
SUCCESSOR **Eugenius I**

Martin was kept under house arrest and frequently denied proper nourishment.

Advised by Paul, the patriarch of Constantinople, Constans decided to abandon the Ecthesis as it had failed to deliver the unity in faith that had been hoped for. He produced another edict, known as the Typos, which, as Theodore had required, abrogated the Ecthesis, but still managed to anger both sides in the controversy by simply banning all discussion of the issue of whether Christ had one or two wills. Theodore died before he could respond to the new situation, and Martin was chosen in his place.

THE CONSECRATION OF MARTIN

Almost two months elapsed between the death of Theodore and the consecration of Martin as bishop of Rome. Such a delay is usually ascribed to the need to receive confirmation from the emperor of the appointment, but that was not the case for Martin. The ceremony raising the former deacon to episcopal rank took place without Constans's permission having been received. It was a clear act of defiance. Martin, from his years as apocrisarius in Constantinople, knew the personalities involved very well. He also understood the theological issues at stake – presumably the reason for his election. He was backed not just by the Roman clergy, but also by the abbot Maximus. Maximus had worked as secretary to Heraclius, then had abandoned this role for the monastic life in Jerusalem, where he had been close to Bishop Sophronius, one of the most vocal and informed opponents of the Ecthesis. Sophronius had died during the Arab siege of Jerusalem, and Maximus was chosen as his successor, but after the capture of the city he fled first to North Africa, and then to Rome.

Though apparently old and certainly ill, Martin acted with considerable energy. As there was no bishop in Jerusalem, he appointed Bishop John of Philadelphia, a man of unimpeachable orthodoxy as far as Monothelitism was concerned, to serve as apostolic vicar, or representative. Martin then called a council in Rome. It began to meet on 5 October 649, and closed on 31 October. It was attended by 105 bishops of the Western Church, including strong representation from northern Italy. The most significant contribution, however, was made by Greek-speaking

A LETTER FROM AN EXILED POPE

EXTRACT FROM A LETTER SENT BY THE EXILED POPE MARTIN I TO THE CLERGY AND PEOPLE OF ROME:

'I am surprised by the indifference and hard-heartedness of my former associates. They have so forgotten me that they not even want to know whether I am alive . . . What fear has seized all these men that it hinders them from fulfilling the commands of God to relieve the distressed? Have I appeared such an enemy to the whole Church, and an adversary to them? However, I pray by the intercession of St Peter they will be preserved steadfast and immovable in the orthodox faith . . . I hope that God in his mercy will not prolong my life.'

exiles, who drew up a written record of
the theological issues which was much
welcomed. When the conclusions were
agreed they were circulated throughout the
church, and a copy was sent to Constans.
The Ecthesis was condemned, and so was
the Typos. Several patriarchs were named,
including Paul, as having supported these
heretical documents, but there was,
diplomatically, no mention of the emperor.

AN EMPEROR ENRAGED

Nonetheless the emperor reacted with fury.
Not only had the pope taken up office
without imperial consent, he had
proceeded to hold a council which rejected
what Constans had decreed. He therefore
sent his chamberlain, Olympias, to Italy, in
the office of exarch, with instructions to
arrest Martin and to force the bishops to
accept the Typos. But on his arrival,
Olympias found that Martin had a very
substantial following, and his arrest was
therefore out of the question. His
alternative strategy was to have the pope
assassinated while at mass, but this likewise
failed. At this point it seems that Olympias
told Martin of Constans's instructions,
made his peace with him, then marched
off south to repel an Arab attack on Sicily.
While in the south he decided that he
would proclaim himself emperor – it was

*A 12th-century manuscript portrayal of Pope Martin I issuing
a papal bull. He fell out with the Emperor Constans and was
forced to go to Constantinople where he was tried and exiled.*

afterwards claimed, as one of the charges against Martin, that the pope had connived in the
plot. Nothing came of the rebellion, however, because Olympias died in an epidemic.

Constans was not ready to give up. He sent another chamberlain, and reinstated a former
exarch. They arrived in Rome from Ravenna with an army in mid-June 653, and on 17 June
seized the pope in the Lateran Basilica, where he had taken refuge. To avoid a violent struggle
the pope agreed to go to Constantinople.

MARTIN'S TRIALS

The pope arrived in the imperial capital on 17 September 653, after an horrendous journey by
sea during which he was extremely sick and was generally very badly treated. The ill-treatment
continued in Constantinople, Martin being kept under house arrest and frequently denied
proper nourishment. So incapacitated was he that, when his trial eventually opened on 19
December, he had to be carried on a litter. There were two charges against him: that he had made

himself pope without imperial permission (so he was not in fact pope at all); and that he had conspired with Olympias against Constans. He was not allowed to bring up the main issue, the status of the Typos. Inevitably the pope was found guilty of treason for having lent his support to Olympias's rebellion, and condemned to death. The death penalty was commuted to exile, however, at the request of the patriarch of Constantinople, and he was sent to Cherson (now Sevastopol) in the Crimea in March 654, after spending three more months in prison in Constantinople.

He died there, some 18 months later, from cold and starvation, and, to his great distress, completely neglected by the clergy and people of Rome (see page 50), who elected a successor, Eugenius I, while Martin was still alive.

ZACHARIAS

Hitherto in the history of the papacy there had been occasional popes of Greek origin, hailing for the most part from Sicily or, like Zacharias, from Calabria, which were still Greek in language and culture, and where the imperial writ continued to hold sway. Zacharias was the last in this line. He had been a deacon under his predecessor, Pope Gregory III, and inherited his problems when he was elected pope in 741. For Zacharias these were solely political, whereas for his predecessor they had been a mix of politics and religion.

The political issues centred on the attempts by the Byzantine emperor Leo the Isaurian (or the Syrian) to reorganize the administration of his domains, and, more particularly, to raise taxation. The increased burden of taxation led to riots in Rome, and although Pope Zacharias was very anxious to maintain good relations with Constantinople, he sympathized with the resistance to imperial tax demands. Moreover, he did not sympathize at all with another of the emperor's policies, that of iconoclasm (see box, page 54). As a punishment for Zacharias's apparently siding with factions that were hostile to Constantinople, Emperor Leo ordered the seizure of papal lands in Calabria and Sicily, part of the papal patrimony which helped to feed the people of Rome.

RELATIONS WITH CONSTANTINE

Though the iconoclast controversy dragged on for well over a century, souring relations between Rome and the imperial capital, rather oddly it was not a major factor in what is reported of the relations between Pope Zacharias and the emperor.

As a matter of course Zacharias sent letters to the patriarch of Constantinople announcing his appointment. He made clear

BIRTH NAME **Zacharias**
BORN **Calabria, date unknown**
PREDECESSOR **Gregory III**
INSTALLED **10 December 741**
DIED **22/23 March 752**
SUCCESSOR **Stephen II**

Pope Zacharias meeting Ratchis, king of the Lombards. The pope allied himself with the Lombards to bring peace to Italy.

his opposition to iconoclasm to the new emperor, Constantine V, though when the pope's envoys arrived in the capital they found a usurper on the throne, a fact which they, and the pope, treated pragmatically. Constantine V himself, once restored, seems to have borne the pope no ill-will, either for his opposition to iconoclasm, or because he had implicitly recognized the usurper. Not only that, but he made up for the loss of the papal territories in the south of Italy by endowing the church with two estates which lay to the north of Rome. The emperor needed the pope's support, because the city of Ravenna, home to the imperial representative in Italy, the exarch, was under increasing threat from the Lombards.

Zacharias's policy towards the king of the Lombards, Liutprand, differed sharply from that of Pope Gregory III (731–41). Gregory had allied himself with the dukes of Spoleto and Benevento, both of them enemies of Liutprand. Zacharias, however, reversed this alliance, even to the extent of committing the army of Rome to aid Liutprand in his attack on Spoleto. The pope then decided to meet the king in person, and in August 742 journeyed to Terni to do so. The two got along extremely well, the king remarking afterwards that he had never enjoyed a dinner as much as the one which he had shared with Zacharias. The treaty that they concluded, to last, they agreed, for 20 years, included handing back to the duchy of Rome four towns which the Lombards had held for 30 years, and the freeing of all prisoners.

> The king said afterwards that he had never enjoyed a dinner as much as that which he had shared with Zacharias.

ICONOCLASM

THE ICONOCLAST CONTROVERSY centred on the propriety or otherwise of venerating images (icons). Those who opposed such veneration were called iconoclasts, those who favoured it were known as iconodules. The emperor Leo III the Isaurian (717–41), in an effort to bring religious unity to the empire, was eager to reconcile not just Monophysites, who played down the human nature of Christ, but also Muslims and, especially, Jews, both of whom were opposed not just to the veneration of images, but to any images at all. In 726 Leo ordered the destruction of all religious images, much to the distress of the patriarch, who appealed to the pope and to many in the empire, especially the monastic communities. The controversy lasted from 725 until 842 in the East, and from time to time there was quite severe persecution of the iconodules, especially monks. The theology of image veneration was expressed at the Second Council of Nicea in 787, which issued three anathemas (literally an excommunication):

1 If anyone does not confess that Christ our God can be represented in his humanity, let him be anathema;

2 If anyone does not accept representation in art of evangelical scenes, let him be anathema;

3 If anyone does not salute such representations as standing for the Lord and his saints, let him be anathema.

RELATIONS WITH THE LOMBARDS

Possibly this agreement encouraged Liutprand to think he might now be free to take Ravenna. He began his campaign in 743, and the exarch, as well as the archbishop of Ravenna, once proud of their independence of Rome, appealed to the pope for help. The pope sent envoys, but they proved ineffectual, so Zacharias went himself. He travelled to Ravenna, where crowds expressed their gratitude for his presence, and then to Pavia, where he again met Liutprand. Once more the Lombard king surrendered at the pope's request the towns he had already occupied.

The king died in January 744, to be succeeded almost immediately by Ratchis, who at first committed himself to keeping the truce, but then was forced by restless nobles to launch an attack on Perugia. This was a strategically important town because it lay between Rome and Ravenna, and if held by the Lombards would cut the road between the two cities, leaving Ravenna even more exposed. Again Zacharias negotiated – and bribed – and again the Lombard king gave way. But then Ratchis became a monk at Monte Cassino, and was succeeded by his aggressive brother Aistulf, who had no scruples about breaking the treaty and seizing both Spoleto and Ravenna. It was effectively the end of imperial influence in Italy. If the pope, now the sole guardian of the Roman tradition in the peninsula, needed the support of a secular ruler, he would have to look elsewhere.

ZACHARIAS AND THE FRANKS

In October 741 the Frankish ruler Charles Martel died. He had not been king of the Franks, but had ruled in the name of a titular king as 'mayor of the palace', or chief administrator of the kingdom. He bequeathed his power to his two sons – Carloman, who entered the monastery of Monte Cassino in 747, and Pepin III. Both men were close to the English monk and missionary Boniface, and they asked him to hold a series of synods to reform the Frankish Church. It was possibly Boniface, always close to the papacy, who suggested to Pepin that he ask Zacharias whether it was appropriate that one man (Pepin, in this case) should rule as the mayor of the palace, and another hold the title of king. Zacharias said that it was not, and Pepin promptly took the title of king, being anointed in a religious ceremony by Boniface in 751. This event marked the end of the Merovingian dynasty, but it also marked – though this would not emerge until after the election of Zacharias's successor, Stephen II (III) – a new and important alliance for the papacy.

FEEDING ROME

In Rome Zacharias concerned himelf with restoring some security to the city's food supplies. He established five estates, known as *domus cultae*, organized around small churches, settled by small groups of clergy and farmed by tenants, whose produce was to feed the city. He also made efforts to return Rome to something of its former glory. The papal residence was moved back to a much improved Lateran Palace from the Palatine Palace, where it had been since the time of John VII (705–7). And he completed the decoration of Santa Maria Antiqua in the Forum, begun by the same Pope John: the mosaics there still display a portrait of Pope Zacharias.

STEPHEN II (III)

he death of Zacharias was followed swiftly on 22 or 23 March 752 by the election of the priest Stephen, about whose previous career nothing is known. He may have been the late pope's envoy to King Liutprand of the Lombards. Given Zacharias's extraordinary diplomatic achievements, this would certainly have recommended him to the clergy and people of Rome. But, already an old man, he died only a couple of days later. There had to be a second election and, confusingly, the choice fell on another Stephen, a deacon.

He styled himself Stephen II, because at that time it was the consecration as bishop that signified the beginning of a pontificate, and the previous Stephen had not been consecrated. A millennium later it became the election which marked the entry into office of a new pope. So Stephen II became in effect Stephen III, and the double accounting of Stephens became the norm – there were ten of them in all.

The new Pope Stephen came from a wealthy family who had a house on the Via Lata (Broad Street), which was the aristocratic area of the city of Rome. He had, however, been left an orphan, and with his younger brother Paul he had been brought up in the Lateran Palace. The two had become deacons under Zacharias, and he was involved in running the hospices that catered for pilgrims to the shrine of St Peter.

THE LOMBARD THREAT

By the time of Zacharias's death, the Lombard king Aistulf had taken Ravenna, home to the Byzantine envoy, the exarch. Aistulf now turned his attention to the duchy of Rome. He laid Rome under siege, the first siege of the city since the sixth century and one which brought great hardship to its inhabitants. Aistulf clearly wanted to govern the whole of the peninsula of what is now Italy, with the exception of the far south. But the papacy was not prepared to be subject to a barbarian people – the Romans still called the Lombards barbarians, even though they were now perfectly orthodox Christians who had long settled to the north of Rome – nor were the Romans prepared to pay the poll tax Aistulf demanded in return for leaving them in peace.

The emperor was also concerned. He wanted Ravenna back, and sent an emissary. The imperial ambassador went to the Lombard court accompanied by Stephen's brother, Paul, but came away empty-handed. Like Zacharias, Stephen then decided to visit the Lombard king himself, but again without success, so he made his way, as possibly he had always intended, to the kingdom of the Franks.

Stephen's dealings with Aistulf are recorded by various chroniclers in great detail.

BIRTH NAME **Stephen**
BORN **Rome, date unknown**
PREDECESSOR **Stephen II**
ELECTED **25 March 752**
DIED **26 April 757**
SUCCESSOR **Paul I**

Stephen was the first pope to cross the Alps. On 6 January 754 he met Pepin, king of the Franks, at Ponthion to beg for assistance against the threat of the Lombards. This engraving shows the pontiff and the king defeating Aistulf in battle.

While their accounts do not always coincide, it is clear that the most important event in Stephen's pontificate was this visit to Pepin, now king of the Franks.

A REQUEST FOR HELP

Stephen was the first pope to cross the Alps, and on 6 January 754 he met Pepin at Ponthion. Or rather, Pepin met him, for although accounts differ, it seems that the king of the Franks came to meet the pope and accompanied him to his quarters as if he were a groom in the papal entourage. The following day Pope Stephen, accompanied by his clergy and wearing penitential dress, begged Pepin to come to the aid of the republic of St Peter.

The king of the Franks must have been expecting the visit, and the request, but though he was moved by the pope's presence, he was not entirely ready to come to his assistance. It seems that there were many among the Frankish nobility who regarded the Lombards as their natural allies, and Aistulf, playing upon that conviction, persuaded the abbot of Monte Cassino to send the monk Carloman, Pepin's brother, to dissuade the king from crossing the Alps to defend Rome. Carloman, however, was not well received: he was arrested and confined to a monastery, where he died soon afterwards.

At Quierzy, near Laon, on 14 April 754, a document was produced in which Pepin committed himself to defending the rights of the pope to certain territories which the Lombards had seized – the document spelt them out – including the territory of the exarchate at Ravenna. Just over three months later, on 28 July 754, at the abbey of St Denis outside Paris, a grateful

The king of the Franks was unmoved. He had, he said, undertaken his campaign for love of St Peter and to gain forgiveness of his sins.

Stephen anointed Pepin and his family, thus confirming the earlier judgement of Pope Zacharias, that Pepin and his heirs were the rightful line of succession to the kingdom of the Franks.

THE 'DONATION OF PEPIN'

Pepin now acted. He sent emissaries to Aistulf, but they were ignored. He then launched, in August 754, an attack on Aistulf in which the Franks swiftly overcame the Lombards, and the first Peace of Pavia was agreed. When Pepin returned home, however, Aistulf simply ignored the provisions of the agreement. Not only that, in January 756 he put Rome, to which the pope had now returned, under siege, and laid waste to the countryside surrounding the city. Pepin took arms for a second time, and once again defeated Aistulf. By the terms of the second Peace of Pavia, in June 756, Aistulf accepted that he had to return to the pope the lands he had captured from the republic of St Peter, and not only those lands but the territory of the exarchate as well.

This agreement, which was at last implemented, is often referred to as the 'Donation of Pepin', but Pepin was giving away nothing of his own. He was forcing Aistulf to give up lands he had captured, which included territory, the exarchate, that was not part of the republic of St Peter, though the papacy had long claimed it. However, there were emissaries from the imperial court present who protested at Pepin giving away the emperor's lands. The king of the Franks was unmoved. He had, he said, undertaken his campaign for love of St Peter and to gain forgiveness of his sins. And as far as the pope was concerned, the fact that Constantine V Kopronymos had just held the iconoclast Council of Hieria without the attendance of a single patriarch, cannot have helped to win the Byzantine emperor sympathy.

Aistulf died in a hunting accident soon afterwards, in December 756, and the papacy could scarcely restrain its delight. Stephen promoted as his successor the Lombard duke of Tuscany with the comfortingly Latin name of Desiderius. In return for papal support, Desiderius handed over further territory to Rome, while two important duchies, Spoleto and Benevento, detached themselves from the Lombard kingdom and, in a somewhat undefined way, attached themselves to Rome. Pope Stephen died having laid, albeit unwittingly, the foundation of the papal states in Italy which were to survive for well over a thousand years.

LEO III

etween the death of Stephen II (III) in 757 and the election of Pope Leo III in 795, there was such confusion in Rome that the papacy threatened to fall prey to the turbulence that would plague it during the tenth century. But for the time being it was rescued by two factors, the election decree of 769, and the role of the Franks.

Stephen II (III) had been followed by his brother Paul I (757–67), but after his death Rome was invaded by Theodore, duke of Nepi, and his brothers, one of whom, Constantine, became pope despite the fact that he was still a layman. One of the late Pope Paul's officials, Christopher, fled Rome for the Lombard court and persuaded the Lombard king Desiderius to overthrow Constantine, which he promptly did. Constantine was first paraded through the streets of the city on a donkey, then sent to a monastery where his eyes were gouged out.

A QUICK ELECTION

Possibly Christopher now expected to be chosen as pope, but by the time he arrived back in the imperial city the Lombards had installed a monk named Philip at the instigation of an influential priest called Waldipert. When Christopher refused to recognize the election of Philip, the erstwhile monk simply returned to his monastery saying he had never wanted to be pope anyway, and Waldipert was assassinated. But by this time Christopher had thought better of being elected himself, and instead engineered the election of Stephen III (IV). At a synod on 12 April 769 the clergy of Rome decreed that in future only Rome's deacons and cardinal priests (see box, page 61) were to take part in the election of the bishop of the city – and this despite the fact that Stephen had been chosen by a popular gathering in the Roman Forum rather than, as had become customary, by a select few in the Lateran. The decree was followed in the elections of Hadrian I (772–95) and Pope Leo III, which were both trouble-free, though the speed with which Leo was chosen, on the very day that Hadrian died, suggests that the electors expected problems.

BIRTH NAME **Leo**
BORN **Rome, date unknown**
PREDECESSOR **Hadrian I**
INSTALLED **27 December 795**
DIED **12 June 816**
SUCCESSOR **Stephen IV (V)**

CHARLEMAGNE RESPONDS TO A PAPAL APPEAL

From Paul I onwards the popes sent news of their election to the Frankish king, to Pepin III and then, after his death in 768, to his son Charles, known more familiarly as Charlemagne or Charles the Great. Stephen III (IV) made ill-advised overtures to the Lombard king Desiderius, but was spurned. He was alarmed by the marriage between Desiderius's daughter and Charlemagne, which seemed to augur an alliance between the Franks and the Lombards that would have been dangerous to Rome. Stephen denounced the marriage, but it went ahead anyway. It did not last, however, as Charlemagne rejected his Lombard wife, thereby putting the Lombards and Franks at odds more

SCS PETRVS

SCISSIMVS DN LEOPP

DNCARVLO REGI

BEATE·PETRE·DONAS VITA·LEONI·PP·BICTO RIA·CARVLO·RECI·DONAS

St Peter gives Pope Leo III the priest's vestment, and Charlemagne the banner of Rome.

effectively than Stephen's complaints had done. When Pope Hadrian appealed to Charlemagne for protection against Desiderius's continued depredation of land belonging to the duchy of Rome, the Frankish king invaded Italy, captured Pavia in June 774, and added the title of king of the Lombards to his own. He also formally repeated the 'Donation of Pepin' (see page 58).

AN IMPERIAL SNUB

One of the recurring problems that attended the election of a new pope was the clash between the Roman nobility, who wanted one of their own in the office, and the Roman clergy. Clearly there were men of aristocratic birth among the churchmen, but Leo was not one of them. He was of humble origins and had worked his way up through the ranks of the clergy to become the cardinal priest of the church of Santa Susanna. He had also become *vestararius*, which required him to look after the papal vestments as well as the papal treasury.

Leo was, as has been remarked, elected with great speed. As was now customary, he then sent news of his appointment to the Frankish king. But he did rather more than that. He also sent him the keys and banner of the city of Rome, thereby symbolizing the subjection of the duchy of Rome to Charlemagne. He also requested that Charlemagne send an envoy to receive the oath of loyalty of the citizens of Rome. Charlemagne replied with a statement that suggested that the pope had very little to contribute apart from his prayers, which he had to undertake for the good of his monarch (see box, page 62). It sounded as if the pope was only one bishop among many in Charlemagne's realm, and regarded by him as little different in status from the rest.

This was obviously not what Leo himself thought, and he expressed what he believed to be the true position in the mosaic decoration of a *triclinium*, or formal dining hall, which he built at the Lateran. It shows Christ sending out his apostles and presenting the keys to Peter, and Peter presenting the pallium to Leo himself and a banner to Charlemagne. It is a pictorial representation of church–state relations that puts the pope very much in command.

A CONSPIRACY AGAINST THE POPE

Leo was not in command, however. On the feast of St Mark, 25 April 799, while he was taking part in a penitential procession, a group of conspirators, who numbered in their ranks high officials from the Lateran as well as one of Pope Hadrian's relatives, pulled him from his horse and carried him off to a monastery. Their intention had been to gouge out his eyes and cut out his tongue, but that did not happen. With the help of a loyal servant Leo managed to escape, and made his way to the court of Charlemagne, then at Paderborn. The conspirators had intended to show that Leo was unfit for office, charging him with both perjury and with adultery. When they failed to do this in Rome, they followed the pope to Paderborn.

> The pope then for the first and last time in history knelt down before the new emperor in an act of homage.

Charlemagne was not prepared to judge Leo, certainly not in Paderborn. And so it was that the pope and his accusers – accompanied by a Frankish escort – returned to Rome. Charlemagne followed, and was received by the pope, the clergy and people of the city on 23 November 800. He had come, he told a gathering of Franks and Roman nobles in St Peter's on 1 December, to hear the charges against Leo, but the assembly pointed out that it was well established that a pope could not be judged by any human tribunal, as had been agreed under Pope Symmachus three centuries earlier. Two days before Christmas Leo purged himself, swearing an oath in St Peter's that he was not guilty of all that had been alleged against him.

CHARLEMAGNE'S CORONATION IN ROME

Two days later, during the third mass of Christmas, Leo picked up an imperial crown and placed it on Charlemagne's head while the crowd shouted out three times 'To Charles the Pious, Augustus, crowned by God. Great and peace-loving emperor, long life and victory'. Then, for the first and last time in history, the pope knelt down before the new emperor in an act of homage. The Roman empire, which came to be called the Holy Roman Empire, was re-established in Rome itself. Maybe Leo was encouraged by the lack of an emperor in Constantinople, where Irene, mother of Constantine VI, had deposed her son, had him blinded, and was herself ruling

CARDINALS

THE ORIGIN OF THE CARDINALATE IS UNCLEAR, but certain of the Roman clergy were designated cardinals by the end of the seventh century. These were the priests who served the main parish churches of the city, the *tituli*. They also appear to have been involved with the pope in deciding major questions concerning the governance of the church at large. Towards the end of the eighth century the term began to be applied to the bishops of the subicarian sees (i.e. those around Rome). The pope was also assisted by deacons. The term 'cardinal' was not applied to this rank, it seems, until the 12th century. The ranks of cardinal bishop, priest and deacon still survive, though now all are priests, and almost all are bishops. In 1049 Pope Leo IX explained in the course of a letter to the patriarch of Constantinople that the cardinals were the hinges or pivots (the Latin for hinge being *cardo*) on which the church turned.

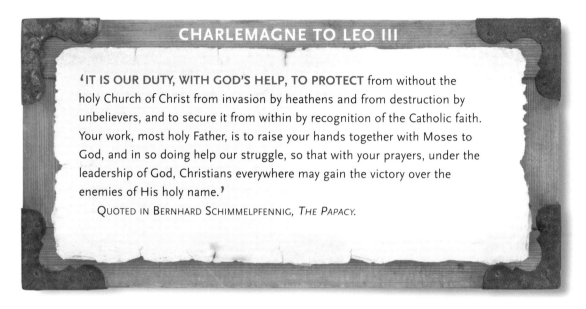

CHARLEMAGNE TO LEO III

'IT IS OUR DUTY, WITH GOD'S HELP, TO PROTECT from without the holy Church of Christ from invasion by heathens and from destruction by unbelievers, and to secure it from within by recognition of the Catholic faith. Your work, most holy Father, is to raise your hands together with Moses to God, and in so doing help our struggle, so that with your prayers, under the leadership of God, Christians everywhere may gain the victory over the enemies of His holy name.'

QUOTED IN BERNHARD SCHIMMELPFENNIG, *THE PAPACY*.

as emperor (she used the masculine title '*basileus*' rather than the femine '*basilissa*'). But Leo also needed an emperor. Traitors could be tried only by the emperor, and those who had laid impious hands on the pope were regarded as traitors. Shortly after Christmas, therefore, Charlemagne sat in judgement on the conspirators, and condemned them to death, but at the pope's behest their sentence was commuted to exile.

Charlemagne continued to involve himself in the affairs of Rome until his death in 814, not long before that of Leo himself. His most striking intervention was his request that Rome should add the so-called *filioque* clause to the Nicene Creed. In the Frankish Church, under the influence of the Visigothic Church of Spain, it was the practice to say of the Holy Spirit in the Creed that it 'proceeded from the Father and the Son' (in Latin, *filioque*). A dispute over these words led to a clash in Jerusalem between Frankish monks and Greek ones, and naturally the king of the Franks sided with the former. Theologians at his court urged the king to support the term. There was no real theological point at issue, just a custom, but when the matter was put to him in 810 the pope resisted. The Creed was a traditional formulary dating back to the fourth century, which he believed (as the Orthodox Church still believes) ought not to be altered. In Rome the Creed was said only in the baptismal liturgy, whereas in the Frankish Church it was repeated at every Sunday worship. Eventually Leo yielded, and also added the Creed to the standard form of the Roman mass.

After Charlemagne's death there was a renewed attempt to overthrow Pope Leo by members of the Roman nobility, but the plot was discovered and this time, without the intervention of any secular ruler, the pope had the plotters put to death in a field near the Lateran. Some reports claim that as many as 300 died, but this is thought to be a wild exaggeration. Nonetheless the tension in Rome between clergy and aristocracy had clearly not gone away during Leo's pontificate (an unusually long one for the time). When Leo died in 816 there was open revolt in the countryside outside the city.

LEO IV

Rome had been invaded by Goths, Ostrogoths and Huns, by Lombards and by Franks – though the last came as protectors of the papacy. Now, in the mid-ninth century, there was a new threat – the Muslim Moors of North Africa, whom the Romans called Saracens.

On 10 August 846, in the last year of the pontificate of Leo IV's predecessor, Sergius II (844–7), a message had come from Count Adalbert in Corsica that a large Saracen force of over 70 ships and some 500 horses had gathered at the mouth of the River Tiber. Two weeks later the invaders landed, and on 26 August they arrived in Rome.

DRIVING OFF THE SARACENS

The city was protected by walls, but St Peter's and the great basilica of St Paul's-Without-the-Walls, as the name of the latter implies, lay outside the safety of the city's boundary defences. The raiders took the bronze doors and the silver altar from St Peter's, among other treasures, and then laid waste to the countryside around the city before being driven away by a Lombard army under Guy of Spoleto. They fled to the coast and took to their ships, but many were lost in a storm, and the bodies of some of

BIRTH NAME **Leo**
BORN **Rome, date unknown**
PREDECESSOR **Sergius II**
INSTALLED **10 April 847**
DIED **17 July 855**
SUCCESSOR **Benedict III**

the looters – together with some of the loot – were washed up on the shore. The lesson from this was that Rome had to look to its army and to its defences. And this is exactly what Leo undertook to do as soon as he was elected in the immediate aftermath of the raid.

Leo was a Roman by birth, but his father was named Radoald, which suggests Lombard ancestry. He had been a monk at the monastery of St Martin, which stood close to St Peter's, then a subdeacon under Pope Gregory IV, and finally became cardinal priest of the church of the Four Crowned Martyrs (the *Quattro Coronati*), appointed by his predecessor Sergius II. Because of the urgency of the situation in the city, he was elected pope even before Sergius had been buried. Sergius had died on 27 January 847, but Leo waited until Easter, which fell on 10 April, to be consecrated. The Roman constitution of 824 required that a pope had to receive imperial consent – now of course from the Frankish emperor, not the Byzantine one – before proceeding to consecration. In the end, however, the ceremony went ahead without any consent being given, and in the absence of any representative of the emperor.

STRENGTHENING ROME'S DEFENCES

Leo's most pressing task was the strengthening of Rome's defences, proposals for which had already been made under Sergius. A new wall was built, still known as the Leonine Wall, extending from Castel Sant'Angelo on the River Tiber, round the back of St Peter's, and back down to the Tiber on the other side of the basilica. It was 40 feet high and had 44 towers but

To strengthen Rome's defences Pope Leo IV built the Leonine Wall. He also restored the ancient church of San Clemente in which his contemporary portrait can still be seen.

only three gates. Constructed by teams of labourers from the *domus cultae*, the papal estates around Rome, it was completed and dedicated in July 852.

Other Italian duchies were also suffering the depredations of marauding Saracens, and long before the wall was completed there was another threat to the peninsula. Early in 849 Leo organized a combined fleet under the command of the son of the duke of Naples to fight off a renewed Saracen attack. The two fleets engaged off Ostia, but when a storm interrupted the battle the Saracen ships had nowhere to run for shelter. Again many were destroyed.

The Saracens had devastated much of the coast. The town of Centumcellae was particularly at risk, and had been destroyed. Leo therefore moved its citizens to a new and more secure site which he named Leopolis. But the inhabitants were not happy there, and eventually moved back to Centumcellae (its modern name of Civitavecchia means 'the old city'). He also settled refugees from Corsica at Porto, just south of Rome, to act as a defence, and promised spiritual benefits to those who took part in the defence of Rome. But such measures would have been inadequate without the support of the emperor. At this time the emperor was Lothair, but effective power in Italy was in the hands of his son Louis II, who was co-emperor and king of Italy (he was

LEO'S DONATIONS

'IN THE CHURCH OF ST PETER the kingdom of heaven's keybearer he provided one fine silver lantern with two wicks, weighing 16 pounds. In St Martin's monastery which adjoins this church of the prince of the apostles, he provided another lantern cast in silver and with two wicks, weighing 27 1/2 pounds, and in SS John's and Paul's monastery he provided another silver lantern like the above one, weighing 22 1/2 pounds; these stand close to the lectern on Sundays and feastdays and shine with very bright light for reading the sacred lesson. This holy pope provided railings cast in silver with lattice-work at the entrance to the presbyterium and in front of the confession of his beloved St Peter the Apostle; radiant with beautiful splendour they provoke admiration in the minds of men; two of them weigh 642 pounds, the other two 630 pounds.'

E.T. RAYMOND DAVIS, *THE LIVES OF THE NINTH-CENTURY POPES*, QUOTING THE LIFE OF LEO IV FROM THE *LIBER PONTIFICALIS*.

crowned and anointed by Leo at Easter 850). At the outset of his pontificate Leo had not waited for Louis's consent before his consecration, but he made every effort to maintain good relations with the king, sometimes under difficult circumstances. One problem concerned the activities of John, archbishop of Ravenna, who was working to separate northern Italy from the domination of Rome, and was turning papal tenants off their lands. When John's brother, Duke Gregory, together with a number of Louis's agents, murdered a papal official, Leo had the imperial officials put to death.

THE ANTIQUARIAN CLERICS

> ... the Leonine Wall extended from Castel Sant'Angelo on the River Tiber, round St Peter's, and back down to the Tiber on the other side of the basilica.

There was also trouble among the clergy in the city of Rome itself. When Leo deposed the priest Anastasius from his church because he was, in Leo's view, neglecting his duties, he fled to Louis, and was later elected an antipope. But there were further issues. Anastasius was among the more learned Roman clerics, a group who were antiquarian in bent and were intent upon reviving some of the old customs and titles of ancient Rome. They also seemed interested in restoring the influence of the Byzantine emperor, something which neither Louis nor Leo was happy about. Their thinking, it seems, was that a distant emperor was preferable to one who was not only close at hand, but was in Rome for long periods and was in any event always represented in the city by his agents.

Leo himself, though respectful of both emperors, Eastern and Western, was perfectly ready to deal with them as he saw fit for the good of the church. He summoned the patriarch of Constantinople to Rome for having deposed the bishop of Syracuse in Sicily when the latter had abandoned his see because of Saracen occupation. He withstood the request of Lothair that he appoint Hincmar of Rheims an apostolic vicar, and give the pallium to the bishop of Autun. He even annulled the decisions of a synod of Frankish bishops, held in April 853 at Soissons, saying that such councils should be presided over by papal legates.

He was also concerned for the education and the spiritual life of his clergy, insisting that priests and bishops should look after their parishes and dioceses, and avoid becoming involved in political affairs. He rebuilt many churches and restored others, replacing some of the treasures that the Saracens had stolen. One of the buildings he restored was the ancient Roman church of San Clemente, where his contemporary portrait can still be seen.

NICHOLAS I

Leo IV's pontificate was followed by the brief reign of Benedict III (855–8), a holy man, but apparently competent. He managed to hold his own against Anastasius, who had fled Rome in Leo IV's time and now returned as an antipope, encouraged by the emperor Louis II. But despite the emperor's support for Anastasius, or perhaps because of it, the clergy and people of the city rejected him. Benedict was released from the prison into which Anastasius had consigned him, and Anastasius himself was locked away in a monastery throughout Benedict's pontificate. When Nicholas was elected, despite the wish of the emperor, who was present in Rome, to have Anastasius reinstated, Anastasius was released and given the post of abbot of Santa Maria in Trastevere. He was later to become librarian of the Roman Church – he is commonly referred to as Anastasius Bibliothecarius for that reason – and a central figure in the pontificate of several popes.

The rehabilitation of so controversial a figure was more a sign of Nicholas's sense of security in his own position, than an effort to reach a compromise with warring parties among the clergy of the city, and between the clergy and the emperor. Nicholas was of relatively humble origins, and had been sent as a youth to the Lateran, where he grew up in the service of the papacy. Leo IV made him a subdeacon, and he was close to Benedict III, but he was not, it would seem, a prominent figure among the Roman clergy.

A THREAT FROM THE SARACENS

Immediately after his election, the new pope wined and dined the emperor at one of the *domus cultae*, or papal estates, outside the city. There was much to talk about. The Italian peninsula was beset by minor wars and – particularly troubling to Nicholas and Louis – there was disunity in the empire as Charlemagne's heirs squabbled over his inheritance. Even more seriously, the Saracens were still a very present threat from their base at Bari. To defend Rome from attack by sea, Nicholas fortified the port of Ostia and created a garrison there.

In Rome itself he soon found he had problems of an entirely different order. In 860 the Tiber burst its banks (see box, page 68), leaving many dead and many more homeless. The pope acted energetically, setting up a hospice for the victims near the basilica of Santa Maria Maggiore. Throughout his pontificate Nicholas took

BIRTH NAME **Nicholas**

BORN **Rome, *c.* 820**

PREDECESSOR **Benedict III**

ELECTED **24 April 858**

DIED **13 November 867**

SUCCESSOR **Hadrian II**

care of the poor – the *Liber Pontificalis* mentions 'the lame, the blind and the totally disabled' – of the city, providing them with weekly food tokens.

A CONTENTIOUS DIVORCE

Disunity in the empire meant that Nicholas had to act as an arbiter in disputes. Charles the Bald of France, youngest son of the former emperor Louis the Pious, turned to him for help when his brother Louis the German invaded his territory in 858, then again when his sons rebelled in 862. But the most problematic issue was that of the divorce of Lothair II of Lorraine. The issue was dynastic. Lothair's wife Theutberga had failed to provide Lothair with a son and heir, whereas a son had been born to the king's mistress Waldrada. Lothair wanted to make his son legitimate by repudiating his wife and marrying his mistress. He claimed that his marriage to Theutberga was incestuous, and therefore invalid, a decision that was upheld by the archbishops of

In 860 the River Tiber burst its banks in Rome and the pope helped the victims with great energy. He set up a hospice near the basilica of Santa Maria Maggiore. He also took care of the poor – even providing them with weekly food tokens.

Trier and Cologne. Even papal legates at the synod of Metz were prepared to back Lothair's second marriage, as they had been bribed to do. The pope, to whom Theutberga had appealed, was having none of it. Nicholas excommunicated the archbishops, threatened the other bishops of Lorraine with the same, and annulled the decisions of the synod. The emperor Louis was Lothair's brother, and he marched in arms to Rome to force Nicholas to agree to the divorce. When Louis's supporters in the city went on the rampage, Nicholas fled for safety to St Peter's. Louis eventually gave way, telling his brother that he had to return to his first – and as far as the pope was concerned his only – wife, while the pope excommunicated Waldrada. Lothair complied with ill grace, but the problem did not go away. It reappeared in the pontificate of Nicholas's successor, the much less effective Hadrian II (867–72).

> Nicholas excommunicated the archbishops, threatened the other bishops of Lorraine with the same and annulled the decisions of the synod.

It was generally accepted in the Western Church that the pope might act as a court of appeal in marriage cases. But some of Nicholas's actions were legally less surely founded. Under Leo IV, as has been seen, John, archbishop of Ravenna, had declared himself independent of Rome, and with his brother was harrying papal tenants in northern Italy. The bishops around Ravenna complained to the pope, and after legates and letters proved ineffective, the rebellious archbishop was summoned to a

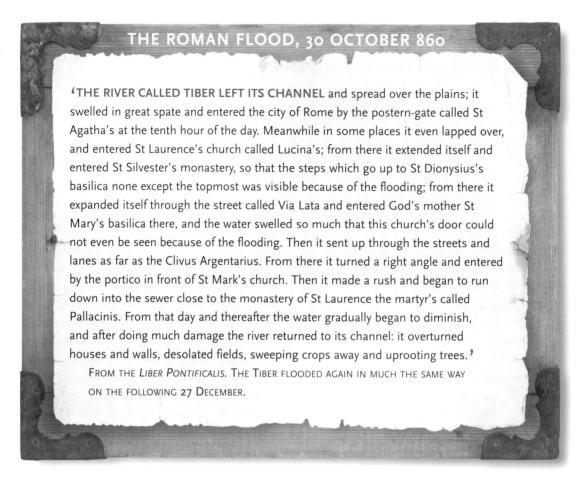

THE ROMAN FLOOD, 30 OCTOBER 860

'THE RIVER CALLED TIBER LEFT ITS CHANNEL and spread over the plains; it swelled in great spate and entered the city of Rome by the postern-gate called St Agatha's at the tenth hour of the day. Meanwhile in some places it even lapped over, and entered St Laurence's church called Lucina's; from there it extended itself and entered St Silvester's monastery, so that the steps which go up to St Dionysius's basilica none except the topmost was visible because of the flooding; from there it expanded itself through the street called Via Lata and entered God's mother St Mary's basilica there, and the water swelled so much that this church's door could not even be seen because of the flooding. Then it sent up through the streets and lanes as far as the Clivus Argentarius. From there it turned a right angle and entered by the portico in front of St Mark's church. Then it made a rush and began to run down into the sewer close to the monastery of St Laurence the martyr's called Pallacinis. From that day and thereafter the water gradually began to diminish, and after doing much damage the river returned to its channel: it overturned houses and walls, desolated fields, sweeping crops away and uprooting trees.'

FROM THE *LIBER PONTIFICALIS*. THE TIBER FLOODED AGAIN IN MUCH THE SAME WAY ON THE FOLLOWING 27 DECEMBER.

synod in 861 and excommunicated. Louis then withdrew his support from John, and the archbishop was forced to accept a humiliating climbdown at another synod in December 861.

NICHOLAS EXTENDS PAPAL POWER

An even more dramatic exercise of papal power was Nicholas's confrontation with the powerful archbishop Hincmar of Rheims, who had deprived of their offices a number of clergy who had been appointed to their posts by his predecessor. The clergy appealed to the pope, and he ordered their reinstatement against the wishes of the metropolitan archbishop. To do so Nicholas relied on a collection of church laws attributed – incorrectly – to the seventh-century St Isidore of Seville. Some of these were genuine enough canons of councils, and had indeed come from Spain, but the significant ones had been composed in France *c.* 850, and exalted the rights of diocesan bishops at the expense of their metropolitans, and of the pope over the whole Western Church.

THE GREEK AND LATIN TRADITIONS COLLIDE

Nicholas was also quite prepared to intervene in the East. When Ignatius, patriarch of Constantinople, was deposed by the Byzantine emperor Michael III, and a layman, Photius, appointed in his stead, Nicholas demanded Ignatius's reinstatement, and sent representatives to Constantinople to support him. Unfortunately they sided with the emperor, at which point the pope excommunicated his own emissaries, and called a Roman synod which also backed Ignatius. Nicholas instructed Anastasius the Librarian, who was Greek-speaking, to send a letter on his behalf, making it very clear that he believed the pope to have jurisdiction over the whole church, the East included.

Relations with Constantinople were further complicated by King Boris of Bulgaria, who, following his conversion to Christianity in 862, wanted to establish his own autonomous church. As the Bulgarians had been evangelized by Greek-speaking missionaries, he naturally turned first to Constantinople, but Photius refused his request. Boris then appealed to the pope. Nicholas sent two missionaries, one of them being Formosus, the bishop of Porto, who was to become pope in 891. Nicholas also sent a letter, describing the differences between the two separate traditions, Greek and Latin. His account was not, as one might presume, sympathetic to the Greek tradition. Photius was furious when he heard of the Roman intervention in a territory which, at least since the iconoclast controversy (see page 54), had been regarded as falling under the jurisdiction of Constantinople, and in 867 called a synod which excommunicated the pope. Nicholas responded by saying that no one could judge the See of Rome, but the matter came to an end with a palace revolution in Constantinople, and the deposition of Photius. The end, that is, as far as Nicholas was concerned, for he died only a couple of months later, but Photius was later to reoccupy the patriarchal see, and the Photian Schism helped to move the two churches towards their final rupture.

FORMOSUS

Up to this point we have been able to provide scant details of the lives of the popes prior to their election as bishops of Rome. For most of the early popes little is known beyond the name of the pope's father and his place of birth, or at least where his family originated. With Formosus it is different. A good deal is known of his career before he was chosen.

His father was called Leo, and that is about all that is known of his family background, but he was clearly highly gifted. In 863 or 864 he became bishop of Porto, which put him into the papal civil service, and was subsequently sent by Pope Nicholas I to Bulgaria, where King Boris, in dispute with the Byzantines, wanted to advance Christianity under the patronage of Rome. As a Roman missionary Formosus was a great success – too great a success, perhaps, because Boris wanted to have him made archbishop. This was impossible. Under the law of the church he was bishop of Porto, and could not become bishop, or archbishop, anywhere else: a bishop was married to his diocese until death did them part. This refusal soured relations between Bulgaria and Rome, and Formosus returned.

A ROMAN TRAGEDY
He came back to a very divided city. Pope Nicholas died in 867, and the election of his successor, Hadrian II (867–72), was highly

BIRTH NAME **Formosus**
BORN **Rome, c. 816**
PREDECESSOR **Stephen V (VI)**
ELECTED **3 October 891**
DIED **4 April 896**
SUCCESSOR **Boniface VI**

contentious. Duke Lambert of Spoleto took advantage of the disorder in the city to sack Rome with a company of Lombards and Franks. To bring peace to Rome after Lambert had withdrawn, Hadrian tried to be friendly to both factions, and brought back from exile people whom Nicholas had expelled. But in the end this caused more problems, because Nicholas's supporters thought Hadrian's policy a betrayal of his predecessor. The leader of the group opposed to Hadrian was a Bishop Arsenius, who proposed a marriage between his son and Hadrian's daughter. When Hadrian refused, she was kidnapped, raped and murdered – and her mother, Hadrian's wife, was also killed. This was the type of situation that called for the strong hand of an emperor, and Louis II duly came to Rome. But Hadrian died soon afterwards, in 872, followed by Louis three years later.

The succession to the imperial title was as problematic as Hadrian's election to the papacy had been. Charlemagne had ruled a territory that covered what is now France and Germany, but these two 'countries' were drifting apart, and it was unclear who should be the emperor to replace Louis. In 875 Pope John VIII (872–82) decided in favour of Charles the Bald of France, rather than the German Carloman (eldest son of Louis the German), who had already been selected by a gathering of nobles at Pavia. Bishop Formosus was sent to negotiate with Charles, who readily accepted the imperial title. He was crowned on Christmas Day 875, and was afterwards crowned king of Italy at Pavia.

THE EXCOMMUNICATION OF FORMOSUS

Rome was now divided, and Formosus became the leader of a faction opposed to Pope John. He was aided by a group of distinguished officials of the Lateran, the seat of the papal administration. The group – apart from Formosus himself, who had a reputation for holiness of life – were not a notably moral crowd, and they were threatened with being hauled in front of a synod to answer charges of corruption and immorality. Before this could happen the Formosans fled with as much of the papal treasure as they could manage, Formosus making his way to France. He was then deposed from his See of Porto and excommunicated.

Italy was by this time in chaos. The emperor Charles was ineffectual, and in any case was absent for much of the time. Formosan sympathizers ravaged Rome, while the Italian peninsula was still under attack from the Saracens. In the midst of all this, in 877, Charles died – it was said he was poisoned – and the pope was left without a protector. The Formosan party now turned to Carloman, whom John had rejected. Although Carloman himself had to return to Germany because of an outbreak of plague, an army sympathetic to Formosus captured the city and brought back many of those exiled by Pope John, who was now powerless. John fled to France, crowning the ineffective Louis the Stammerer as emperor at Troyes, where he was attending a council, in 878. At the same time he forged an alliance with the more vigorous Duke Boso of Provence. Formosus himself, however, had not returned to Rome. His excommunication was lifted at Troyes, but he returned to the lay state, and had to undertake not to re-enter Rome.

POPE FORMOSUS AND EMPEROR ARNULF

Pope John was followed by Pope Marinus (882–c.884), who decided to allow Formosus to return to Rome, and gave him back his bishopric. Despite his party being in the ascendant in Rome, Formosus does not seem to have been very active, though he was one of those who, in 885, consecrated the new Pope Stephen V (VI) (885–91), and then, at the death of Stephen, was himself chosen to succeed. The election seems to have been popular enough, but there was

Pope Formosus was more famous for his posthumous trial, shown in this painting, than for anything he did in his lifetime. His successor, Pope Stephen V (VI), had his body disinterred and put on trial for breaking an oath.

some violence. There was no protest at the fact that the man elected bishop of Rome was already bishop of Porto, and that the appointment was therefore illegal. Certainly Formosus did not need to be consecrated: instead he was enthroned.

He was immediately faced with huge political problems. The Formosan party had made common cause with the duchy of Spoleto, but Formosus's rival in the election was the leader of the Spoletan party in Rome, whom the pope created bishop of Cere. (This should have made him ineligible for the papacy, although of course that had not stopped Formosus himself.) Guy, duke of Spoleto, already king of Italy, had been crowned emperor by Formosus's predecessor Stephen, and now Formosus crowned Guy's son Lambert as co-emperor. But the pope felt threatened by having so powerful an ally close at hand. The pro-German party in the city wanted him to turn to Arnulf, king of Germany.

Guy died in December 894 and Arnulf took the opportunity to invade Italy. He reached Rome, where the Spoletans were led by Guy's widow Ageltrude. The redoubtable Ageltrude not only organized a sturdy defence, she also arrested Formosus and appointed an antipope, Boniface VI. The city fell to Arnulf in February 896, however, and Formosus crowned him in St Peter's. The people of Rome swore an oath to the new emperor (see box, page 72). But Arnulf's triumph, and that of Formosus, was brief. He suffered a stroke and returned to Germany, while Formosus died soon afterwards. Antipope Boniface promptly reappeared, but after only a fortnight he too died, from gout.

Though politics had dominated Formosus's pontificate, he was nonetheless busy as well on more directly religious matters. Both as a missionary in Bulgaria and then as Hadrian II's legate to Constantinople, he had acquired some knowledge of the Eastern Church. As pope he sought better relations with the patriarchate of Constantinople, but his efforts came to little. The issue that prevented a rapprochement between Rome and Constantinople was that of the

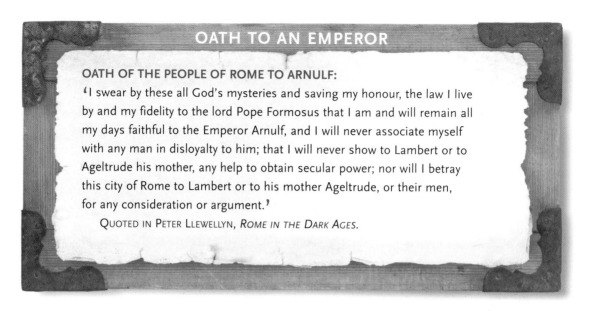

legitimacy of the orders of Patriarch Stephen, which were contested because the latter had been ordained by Photius (see page 68). Formosus suggested that while Photius's first term of office had been illegal because he had been intruded, and that therefore his ordinations were invalid, his second term was entirely legitimate. This solution did not, however, find favour with Patriarch Stephen's opponents. Formosus also involved himself in the affairs of the church in England, France and Germany.

THE 'SYNOD OF THE CADAVER'

In the story of the popes, Formosus is a good deal more famous for what happened after his death than during his life. He was succeeded by Stephen VI (VII) (896–7), who had been made bishop of Anagni by Formosus. This should, of course, have made him ineligible for the papacy, but that fact was ignored. Nonetheless Stephen appears to have been troubled by it. Early in 897 Formosus's body was disinterred, clothed in papal vestments and put on trial. Defended by a deacon, he was accused of having broken the oath he made at Troyes not to seek ecclesiastical preferment, and to stay out of Rome. Inevitably found guilty at this macabre 'synod of the cadaver', as it became known, his vestments were stripped from him, the fingers he had used in blessing were cut off, and his body was thrown into the River Tiber (though it was later recovered and given honourable burial). Most importantly from Pope Stephen's perspective, all Formosus's acts as pope were declared void – which meant that Stephen had never been licitly made bishop of Anagni, and could therefore rule as bishop of Rome with good conscience.

Not that Stephen had long to enjoy his new sense of security. Formosus's supporters rose in revolt against him, flung him in prison, or possibly exiled him to a monastery, where, in August 897, he was strangled. The papacy was falling into chaos.

> ... found guilty at the macabre 'synod of the cadaver', his vestments were stripped from him ... and his body was thrown into the River Tiber.

THE TENTH-CENTURY PAPACY

he demise of Formosus ushered in a confused and chaotic period in the history of the papacy. From his death in 896 to the election of Pope Gregory V in 996 there were 27 popes and one antipope, and two of the popes, having been deposed, were returned to power. Of the 27, no fewer than 9 met violent deaths. Hereafter the only pontiff to meet with a violent end was Pope John XXI in 1277, and that was death from an accident, not by assassination.

As has been seen, Formosus was followed by Stephen VI (VII) (896–7), who was strangled, and Stephen was followed by Romanus (897), who was deposed after four months and apparently imprisoned in a monastery. Theodore II (897) served for only 20 days, dying of natural causes, to be followed by John IX (898–900) who was pope for two years, while Benedict IV (900–3) managed three. Benedict may have been murdered, though that is not certain, but Leo V (903), who followed him, almost certainly was. Leo was imprisoned by the priest Christopher who proclaimed himself (an anti)pope. He was then put to death, along with Christopher, by Sergius III (904–11).

CONFLICT IN ROME

These bloody events took place in the context of conflict within Rome between the followers of Formosus and their opponents. Christopher had been of the Formosan party, but they had split, leaving the way for Sergius, who had first been elected in December 897, from which election he continued to date his pontificate. After being driven out of the city in January 904, Sergius was only able to return with the backing of the army of Duke Alberic I of Spoleto and the support of the nobility of Rome. And chief among the nobility was a man named Theophylact.

Theophylact is a Greek name. It is not clear what his family background was, but by the beginning of the tenth century he was not only *vestararius*, which gave him control of the papal treasury, he was also *magister militum*, or head of the city militia. Theophylact was a family man. He was married to a pious woman called Theodora, by whom he had two daughters. His elder daughter Marozia was married to Duke Alberic, but she may have been the lover of Pope Sergius, and possibly the mother of Pope John XI (931–6). Sergius himself was, it would seem, not otherwise an immoral pope, so the story may simply be a concoction of his enemies, of whom there were many.

His ecclesiastical acts appear to have been few, but he rebuilt the Lateran Basilica, which had been badly damaged by an earthquake during the Synod of the Cadaver (the people of Rome interpreted the quake as an omen demonstrating God's anger with Pope Stephen). He also added the dedication to St John to the Lateran Basilica, which is known as St John Lateran to this day.

A dispute amongst cardinals.

JOHN X – A VIGOROUS POPE

After the death of Sergius, and the two short pontificates that followed, the Theophylact faction took the remarkable step of bringing Archbishop John of Ravenna to Rome to take over the papacy. Roman gossip believed that John X (914–28), who as a deacon had been a frequent visitor to Rome as an emissary of his archbishop, had been a lover of Theodora, Marozia's younger sister, but the truth was that Rome needed a vigorous leader, and vigorous leadership was what he supplied. In 915 a papal alliance of Italian dukes, supported by the Byzantine fleet, finally defeated the Saracens at the Battle of Garigliano and drove them from the peninsula. The pope himself took part in the battle, a fact of which he was proud. His political standing was at its height when, in December 915, he crowned Berengar, the king of Italy, as emperor. Berengar died in April 924, to be succeeded in 926 by Hugh of Provence, with whom John X sought to ally himself.

But the pope was beginning to act too independently for the Theophylact family (Theophylact himself had died *c.* 920) and for the Roman nobility with whom they were linked. Moreover, he appeared to be trying to give his brother Peter power over offices which the Theophylacts themselves had controlled. In 927 Peter was killed in the Lateran, in the presence of the pope, and the following year John himself was locked up in Castel Sant'Angelo, where he was smothered to death in 929.

There followed two papacies, Leo VI (928) lasted six months, Stephen VII (VIII) (928–31) little more than two years, while Theophylact's daughter Marozia waited for her son, also called John, to be old enough to be elected as John XI. Despite his youth (he was aged only 25 at his appointment in 931), and the doubtful nature of his succession, he turned out to be not at all a bad pope. However, he shocked the Eastern Church when he gave his approval for the 16-year-old son of the Byzantine emperor Romanus to be consecrated patriarch of Constantinople, and even sent representatives to the ceremony. This may have been his mother's doing, as Marozia was trying to marry her daughter Bertha into the Byzantine royal family. Marozia herself had remarried following the death of Alberic of Spoleto. Her second husband was Guy, count of Tuscany, with whose help she regained her family's domination of the city of Rome. Guy did not long survive, however, and in 932 she determined to marry for a third time. On this occasion her choice fell on Hugh of Provence, the king of Italy.

ALBERIC II'S CONTROL OF THE PAPACY

For her son Alberic II, duke of Spoleto, this was a stepfather too far, and apparently the Roman people thought similarly: having the king of Italy on one's doorstep threatened the independence of Rome. During the wedding reception in Castel Sant'Angelo Alberic arrived in arms, and drove Hugh out of the city. He threw his mother and his half-brother Pope John into prison, where John was suffocated. Marozia, whom he eventually consigned to a nunnery, spent the rest of her days writing bitter letters to her rebellious son. But it was now Alberic II who controlled Rome and appointments to the papacy, much as his mother, and before her his grandfather, had done.

Not that he made bad choices, quite the contrary. The popes he selected for the most part stayed out of politics and got on with ecclesiastical matters: monastic reform, under the influence of the French abbey of Cluny, was high on the agenda.

> Alberic had done a great deal for the city of Rome. The Saracens had been driven away … and the countryside was at peace, enabling agriculture to flourish.

But Alberic was firm. When Stephen VIII (IX) (939–42) stepped out of line he was imprisoned and mutilated. Agapitus II (946–55), who was Stephen's successor but one, was also rather more independent, at least until the last year or so of his pontificate. By that time Alberic II was dying. Anxious to ensure that control of Rome remained with his family, he persuaded the Roman clergy and nobility, along with the pope himself, to swear that his son Octavian, who became secular ruler of the city on his father's death in 954, would be elected pope after Agapitus.

Alberic had done a great deal for the city of Rome. The Saracens had been driven away, though admittedly not by him, and the countryside was at peace, enabling agriculture to flourish. Under Alberic, who took the ancient Roman title of *Princeps*, religious life was reformed with the aid of Cluniac monks. Rome was safe, and relatively prosperous, but this prosperity was gained at a price. The city was virtually isolated, and pilgrims had ceased to travel there. It lay outside the politics of Europe.

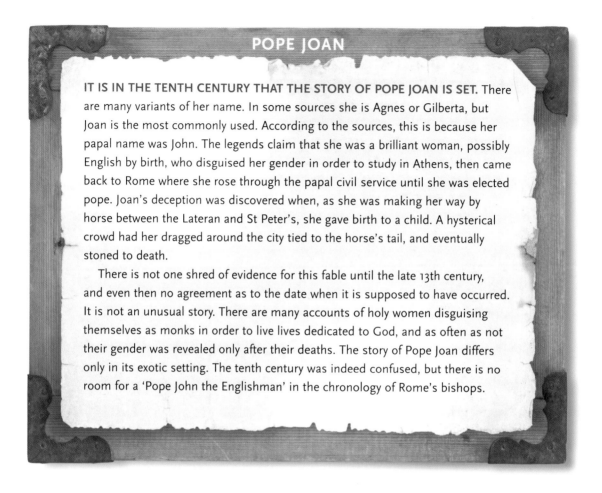

POPE JOAN

IT IS IN THE TENTH CENTURY THAT THE STORY OF POPE JOAN IS SET. There are many variants of her name. In some sources she is Agnes or Gilberta, but Joan is the most commonly used. According to the sources, this is because her papal name was John. The legends claim that she was a brilliant woman, possibly English by birth, who disguised her gender in order to study in Athens, then came back to Rome where she rose through the papal civil service until she was elected pope. Joan's deception was discovered when, as she was making her way by horse between the Lateran and St Peter's, she gave birth to a child. A hysterical crowd had her dragged around the city tied to the horse's tail, and eventually stoned to death.

There is not one shred of evidence for this fable until the late 13th century, and even then no agreement as to the date when it is supposed to have occurred. It is not an unusual story. There are many accounts of holy women disguising themselves as monks in order to live lives dedicated to God, and as often as not their gender was revealed only after their deaths. The story of Pope Joan differs only in its exotic setting. The tenth century was indeed confused, but there is no room for a 'Pope John the Englishman' in the chronology of Rome's bishops.

John XII

When Alberic's son Octavian became pope in December 955 he took the name John XII (955–63). He was not the first pope to change his name, but he started a trend, and by the end of the century it had become the usual practice. He also changed his father's policy of isolation. Since 951 the German king Otto I had been king of Italy, having defeated Berengar II of Ivrea who had claimed the throne after abducting Adelaide, who had inherited it, but Alberic had not wanted Otto in his city. John XII was just 18 when he became bishop of Rome. Though reputedly dissolute, he was active in ecclesiastical affairs and, like his father, a promoter of monastic reform. But he was also ambitious to extend the temporal power of the papacy. When he embarked on a disastrous campaign to capture Benevento and Capua, Berengar ravaged his northern territories, and John was forced to turn to Otto for help. This was perhaps not his own decision: he was under pressure from the powerful Roman nobility, particularly from the Tusculani and the Crescentii families, to whom he was probably distantly related. Otto was ready to come to John's assistance: he had sought the imperial crown in 951, but it had been denied him. Now he marched on Rome, defeating Berengar en route, and the man who had modelled his career on that of Charlemagne was crowned emperor alongside Queen Adelaide (whom he had married in 951) on 2 February 962.

A synod was called, which dealt with a number of matters concerning the church in Germany to Otto's satisfaction. Otto then issued what came to be called the 'Ottonian Privilege', guaranteeing the 'Donation of Pepin' (see page 58) and adding even more lands to the papal estates. He later issued a new constitution for papal elections – they were to be free of political pressure, but before a new pope was consecrated he had to take an oath of loyalty to the emperor, and to recognize him as overlord. The papacy, in these terms, was being reduced to little more than a German bishopric.

... he had what seems to have been a heart attack while consorting, or just after consorting, with a married woman ...

This did not suit John. The moment Otto left Rome he started to intrigue against him with Berengar and others. Furious, Otto stormed back in November 963, and at a hastily convened synod had John deposed for immorality. John fled, taking with him as much as he could carry of the papal treasure, and Leo VIII (963–65) was elected in his stead. But again, once Otto was out of the way, John returned, deposed Leo and wreaked terrible vengeance on those who had supported the antipope. John died shortly afterwards, in 964. Reports of the circumstances of his death vary, but they all seem to concur that he had what seems to have been a heart attack while consorting, or just after consorting, with a married woman – though one version has him stabbed to death by the woman's husband.

For the rest of the century there was a struggle for control of the papacy between the emperors Otto I and Otto II on one side and, on the other, the nobility of Rome, particularly the Crescentii family, which was in the ascendent. Pope John XV, who was elected in August 985, was the nominee of John Crescentius, the German royal family being otherwise occupied at the time. During John XV's pontificate (985–96), Crescentius acted as the political overlord, while John dealt with ecclesiastical affairs. After the death of John Crescentius, John XV's position weakened and in 995 he fled to Sutri, about 30 miles from Rome, leaving the city in the hands of the Crescentii. He appealed for help to the German king Otto III, the 16-year-old grandson of Otto I. The young monarch marched south, and the Roman nobility panicked, begging the pope to return. He did so, but Otto continued to approach Rome. By the time he arrived, however, Pope John XV had caught a fever and died in March 996. Otto was in a position to decide upon the next pope. His choice would take the Romans by surprise.

GREGORY V

ews of the death of Pope John XV reached the young Otto III at Pavia at Easter 996, as he made his way through Italy to come to the assistance of the Roman pontiff. At Ravenna he was met by a group of Roman nobles who, worried that he might still exact vengeance for their treatment of John XV, asked him to nominate a new pope. Otto's choice was to be the cause of some astonishment.

Any list of bishops of Rome that gives their place of origin includes Greeks, Syrians and others, but what they all had in common was that they were clergy of the city of Rome. There were one or two exceptions to this general rule, but all popes hitherto had been either Roman by birth or by adoption, or at the very least had been born in what is now Italy. Otto III, however, nominated his second cousin Bruno, a member of his entourage. Bruno was not only just 24 years of age, he had been born in what is was now Austria, and had studied at Worms, where he had enjoyed a very good education. He was much immersed in the study of the Fathers of the Church, which is why he chose the papal name Gregory.

OTTO III, HOLY ROMAN EMPEROR

From Ravenna Otto's party moved on to Rome. Bruno was consecrated pope, and two weeks later, on 21 May 996 – it was Ascension Day – he anointed Otto as Holy Roman Emperor. The trouble with Otto was that he took the title too seriously. He wanted to build up the imperial dominions, even at the expense of the papacy, and to rule from Rome itself (he was, after all, the son of a Byzantine princess). But this was not a proposition that appealed to the Roman nobility. Pope

BIRTH NAME **Bruno of Carinthia**
BORN **Steinach,**
   near Salzburg *c.* **972**
PREDECESSOR **John XV**
ELECTED **3 May 996**
DIED **18 February 999**
SUCCESSOR **Sylvester II**

Gregory V, who realized that he would have to remain in Rome when, inevitably, the emperor withdrew, began to make common cause with the nobility, thereby displaying a degree of independence from Otto. Crescentius Nomentanus, who had been the enemy of John XV, was put on trial and sentenced to exile, but was pardoned by Gregory, against Otto's wishes, in a show of conciliation towards the Roman aristocracy. For his part, Otto not only refused to renew the 'Ottonian Privilege' bestowed by his grandfather, but also declined to hand back to the pope the territory known as the Pentapolis, five strategic towns on the Adriatic coast, from Rimini down to Ancona. And there were further causes of friction between pope and emperor. The new pope was unwilling to overturn judgements made by John XV, one of which had been to cite Gerbert of Aurillac as an intruder in the See of Rheims, and to reinstate his predecessor. The problem for Gregory was that Gerbert, who would succeed him as Pope Sylvester II, was a close friend of Otto.

When Otto demanded that Gerbert be made archbishop of Ravenna, he could not refuse him.

A COUP AGAINST GREGORY

In June 996 Otto left Rome for cooler climes. Gregory immediately began to feel the resentment in the city at the appointment of a foreigner by the emperor, and asked him to come back. Otto refused on health grounds. It was not long before Crescentius Nomentanus organized a coup against Gregory and drove him out of the city. He made two attempts to recover Rome by force of arms, but they failed. Gregory excommunicated Crescentius at a synod held in Pavia in 997. Although Gregory did not know it at the time, in Rome they had elected the archbishop of Piacenza, John Philagathus, as pope in his stead. He styled himself John XVI.

While Otto's relationship with his cousin had not been easy, and the emperor had refused to come to Gregory's help in 996, in February

Pope Gregory V was second cousin to the Holy Roman Emperor, Otto III, but maintained his independence from him. Gregory was a zealous reformer who spoke out against simony – the sale of ecclesiastical offices.

998 he again marched on Rome, alarmed perhaps that the rebels there were turning to the Byzantine emperor for support. Crescentius took refuge in Castel Sant'Angelo, which was besieged and eventually captured. He was beheaded. John XVI was blinded, and his mouth, ears and tongue mutilated. He was then imprisoned until his trial, at which he was found guilty. His papal garments were stripped off him, he was mounted on a donkey, facing backwards and clinging to its tail, and paraded through the streets in front of jeering crowds.

A REFORMING PAPACY

Though these events dominated Gregory's short pontificate, it is clear from his other actions that he was a reformer, with the good of the church at heart. The synod held at Pavia in 997 did more than issue excommunications. It also re-enacted rules going back to Pope Symmachus at the end of the fifth century which forbade discussion about the papal succession during the lifetime of a reigning pope, and also forbade simony, the sale of ecclesiastical offices. Gregory personally took a firm stand against the king of France, Robert II (996–1031), who had entered an illegal marriage, as far as the law of the church was concerned, with his cousin Bertha of Burgundy. When Gregory excommunicated Robert, the French bishops who had backed the king rejected the idea of an appeal against the pope's decision. The fact that Gregory took such a

> John XVI was blinded, and his mouth, ears and tongue mutilated. He was then imprisoned until his trial, at which he was found guilty.

decision when he was politically very weak is evidence of his committed zeal.

Gregory's death in 999 was sudden. There were rumours that he had been assassinated, which might not have been surprising, given the hostility shown to him by the Roman nobles on the one hand, and his own fraught relations with the emperor on the other. But the truth is much more prosaic. He died of malaria.

SYLVESTER II

At the early death of Gregory V, Otto III suddenly had to find a new pope. He took advice. It was, it seems, Abbot Odilo of the monastery of Cluny who suggested Gerbert of Aurillac, who was by then archbishop of Ravenna. Gerbert chose the name Sylvester, the first of that title having been bishop of Rome under Constantine. The implication was that he intended to work closely with the emperor, which, after Otto's problems with Pope Gregory, must have come as a relief.

A great deal is known about the remarkable life of Gerbert. He came from a humble family, and at an early age, as was then the custom, he was sent to the monastery of Saint-Géraud d'Aurillac, where he showed signs of an unusually high intelligence. His abbot, after a visit to the abbey by the count of Barcelona, put the young monk into the care of the count and sent him to Catalonia for further studies. He spent three years there, before travelling to Rome in 970. In Rome he encountered both the pope and the then emperor, Otto II, but rejected the idea of joining either the imperial or the papal civil service, and went off to Rheims for yet more studies. He soon rose to be head of the cathedral school and became celebrated for his scientific and mathematical expertise, learnt in Spain from the Arabs.

FROM ABBOT TO ARCHBISHOP

Otto III bestowed on him the abbacy of Bobbio in northern Italy. Local hostility forced him to return to Rheims, but he never gave up his claim to Bobbio. At Rheims he became embroiled in the struggle of Hugh Capet with the Carolingians, which ended with Hugh's election as king of France in 987 and the end of the Carolingian line. As a supporter of Hugh Capet, on the death of the archbishop of Rheims Gerbert might have expected to succeed him, but the new king wanted to give the see to a Carolingian as a sop. He therefore appointed Arnoul, who almost immediately betrayed the king. Arnoul was flung into prison and, after a long delay while the bishops tried

BIRTH NAME **Gerbert of Aurillac**
BORN **Beillac, Auvergne c. 945**
PREDECESSOR **Gregory V**
INSTALLED **9 April 999**
DIED **12 May 1003**
SUCCESSOR **John XVII**

and failed to get a ruling from the pope, was put on trial before a synod of bishops. At this synod another Arnoul, the bishop of Orleans, argued that the papacy was so immoral and corrupt that it was an unsuitable judge – the indictment against the popes is thought to have been composed by Gerbert – and that therefore the French bishops were quite within their rights to judge Arnoul of Rheims, and to depose him. This they did, and Gerbert was finally created archbishop of Rheims in Arnoul's stead.

GERBERT BECOMES POPE

The intrusion of Gerbert did not go unnoticed by Pope John XV. He sent an emissary to France and a synod was held at Mouzon in June 995, the papal legate now vindicating Arnoul and suspending Gerbert from his office of archbishop. Gerbert decided to go to Rome to defend himself, and there he met, and became close friends with, Otto III. The emperor kept Gerbert beside him as his tutor before, in April 998, making

A brilliant man, Pope Sylvester II was noted for his learning in the fields of music, mathematics and astronomy.

him archbishop of Ravenna and then, on the death of Gregory V, elevating him to the papacy.

As pope, Sylvester was as vigorous a defender of the papacy's rights as he had hitherto been a stern critic. He reinstated Arnoul at Rheims, on the grounds that John XV had never approved of his deposition, and he made Leo, the legate who had presided at his own deposition at Mouzon, the archbishop of Ravenna. He finally ceded the abbey of Bobbio and tried to insist that in future abbots be freely elected by the monks, as the Rule of St Benedict required. He prevailed upon the emperor to establish a national church in Poland independent of Germany, with the archbishopric of Gniezo, founded in the year 1000, as the primatial see. (In theory Gniezo remains Poland's primatial see to this day, though it is now combined with the See of Warsaw.) On the conversion of King Stephen I of Hungary, Sylvester sent him a royal crown in 1001, thereby extending the reach of the papacy into new territory.

SYLVESTER DEMANDS CLERICAL CELIBACY

Sylvester remained close to Otto III, who, although he declared the Ottonian Privilege of his grandfather a forgery, nonetheless returned to the papacy the cities of the Pentapolis, which the emperor had pointedly refused to hand over to his predecessor. He was also active against corruption, condemning simony and demanding that the clergy observe celibacy. But none of this went down well with the Romans. In February 1001, led by John II Crescentius, the Roman nobles revolted against pope and emperor and both had to flee Rome. Otto died of malaria a year later, before he could re-establish his authority in the city. Without him Sylvester posed no challenge, and he was allowed to return to the Lateran, where he housed the vast and much-loved library that he had brought with him from Rheims.

Sylvester II did not live long enough to achieve a great deal as pope. His pontificate was short, and it may be that without the support of the emperor Otto III he was not a powerful enough character to face down the inevitable local opposition to a French-born pope ruling the city of Rome. However, his eminence in European scholarship, gained before his elevation to the papacy, is immense. He was not simply a highly cultured man with a delight in music, mathematics and astronomy, he was also a collector of manuscripts of classical authors. Such was his brilliance that people came to wonder whether he was not a magician, who had made a pact with the devil. And in an even later generation, Protestant scholars of the 17th century were able to re-use the ammunition against the papacy with which, as plain Gerbert, he had once furnished the bishop of Orleans.

LEO IX

Between the death of Sylvester II in 1003 and the intervention of the German king, Henry III, in December 1046, the papacy remained under the control of one of two families: the Tusculani, whose base was near modern Frascati, southeast of Rome; or the Crescentii in Rome itself. For most of the time it was the Tusculani who were in the ascendant. The situation was not, however, as dire as it had been during the previous century; even Benedict IX, elected in 1032 when still a layman (and according to some reports only 12 years old, though that is not now believed) and who owed his elevation to the largesse of his father, Alberic III, count of Tusculum, seems to have carried out his public duties well, even if his private life was as scandalous as it was reputed to have been.

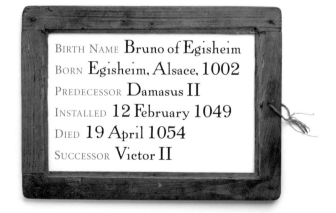

BIRTH NAME **Bruno of Egisheim**
BORN **Egisheim, Alsace, 1002**
PREDECESSOR **Damasus II**
INSTALLED **12 February 1049**
DIED **19 April 1054**
SUCCESSOR **Victor II**

Benedict's pontificate is remarkable, however, because he left office no less than three times. The first occasion was in September 1044, when he had to flee Rome because of an uprising against him, which led to the imposition by the Crescentii of Sylvester III. But by the following March he was back again. He did not remain long. Possibly alarmed at the thought that Henry III was on his way to Rome in search of an imperial coronation, or possibly because he had simply had enough of the office – he had held it since October 1032 – in 1045 he apparently sold the papacy to his godfather, one John Gratian, for a very large sum of money. It seems an out-of-

THE ABDICATION OF GREGORY VI

BONIZO, BISHOP OF SUTRI, DESCRIBES THE ABDICATION OF GREGORY VI AT THE SYNOD OF SUTRI, 1046:

'I call God to be witness on my soul, brothers, that I thought by this act [buying the papacy from Benedict IX] to win the remission of sins and deserve God's grace. But now that I see the snares of the Devil in the deed, tell me what should be done with me.' They replied: 'You should turn over the business in your own mind, and judge yourself with your own mouth. For it is better for you that you should live here as a poor man with St Peter, for love of whom you did this, so that you may be rich in the life to come, than enjoy present riches with Simon the Mage [Simon Magus, from whom the term 'simony' derives] who deceived you, and then perish eternally.'

Having heard these things he passed sentence on himself in this manner: 'I Gregory the bishop, servant of the servants of God, because of the disgraceful venality of Simoniac heresy, which through the cunning of the Devil has tainted my election, judge that I should be removed from the Roman see.' And he added: 'does this please you?' And they responded: 'What pleases you we confirm.'

character transaction because Gratian, who took the title Gregory VI, was a devout man, and a member of the reforming party among the Roman clergy.

So when a synod was held at Sutri in 1046 there were three popes claiming the title – Benedict, Sylvester and Gregory. At the synod Henry III deposed the last two, then four days later called another synod, this time in Rome, deposed Benedict and appointed Suidger, bishop of Bamberg, who took the title Clement II – the choice of a name from the very early church seemed to presage a fresh start. Soon afterwards Henry withdrew to Germany, and Benedict made a final bid for power when Clement died after only ten months in office. He managed to remain in Rome as pope from November 1047 until the July of the following year. When Henry put pressure on Benedict's supporters, however, they accepted the imperial nominee, Poppo, bishop of Brixen, who took the papal name, again from the early church, of Damasus II. Poppo, or Damasus, unsure of his ability to hang on to the papacy, kept the bishopric of Brixen alongside that of Rome until his death, which came quickly, in August 1048, less than a month after his installation. Benedict, meanwhile, survived, still claiming the title of pope, until 1055 or 1056, outliving five of his successors, including the most influential of them all, Bruno of Toul, who took the name Leo IX.

When Bruno was born, the son of Count Hugo of Nordgau, legend has it that his body was covered in crosses. At the age of five he was put into the care of the bishop of Toul, rising in his service to the rank of deacon and commander of the bishop's troops in the service of the emperor Conrad II. He was in Italy on military service when the bishop died, and he was promoted to the bishopric by popular acclaim in September 1027. After the death of Damasus II in 1048, when the Roman delegates travelled to Worms to ask the emperor Henry III to designate a new pope, he chose Bruno, who was his cousin.

BRUNO DENOUNCES SIMONY

While Bruno accepted in principle, he would not take up the office as Pope Leo IX without the approval of the people of Rome. He therefore journeyed to the city and entered its gate barefoot, as a pilgrim and weeping, according to some accounts. If he had hoped by this display of humility to reconcile the warring factions in Rome, he was disappointed. When the conflict continued despite his attempts to put an end to it, he resorted to force, laying waste the lands of both the Tusculani and the Crescentii. But his main concern was church reform, and, in particular, the practice of simony. (Simony is the name given to the selling of ecclesiastical offices and, strictly speaking, other holy things, but ecclesiastical preferments were the chief object of the reformers of whom Leo was a major figure.) At a synod held at Easter 1049, Leo strongly attacked the practice. The synod also condemned what came to be called Nicolaitism, or the marriage or concubinage of senior clergy – those, that is, from the rank of subdeacon upwards. Clerical celibacy had been an aspiration from the earliest centuries of Christianity but, except for those who chose the life of monks, had not been widely observed.

After the synod of Rome Leo went on his travels, conducting synods elsewhere in Italy, and in France and Germany, always with the same message – the abolition of simony and of clerical concubinage. He also upheld the ancient principle that bishops should be freely elected by the clergy and people of the diocese. And likewise, he insisted that abbots be elected by the community that they were to govern: he was a great supporter of monastic life, always staying in monasteries wherever possibly on his extensive travels, and issuing bulls (see box) granting privileges to many of them.

Leo also made important reforms in the administration of the papacy, in the papal court, or curia. He brought in to advise him many men from different regions of Europe, an approach that was unpopular in Rome, where the Romans had hitherto supplied almost all the papal officials and cardinals. Two of these advisors were themselves shortly to become popes and one of them, Hildebrand, later Gregory VII, gave his name to the whole programme of reform.

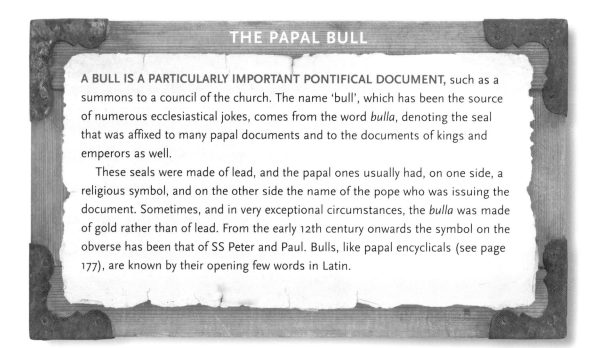

THE PAPAL BULL

A BULL IS A PARTICULARLY IMPORTANT PONTIFICAL DOCUMENT, such as a summons to a council of the church. The name 'bull', which has been the source of numerous ecclesiastical jokes, comes from the word *bulla*, denoting the seal that was affixed to many papal documents and to the documents of kings and emperors as well.

These seals were made of lead, and the papal ones usually had, on one side, a religious symbol, and on the other side the name of the pope who was issuing the document. Sometimes, and in very exceptional circumstances, the *bulla* was made of gold rather than of lead. From the early 12th century onwards the symbol on the obverse has been that of SS Peter and Paul. Bulls, like papal encyclicals (see page 177), are known by their opening few words in Latin.

ENTER THE NORMANS

The end of Leo's pontificate was unhappy. Norman adventurers, who had invaded southern Italy and established themselves there, began raiding the papal states, and the pope determined to lead an expedition against them. At Civitella, on 18 June 1053, Leo's coalition army was defeated, and he himself was taken prisoner. Part of the reason for the defeat was the papal army's failure to link up with its Byzantine allies.

This military debacle took place against a backdrop of worsening relations between the papacy and Constantinople. The Byzantines, who had been established since the sixth century in the areas of southern Italy now threatened by the Normans, still considered parts of the region to belong to their sphere of control. And despite the papacy's military assistance in the struggle against the Normans, the Byzantines resented what they regarded as papal interference in the ecclesiastical domain. A particular cause of bitterness was Leo's holding of a synod in Sicily, and appointment of a bishop there, without consulting the Byzantine emperor Constantine. The patriarch of Constantinople, Michael Cerularius, shut the Latin churches in his city in 1053, and attacked Latin practices, particularly that of using unleavened bread in the Eucharistic wafer. One of Leo's closest advisors, the

Pope Leo IX was anxious to reform abuses in the church. He also led an army against the incursion of the Normans into the papal states. After his defeat at the Battle of Civitella, 18 June 1053, he was placed under arrest by Robert Guiscard.

French cardinal Humbert of Silva Candida, wrote an antagonistic response.

Leo, held prisoner by the Normans following his defeat at Civitella, decided to send a legation to Constantinople, led by Humbert. The legation arrived in January 1054, and negotiations between the cardinal and the patriarch dragged on with increasing acrimony. On 16 July 1054, Humbert laid a bull excommunicating Michael Cerularius on the altar of Hagia Sophia, the great church of Constantinople. Cerularius issued a counter-excommunication against the pope eight days later. But by the time Humbert's excommunication was issued Leo had been released by the Normans and had returned to Rome a broken man, to die after only a month. Humbert had issued his excommunication in the name of the pope, but at the time he did so there was no pope, so it was technically invalid. Nonetheless the excommunications of 1054 marked a definitive break between the church of the East and that of the West.

Victor II 1055–57	Clement III 1187–91
Stephen IX (X) 1056–58	Celestine III 1191–98
Nicholas II 1059–61	*Innocent III 1198–1216
Alexander II 1061–73	Honorius III 1216–27
*Gregory VII 1073–85	*Gregory IX 1227–41
Victor III 1087	Celestine IV 1241
*Urban II 1088–99	Innocent IV 1243–54
*Paschal II 1099–1118	Alexander IV 1254–61
Gelasius II 1118–19	Urban IV 1261–64
*Callistus II 1119–24	Clement IV 1265–68
Honorius II 1124–30	*Gregory X 1272–76
Innocent II 1130–43	Innocent V 1276
Celestine II 1143–44	Hadrian V 1276
Lucius II 1144–45	John XXI 1276–77
*Eugenius III 1145–53	Nicholas III 1277–80
Anastasius IV 1153–54	Martin IV 1281–85
*Hadrian IV 1154–59	Honorius IV 1285–87
Alexander III 1159–81	Nicholas IV 1288–92
Lucius III 1181–85	*Celestine V 1294
Urban III 1185–87	*Boniface VIII 1295–1303
Gregory VIII 1187	Benedict XI 1303–04

Denotes popes featured within this section

OPPOSITE *A 15th-century manuscript illumination showing a view of Rome as the City of God, and St Augustine of Hippo writing.*

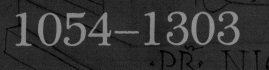

1054–1303

REFORMERS AND CRUSADERS

The high Medieval papacy

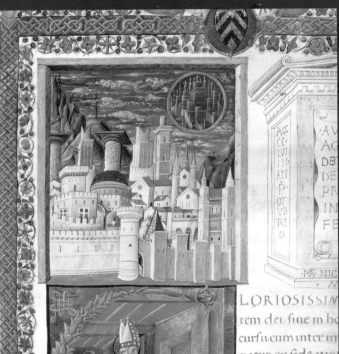

GREGORY VII

s can be seen from the life of Pope Leo IX, Hildebrand was a major player in the reform movement which took hold of the papacy in the middle years of the 11th century. He was particularly close to Pope Gregory VI (1045–6), with whom, after the latter's deposition, he went into exile in Germany.

Hildebrand came from a fairly humble background, though one of his uncles had risen to become abbot of the monastery of St Mary on Rome's Aventine Hill where he was sent as a boy, and it is likely that he also became a monk there, though that is not certain. He came to know many of the powerful figures in papal Rome, including John Gratian, the future Gregory VI, who was related to the Pierleoni banking family and who became archpriest of the Lateran.

NICHOLAS II

After Gregory VI's death in exile, late in 1047, Hildebrand may have entered the monastery of Cluny, in Burgundy, but he returned to Rome at the behest of Pope Leo IX, who ordained him subdeacon, and made him prior of the monastery at St Paul's-Without-the-Walls. Leo IX made him his legate to France. Under Leo's successors, the German Victor II (1055–7) and the short-lived Stephen IX (X) (1057–8), he was given a similar task in Germany. He was still in Germany when Stephen died, but Stephen had asked that no election be held until Hildebrand returned to Rome, probably in an effort to avoid the choice of someone from the Roman nobility who was out of sympathy with the reform movement.

BIRTH NAME **Hildebrand**

BORN **Savona, Tuscany, c. 1020**

PREDECESSOR **Alexander II**

INSTALLED **30 June 1073**

DIED **25 May 1085**

SUCCESSOR **Victor III**

The new pope was Nicholas II (1058–61), formerly the bishop of Florence, who promoted Hildebrand to the rank of archdeacon of the Roman Church, with responsibility for papal finances. This was a high-profile post, and one that would later provide ammunition for his enemies when they accused him of the very crime of simony against which he was campaigning.

TWO POPES IN ROME

Hildebrand was also instrumental in the election of Nicholas's successor, Anselm, bishop of Lucca, who had been a monk at Bec in Normandy under Lanfranc, a future archbishop of Canterbury. He took the name Alexander II. During Nicholas's pontificate a new election decree, drafted by Hildebrand, had been agreed. It gave the responsibility of electing a pope to the cardinal bishops alone, who then were to get the agreement of the rest of the cardinals, and the clergy and people of Rome were afterwards to give their assent. The emperor simply had the task of confirming the decision the cardinal electors had made. This was the procedure followed in the election of

A dramatic woodcut telling the story of the difficulties of Pope Gregory VII's pontificate. It shows King Henry IV and the antipope Clement III. Henry imprisoned Gregory in 1084 in the Castel Sant'Angelo, whence he was freed by the Norman Robert Guiscard.

Alexander, causing a breach with the German court, a breach which the Roman nobility tried to exploit to regain the ascendancy in Rome over the reform movement. With the connivance of the empress Agnes, acting as regent for King Henry IV, who was still a minor, an antipope was indeed elected in 1061. He took the name Honorius, though he eventually fell out of favour.

The experience of having two popes in Rome – Honorius managed to occupy Castel Sant'Angelo for a few months in 1063 – was chastening. When Alexander died in 1073, the Roman crowd called immediately for the election of Hildebrand. A meeting of electors was hastily summoned by Cardinal Hugh the White, and Hildebrand was formally and unanimously given the office of pope. He took the name Gregory VII, partly out of admiration for the great Gregory I, and partly out of respect for his late patron Gregory VI. He informed the German court of his election, though he did not seek its permission.

THE GREGORIAN REFORMS

In the Lenten synods of 1074 and 1075 Gregory embarked upon the reform of the church which now bears his name, either the Hildebrandine reform or, more commonly, the Gregorian reform. In 1074 he launched an attack, as his predecessors had done, on simony and clerical concubinage, and he sent out legates to ensure that the synod's decrees were implemented. It caused wide disruption in the church as unworthy bishops were deposed, and, since bishops were very often closely linked to the secular power, it likewise frequently upset the civil authorities. The link between the civil and the religious was a major stumbling-block in the whole reform movement. About the year 1060 Cardinal Humbert of Silva Candida had written a treatise, in the spirit of the reform, attacking simony. In the third book of that treatise he criticized the customary practice of lay rulers bestowing the symbols of episcopal office upon bishops, known as lay investiture. Humbert's criticisms had made little impact at the time, and lay investiture did not figure in Gregory's first Lenten synod. The forceful condemnation of the practice by the synod of 1075, however, marked the beginning of what became known as 'the investiture contest'. In essence, investiture was about the right of kings to control bishops, something which monarchs were loath to abandon. That was particularly true of the young Henry IV in Germany, who was concerned not only about his influence over the German episcopate but over that of northern Italy as well, where there were signs of resistance to the Gregorian reform. Emboldened by military success over the Saxons, Henry proceeded to nominate new bishops in Germany and Italy. Gregory strongly objected.

The German king marched on Rome in March 1084, Gregory was locked up, and antipope Clement crowned Henry as emperor.

HENRY IV AT CANOSSA

In response, Henry called a synod at Worms for 24 January 1076. It was attended by 24 German and two Italian bishops. The synod claimed that the election of the 'false monk Hildebrand' had been invalid, and that he was to abdicate. He was in any case declared deposed. Gregory responded in like manner. In his Lenten synod of that year he declared Henry excommunicate and deposed, and released his subjects from their allegiance to the king. The synod also deposed the bishops who were supporting Henry. At this point German politics took over. Gregory's actions had a significant impact in Germany, and, though few of the princes were inclined to the reform movement, they were rivals to Henry for the German throne. The German king therefore decided to seek pardon. Gregory was staying at the castle at Canossa belonging to his ally the countess Matilda when, in January 1077, Henry arrived dressed as a penitent, and stood outside in the snow asking for forgiveness. This Gregory felt obliged to deliver. A penance was imposed, and the king was freed from his excommunication.

BLUFF AND BLUNDER

If Henry believed that this act would not only reconcile him to the pope but also put an end to disturbances in Germany, he was mistaken on both counts. The rebellious princes put up an alternative king, Rudolph of Swabia, and Gregory, although he attempted to remain neutral between the two claimants to the kingship, eventually decided that Henry was too intransigent. The king was attempting to impose his authority once again over the German bishops, so Gregory came down on Rudolph's side, excommunicating and deposing Henry for a second time. Supporting Rudolph was a political blunder, not least because Rudolph was defeated by Henry and killed in battle in 1081, but more importantly because it deeply antagonized the German king. Henry called a synod at Brixen in June 1080 at which Gregory was declared deposed and an antipope chosen, who took the title Clement III.

To some extent it was a game of bluff. Henry wanted to be crowned emperor in Rome, and he might have been amenable to a compromise with Gregory, but Gregory was not amenable to a compromise with Henry. The German king marched on Rome in March 1084, Gregory was locked up in Castel Sant'Angelo, and antipope Clement crowned Henry as emperor in the Lateran Basilica. Gregory was fairly promptly rescued from Castel Sant'Angelo by the Norman Robert Guiscard, but in the process Guiscard's troops pillaged the city and so antagonized the Romans that they turned against Gregory himself – as indeed 13 of his cardinals had already done. The pope fled the city, going first to the abbey of Monte Cassino and then on to Salerno, where he died. His last words were 'I have loved justice and hated iniquity, therefore I die in exile'.

THE POPE AND THE PRINCES

Any account of Gregory must concentrate on the investiture contest, which looms large in medieval history but was all but resolved by the 1120s. Although his energy was largely taken up with the affairs of Germany, he had enough left over to enter into correspondence with Christian

THE *DICTATUS PAPAE*

That the Roman church was founded by God alone.

That the Roman pontiff alone can with right be called universal.

That he alone can depose or reinstate bishops.

That, in a council his legate, even if a lower grade, is above all bishops, and can pass sentence of deposition against them.

That the pope may depose the absent.

That, among other things, we ought not to remain in the same house with those excommunicated by him.

That for him alone is it lawful, according to the needs of the time, to make new laws, to assemble together new congregations, to make an abbey of a canonry; and, on the other hand, to divide a rich bishopric and unite the poor ones.

That he alone may use the imperial insignia.

That of the pope alone all princes shall kiss the feet.

That his name alone shall be spoken in the churches.

That this is the only name in the world.

That it may be permitted to him to depose emperors.

That he may be permitted to transfer bishops if need be.

That he has power to ordain a clerk of any church he may wish.

That he who is ordained by him may preside over another church, but may not hold a subordinate position; and that such a one may not receive a higher grade from any bishop. That no synod shall be called a general one without his order.

That no chapter and no book shall be considered canonical without his authority.

That a sentence passed by him may be retracted by no one; and that he himself, alone of all, may retract it.

That he himself may be judged by no one.

That no one shall dare to condemn one who appeals to the apostolic chair. That to the latter should be referred the more important cases of every church.

That the Roman church has never erred; nor will it err to all eternity, the Scripture bearing witness.

That the Roman pontiff, if he have been canonically ordained, is undoubtedly made a saint by the merits of St Peter; St Ennodius, bishop of Pavia, bearing witness, and many holy fathers agreeing with him. As is contained in the decrees of St Symmachus the pope.

That, by his command and consent, it may be lawful for subordinates to bring accusations.

That he may depose and reinstate bishops without assembling a synod.

That he who is not at peace with the Roman church shall not be considered catholic.

That he may absolve subjects from their fealty to wicked men.

princes across Europe and beyond – and even with one Muslim ruler in Africa. He tried to persuade the king of Denmark that he held his lands only as a vassal of the pope, and similarly laid claim to Spain – where the king of Aragón abandoned the local liturgy (the Mozarabic rite, as it is called) in favour of the Roman form – and to Hungary. He maintained good relations with the king of France, Philip I, and with William the Conqueror in England, even though both these monarchs ran their churches in much the same way as Henry IV did in Germany. Because of his long struggle with the German king, Gregory could not risk alienating other European monarchs with whom he had less leverage. His relations with the Byzantine emperor Michael VII were good. He thought that because of the Muslim threat to the Byzantine empire there might be hope of a reunion of the two churches, especially if the West went to the aid of the beleaguered Byzantines. At Manzikert, in 1071, in what is now eastern Turkey, Byzantium had suffered its worst ever defeat at the hands of the Muslims, and the emperor Romanus IV had been captured. The pope therefore proposed a crusade (though that word was not used) to recover the church of the Holy Sepulchre in Jerusalem, and he also proposed leading the expedition himself. Gregory did not have time to put into practice either this proposal or another idea of his, broached in a letter to the abbot of Cluny, that the knights of Europe be organized into a holy militia that might be used to recover Jerusalem as well as against clerics who opposed his reforms.

And there were many such. Gregory was a great centralizer, and a good many of the senior clergy did not approve. They liked their independence. But Gregory insisted, for instance, that all appeals come to him, and that all metropolitan archbishops journey to Rome to receive the pallium, rather than have it sent to them. The ideals espoused by Gregory were encapsulated in a document known as *Dictatus Papae* (see page 91), found in the papal register of official documents at the year 1075, although it is itself not dated. It is not clear what its purpose was – it is possible that it was a series of headings for a collection of church (canon) law. But, whatever its precise nature, it expressed the aspiration of the reformers for a papacy to which all Europe was subject.

URBAN II

n the official list of popes, Gregory VII is followed by Victor III (1086–7), who in turn was succeeded by Pope Urban II. It probably did not seem quite such a smooth progression at the time. There was almost a year between the death of Gregory at Salerno and the election by the cardinals of the reform party of Cardinal Desiderius, the abbot of Monte Cassino. Desiderius, who took the name Victor III, was a reluctant pontiff. He retained his abbacy, and after his short reign of a few days less than a year, hurried back to die in his monastery. In all that time he had scarcely been able to set foot in Rome because it was occupied by the supporters of the antipope Clement III, who managed to survive not only Victor, but Victor's successor, Pope Urban II. And even Urban was only able ever to gain control of parts of Rome late on in his pontificate.

Urban was born into a noble family at Châtillon-sur-Marne, in northeastern France, and was baptized Odo. He was sent to study in Rheims, at the school then under the charge of Bruno, the future founder of the Carthusian order of monks. At Rheims he became a canon, and then archdeacon, but resigned those posts to become a monk at Cluny, where he became prior sometime in the late 1070s. Gregory VII, before he became pope, is thought to have spent some months at Cluny after the death in exile of Pope Gregory VI. In about 1080 he summoned Odo to Rome and appointed him cardinal bishop of Ostia, the most senior title of all the cardinals.

Gregory made him his papal legate to Germany, an extremely tricky position given the conflict between Henry IV and Gregory VII over investiture. At Quedlinburg in 1085, Odo presided over a synod which excommunicated the German king and his antipope Clement.

A FLEXIBLE REFORMER

On the death of Gregory's successor, Victor III, the cardinals were unable to gather in Rome, because the city was still in the hands of the excommunicated emperor. After a long delay they met

BIRTH NAME Odo of Châtillon
BORN Châtillon-sur-Marne,
c. 1035
PREDECESSOR Victor III
INSTALLED 12 March 1088
DIED 29 July 1099
SUCCESSOR Paschal II

instead at Terracina, south of Rome, and there chose Odo. Though unwavering in his support for the Gregorian reform, he understood the issues as perhaps Gregory himself had not done. He was committed to eradicating lay investiture, but he preferred a less confrontational approach. He was as opposed to simony, clerical concubinage and lay investiture as Gregory had been – and, for that matter, as antipope Clement was – but he allowed his legates more latitude in dealing with the issue, especially in Germany. In doing so he went against many of the reformers

Pope Urban II preaches the first crusade at the church council in Clermont in 1095.

by being prepared to recognize the validity of the orders of bishops who had been invested by laymen provided they had been canonically elected.

One of the factors which helped Urban was the increasing political isolation of Emperor Henry IV. From 1090 to 1092 Henry led a campaign in Italy which at first went well, forcing Urban to abandon Rome to antipope Clement and flee to Norman-held southern Italy. But Urban had helped to build up an alliance against Henry, not least by promoting the unlikely match between Gregory's old ally the countess Matilda and the son of Duke Guelph IV of Bavaria, whom Henry had deposed. In 1093 Henry's son Conrad defected to the papal side and was crowned king of Italy in Milan, later taking on the role, though not the title, of emperor in undertaking to protect the pope. Even Henry's wife eventually sided with Urban. While Henry was struggling to control northern Italy, Urban returned to Rome with Norman support, and was able to take possession of the Lateran in 1094 and of Castel Sant'Angelo in 1098 – the latter probably through bribery.

URBAN PROCEEDS WITH CAUTION

Elsewhere Urban was constrained by the need to prevent other rulers from backing Henry or, more significantly, supporting the antipope. He had therefore to tread carefully. In 1092 the French king Philip I had married, against church law, Bertrada, the wife of the count of Anjou. He was not immediately excommunicated, even though the king put one of the bishops who protested into prison. It was not until the synod of Autun, two years later, that Philip was condemned, a judgement Urban himself repeated at the council of Clermont the following year. The pope may have alienated the king, but it had become clear that the all-important bishops were siding with the pope. This was uncomfortable for Philip and in 1095 he undertook to separate from Bertrada. The excommunication against him was lifted, albeit only for a while.

In England, King William II remained at first neutral in the conflict between Urban and Clement. His father, the Conqueror, had been able to run the church as he wished, but in the learned (St) Anselm, the archbishop of Canterbury, the English king came up against a reformer of stern temperament. Anselm was eventually given permission to leave the country and he went to Rome to consult the pope, taking part in the councils at Bari in 1098 and at Rome in 1099. He returned to England convinced of the need to end lay investiture, but his subsequent career belongs to another pontificate.

There were other deals to be struck. In Spain, which was gradually being won back from the Moors, Urban bestowed the pallium on the archbishop of Toledo as the primate, or chief bishop, of all Spain – a title that the archbishop of Toledo holds to this day. In Sicily he granted Roger I, count of Sicily, authority over the church in a form which survived until the mid-19th century.

THE 'TRUCE OF GOD'

As Urban grew more secure in his role, he was able to hold important synods to bring his authority to bear. At the synod of Melfi in September 1089 he started talks with the Greeks, which he continued – with the assistance of Anselm of Canterbury – at the synod of Bari in 1098. There he was able to persuade the bishops of southern Italy, still influenced by Byzantium, of at least one of the theological issues which divided East from West, the question of the *Filioque* (see page 62). But he also extended to southern Italy the French notion of the 'Truce of God', in an attempt to moderate the violence of contemporary society. The 'Truce of God' was a complex idea, but basically it limited the days on which wars might be fought, gave protection to non-combatants, including clerics, and was backed up by oaths and the threat of ecclesiastical censures.

At the synod of Melfi Pope Urban also renewed Pope Gregory VII's condemnation of lay investiture, and he repeated it more forcefully at the Council of Clermont on 18–28 November 1095. The council forbade bishops, or any clergy, from doing homage to anyone, whether king or not. But Clermont is remembered for an entirely different reason. On 27 November Urban preached a sermon. No text survives, but there are several accounts of it, at least one of them by an eye-witness. The sermon was addressed specifically to the French, and called upon them to take up arms to rescue the pilgrim sites in the Holy Land from domination by Muslims (see box).

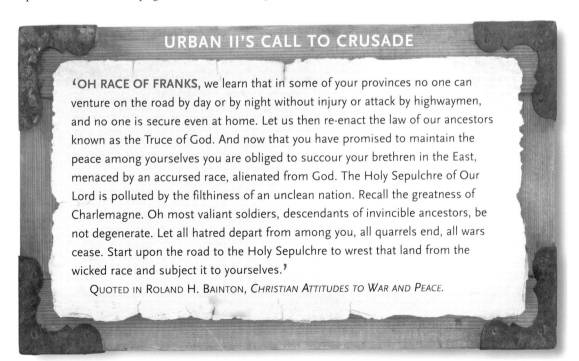

URBAN II'S CALL TO CRUSADE

'OH RACE OF FRANKS, we learn that in some of your provinces no one can venture on the road by day or by night without injury or attack by highwaymen, and no one is secure even at home. Let us then re-enact the law of our ancestors known as the Truce of God. And now that you have promised to maintain the peace among yourselves you are obliged to succour your brethren in the East, menaced by an accursed race, alienated from God. The Holy Sepulchre of Our Lord is polluted by the filthiness of an unclean nation. Recall the greatness of Charlemagne. Oh most valiant soldiers, descendants of invincible ancestors, be not degenerate. Let all hatred depart from among you, all quarrels end, all wars cease. Start upon the road to the Holy Sepulchre to wrest that land from the wicked race and subject it to yourselves.'

QUOTED IN ROLAND H. BAINTON, *CHRISTIAN ATTITUDES TO WAR AND PEACE*.

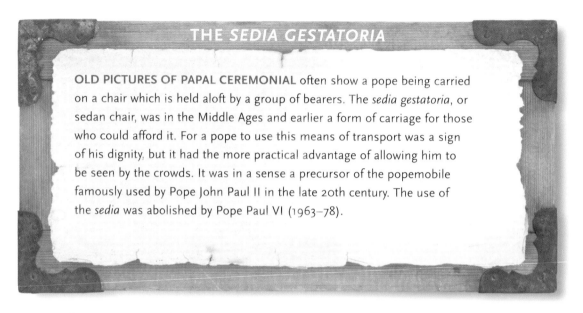

It perhaps seems nowadays unsurprising that such an expedition was launched, but it represented a remarkable change in the church's attitude. Christianity had from its earliest centuries been steadfastly opposed to the shedding of blood, but, as has been seen, Pope Gregory VII considered raising an army to come to the aid of the Byzantine emperor, and later, in a letter to the abbot of Cluny, had suggested a form of Christian militia. Gregory's close advisor, Anselm of Lucca, departed so far from traditional teaching as to propose that those who killed committed no sin, provided they did so with the right intentions. Gregory himself does not seem to have approved of this. A synodal decree of 1078 insisted that the career of a knight, because it involved the shedding of blood, could not be one which men might follow without committing sin.

What Urban did, however, was to appear to claim that anyone who fought to defend the Byzantine empire, and met death at the hands of the Muslims, would go straight to heaven, because they would have died a martyr's death. This was not an entirely new idea. Earlier popes, including Leo IV in the ninth century, had suggested a similar notion as they tried to raise troops to defend the papal states from the Saracen invaders. On his return to Rome from Clermont, Urban stopped at the Cluniac abbey of Moissac. There, shortly afterwards, a letter was forged, claiming to be from Pope Sergius IV – who had died in 1012 – and calling upon Christians to drive the enemies of God from the Holy Land.

THE CRUSADING OATH

There was in all this a curious amalgam of ideas. On the one hand Urban was preaching the Truce of God, and imposing it right across Christian Europe. On the other hand he was sending a Christian army to wreak violence on Muslims in the Middle East. And he was calling upon them to shed the blood of Muslims, while at the same time declaring, in the church's traditional teaching, that the spilling of blood was a grievous sin, for which knights had to do penance. And one way of doing penance was, of course, to go on pilgrimage. This was acknowledged to be a dangerous enough enterprise in itself, from which one might not return. The church therefore promised protection to the families and property of pilgrims, as it then promised safety to the families and property of those who took the crusading oath.

Very many knights, their consciences guilty with the shedding of blood, as successive popes had told them, made their armed pilgrimage to Jerusalem. They included knights from England, Normandy, Lorraine, southern France, and Sicily. Jerusalem fell to the crusaders on 15 July 1099, just two weeks before the death of the pope who had launched the Christian army on its way.

PASCHAL II

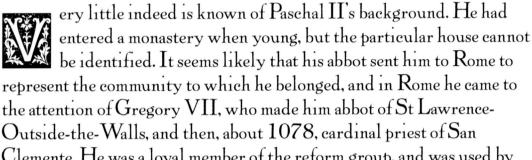

ery little indeed is known of Paschal II's background. He had entered a monastery when young, but the particular house cannot be identified. It seems likely that his abbot sent him to Rome to represent the community to which he belonged, and in Rome he came to the attention of Gregory VII, who made him abbot of St Lawrence-Outside-the-Walls, and then, about 1078, cardinal priest of San Clemente. He was a loyal member of the reform group, and was used by Urban II as his legate at synods in Léon and in Toulouse. He was elected pope, in his own church of San Clemente, just a fortnight after Urban's death, took possession of the Lateran on the same day, and the following day was consecrated in St Peter's. It was shortly after his enthronement that the news reached Rome of the fall of Jerusalem to the crusaders.

Though the capture of Jerusalem may have seemed a good omen for his pontificate, Paschal inherited from his predecessor all the problems over investiture, a hostile emperor, Henry IV, and an unexpectedly successful antipope, Clement III. Clement's authority, however, was in decline, and he died in Civita Castellana in September 1100. He was succeeded by others, but they did not have the support of the emperor – who was actively seeking a solution to the problems over investiture and posed no threat to Paschal.

Pope Paschal was not one for compromise, at least not at first. In a synod of March 1102 he again banned the practice of investiture, and renewed the excommunication on the emperor which Gregory had been the first to issue.

Then, in 1105, he lent his support to Henry's son, another Henry, who had rebelled against his father. Henry IV died the following year, and to the pope's dismay the new king showed himself no less intransigent over lay investiture than his late father had been. Paschal renewed the prohibition at a series of synods. An end to the controversy was in sight, however, if not in Germany then first in England and afterwards in France.

BIRTH NAME **Rainero**
BORN **Bieda di Galeata, near Ravenna, date unknown**
PREDECESSOR **Urban II**
INSTALLED **14 August 1099**
DIED **21 January 1118**
SUCCESSOR **Gelasius II**

After many disagreements with the German king, Henry V, Pope Paschal finally agreed to crown him emperor at St Peter's on 13 April 1111.

RECONCILIATION WITH ENGLAND AND FRANCE

The idea for a solution to the crisis over investiture came from France. Hugh of Fleury, in his *Treatise on the Royal Power and the Priestly Dignity*, which he wrote in the early years of the 12th century and dedicated to King Henry I of England, suggested that a distinction could be drawn between the religious function of bishops and their secular function within the state (see box, page 99). This took concrete form at the diet of London of 1107, when King Henry agreed to renounce the right of investiture provided that the bishops did homage before they were consecrated, and that the king might be present at the election.

In France the issue was complicated by the presence of a rigorist, Archbishop Hugh of Lyon, as papal legate, but Paschal relieved him of his post and sent him off to the Holy Land. Then there was the issue of King Philip I's adulterous marriage to Bertrada (see page 94). Philip had been king of France since 1060, and was advancing in years (indeed he was to die in 1108). It was perhaps this that made him both eager to settle the status of his relationship with Bertrada and to consider an accommodation with the papacy over investiture. His son, the future Louis VI, was also keen to see a resolution to the conflict. There was never a formal agreement on the issue, as there had been in England, but the reconciliation between the pope and the king of France was effected in a visit by Paschal to the royal court at Saint Denis. From then on the French king ceased to demand the right not only of investiture but, unlike the king of England, the right to receive homage from his bishops, though they were still required to swear an oath of loyalty to the monarch. This arrangement was brokered by Bishop Ivo of Chartres, who had been the teacher of Hugh of Fleury.

A STAND-OFF WITH HENRY V OF GERMANY

But nothing similar was accepted by Henry V in Germany. Quite the contrary. At a meeting at Châlons-sur-Marne, possibly in May 1107, there was a stand-off between Paschal and representatives of the German monarch. At regular synods the ban on lay investiture was repeated, and punishments of increasing severity were imposed on clerics who took part in investiture ceremonies. In 1110 Henry V invaded Italy with a large army, and at Sutri on 9 February 1111 king and pope hammered out a compromise. The proposal was that, at Henry's coronation as emperor, he would renounce all rights over the investiture of bishops, while the bishops were to hand back all that they had received from the empire, which meant all income except that derived from purely ecclesiastical sources. The coronation, set to take place in St Peter's on 12 February, never happened. When the agreement that had been reached at Sutri was read out in

HUGH OF FLEURY ON INVESTITURE

'THEREFORE I THINK THAT A KING can indeed by the inspiration of the Holy Spirit grant a prelacy to a religious cleric. The archbishop ought to convey the care of souls . . . When a bishop is chosen by the clergy and people according to ancient custom, the king ought by reason to bring no kind of force or disturbance against those who are electing – that would be tyrannous – but give his lawful consent to the ordination. And if he who is elected is found to be unworthy, then not only the king but the people also ought not to agree to his election . . . After the election, he should not take the ring and staff from the hand of the king, but the elect should receive investiture of the temporal goods of the bishopric, and then receive the care of souls and his ordination with the ring and staff from the archbishop, so that the whole thing may be carried out without dispute and both earthly and spiritual powers may preserve the rights due to their authority.'

TRANSLATED BY PROFESSOR TIMOTHY REUTER, UNIVERSITY OF SOUTHAMPTON.

church, there was uproar. The deal was rejected by everyone, clergy and laity alike – and then by Henry himself. There were renewed talks, and when they went nowhere Henry had Paschal and his cardinals arrested and flung into prison. On 12 April an agreement was made near Tivoli which came to be known as the 'privilege of Ponte Mammolo'. According to this, Henry himself might invest bishops before their consecration with crozier and ring, provided they had been freely elected. The pope also undertook never again to excommunicate Henry, whom he then crowned emperor in St Peter's on 13 April.

Paschal instantly regretted the agreement. In the months that followed he was so ashamed at having betrayed the basic principle of the reform movement that he considered resigning his office. He withdrew the privilege at the Lateran Synod of 1112, and four years later again condemned investiture. The year after, in 1117, Henry again marched on Rome, but the pope left the city and never met him. In 1116, an outbreak of rioting among the city's powerful families had forced Paschal to seek shelter with the Pierleoni family in Trastevere, before escaping as the emperor approached. In the last year of his life he was able to return to Rome, personally taking part in fortifying Castel Sant'Angelo, where he took refuge, and where he died. He was buried in the Lateran, because St Peter's was in rebel hands.

Paschal . . . was so ashamed at having betrayed the basic principle of the reform movement that he considered resigning his office.

CALLISTUS II

aschal's successor, Gelasius II, had only a short, but particularly troubled, pontificate (1118–19). Like his predecessor, he was compelled to flee Rome by unrest in the city and by a renewed march on Rome by the emperor Henry V. He retired to Gaeta, where he was ordained priest (he was a cardinal deacon at his election) and consecrated bishop. Henry appointed the archbishop of Braga as antipope, and he took the title Gregory VIII. Although Gelasius managed to return to Rome after Henry left, he found most of the city in the hands of supporters of the antipope. Despairing of establishing himself in Rome, he left for France with two of his cardinals. In January 1119 he held a synod at Vienne, but he fell ill and retired to Cluny (he had been a monk of Monte Cassino), where he died and was buried.

The two cardinals with him held an election of their own and chose a non-cardinal, Guy of Burgundy, archbishop of Vienne since 1088. They sent word of this to Rome, where their choice was approved as required by the remaining cardinals, and by the clergy and people, but by this time Guy had already been crowned Callistus II in his own cathedral church.

CALLISTUS OVERTHROWS THE ANTIPOPE

Unconventional though his election may have been, Callistus was a good choice. He had been an ardent reformer, but as the son of the count of Burgundy he was also related to the emperor (and, for that matter, to the royal houses of France and England as well). Callistus knew that an agreement had to be reached before too long over the investiture crisis, but he was also aware that there was pressure on Henry, expressed by German bishops at the imperial diet held in Mainz in June 1119, to bring an end to the stand-off.

Shortly after his installation, therefore, Callistus sent off emissaries to Henry. A draft agreement was drawn up, and it was to have been signed at Mouzon, on the River Meuse, but its terms turned out to be too vague, and Callistus finally refused the deal. At the end of October, in Rheims, the pope repeated the anathemas against the emperor, as well as the rejection of lay investiture. He then journeyed to Rome, arriving there in mid-June 1120. Henry, under pressure from his bishops, had ceased to support the antipope Gregory VIII, who had fled to Sutri in 1119. He was besieged there by Callistus, capitulated, and was then locked away in a series of monasteries for the rest of his life. Such was the obscurity into which he fell that

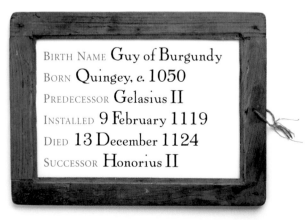

BIRTH NAME **Guy of Burgundy**

BORN **Quingey, c. 1050**

PREDECESSOR **Gelasius II**

INSTALLED **9 February 1119**

DIED **13 December 1124**

SUCCESSOR **Honorius II**

it is not even known when or where he died.

AGREEMENT AT LAST WITH THE EMPEROR

Henry sent representatives to Rome early in 1122. Callistus responded to the emperor's approach by sending his own representatives – including one destined to succeed him as Pope Honorius II. An agreement was reached as early as February, though the final terms were hammered out only in September 1122 at Worms (see box, page 102). The Concordat, signed on 23 September, laid down that there should be free elections to bishoprics, but that in Germany the emperor might be present – though not elsewhere in the empire – and that the chosen candidate would then swear allegiance, a detail which effectively gave the emperor a veto over appointments. The

The high point of Callistus's pontificate was the Concordat of Worms in 1123, which restored powers of ecclesiastical investiture to the papacy.

emperor could invest the new bishop (or abbot) with a sceptre, because that was a symbol of temporal authority, but not with the ring or crozier, symbols of spiritual authority. This was not all that the most rigorous members of the Gregorian reform party might have wanted, but the Concordat nonetheless was a major concession by the emperor, and in practice worked in favour of the church rather than the empire.

THE FIRST LATERAN COUNCIL

The Concordat was formalized at what has become known as the First Lateran Council. It met between 18 and, probably, 27 March 1123, though it had been summoned the previous June, well before the Concordat was finally agreed. The Concordat was referred to in three of the canons, most expressly in canon 8: 'If any prince or other lay person should arrogate to himself the disposition or donation of ecclesiastical things or possessions, let him be regarded as sacrilegious.' The Council marked the apogee of Callistus's pontificate. There had been many Lateran, and other, synods before, but possibly none quite as large – at least 300 bishops attended. Callistus referred to it as a 'general council' of the church, and it has come to be regarded by the Roman Catholic Church as ecumenical, that is, a binding council of the whole church, though there was no one present from the Eastern church. Hitherto all general councils of the church had taken place in the East. This was the first in the West and has been followed by a dozen more, five in all being termed Lateran Councils, from the location in Rome where they have been held. 'Lateran I' was of course not entirely taken up with settling the question of investiture. Most of its provisions were concerned with reform of the church in a wider sense –

The Council marked the apogee of Callistus's pontificate.

CONCORDAT OF WORMS

WHAT FOLLOWS IS THE TEXT OF HENRY V'S EDICT. It had been preceded by a 'Privilege' granted by Pope Callistus II making concessions to the emperor in relation to his involvement in elections:

'In the name of the holy and indivisible Trinity, I, Henry, by the grace of God august emperor of the Romans, for the love of God and of the holy Roman church and of our master pope Calixtus, and for the healing of my soul, do remit to God, and to the holy apostles of God, Peter and Paul, and to the holy catholic church, all investiture through ring and staff; and do grant that in all the churches that are in my kingdom or empire there may be canonical election and free consecration. All the possessions and regalia of St Peter which, from the beginning of this discord unto this day, whether in the time of my father or also in mine, have been abstracted, and which I hold: I restore to that same holy Roman church. As to those things, moreover, which I do not hold, I will faithfully aid in their restoration. As to the possessions also of all other churches and princes, and of all other lay and clerical persons which have been lost in that war: according to the counsel of the princes, or according to justice, I will restore the things that I hold; and of those things which I do not hold I will faithfully aid in the restoration. And I grant true peace to our master pope Calixtus, and to the holy Roman church, and to all those who are or have been on its side. And in matters where the holy Roman church shall demand aid I will grant it; and in matters concerning which it shall make complaint to me I will duly grant to it justice.'

QUOTED IN ERNEST F. HENDERSON, *SELECT HISTORICAL DOCUMENTS OF THE MIDDLE AGES.*

against simony and clerical concubinage as usual, against marriage between close relatives (participants in such relationships were to be deprived of their inheritance), on safeguarding pilgrims and the Truce of God, and promising remission of sins to all who went to Jerusalem to 'offer effective help towards the defence of the Christian people'.

A SHORT BUT IMPORTANT PONTIFICATE

Callistus's pontificate was relatively short, but in settling the investiture conflict it was of immense importance in the history of the church in the Middle Ages. The pope had little time for anything else, but he also intervened in a clash between the Cluniac monks and the bishops over the collection of revenues which the bishops believed ought to come to them, and the monks thought were rightfully theirs. The pope, who was not a monk, came down on the side of the bishops, causing a major crisis in the Cluniac order from which it never fully recovered. The Cluniacs had played a major part in the reform of the church, but the future belonged to another order of monks who sought, at least at first, a much simpler style in their lives, in the monasteries they erected and in their liturgy. This was the order of Cîteaux, the Cistercians, under their great protagonist St Bernard of Clairvaux.

EUGENIUS III

In the year 1112 a Burgundian nobleman named Bernard entered the recently founded monastery of Cîteaux, a few miles south of Dijon. The abbey had been struggling and might possibly have gone out of existence but for the group of 31 young men whom Bernard brought with him. Instead it flourished as the home of the Cistercian order, or White Monks, so called from the colour of their habit. Four houses of the order were then established in quick succession, one of them, in 1115, at Clairvaux, where Bernard became abbot. By the time of his death in 1153 there were no fewer than 345 houses, and the number eventually rose to well over 700.

In some ways the order of Cîteaux had been created in opposition to the elaborate monastic ritual of the abbey of Cluny. The monks were to live simple lives of silence, prayer and manual labour. They lived in seclusion – as the locations of the ruins of the great Cistercian monasteries of Rievaulx and Fountains in Yorkshire, in northern England, still bear witness.

THE TWO BERNARDS

Bernard himself led anything but a secluded life. He was heavily committed to preaching the crusades, and was closely involved in the establishment of the Knights Templar, but when Bernardo Paganelli was elected pope in 1145, he was dismayed. It is usually said that he did not think that Bernardo, or Pope Eugenius III as he became, was sufficiently competent for the office. But it may also have been that he did not wholly approve that a monk, whose life was supposedly lived in isolation from the world, should accept so high profile a role in medieval society.

Eugenius was not originally a Cistercian, but had joined another order, the Camaldolese, at their monastery of St Zeno in Pisa (in all probability Pisa was his home town). He had not only become prior of the monastery, but had also served as a canon of the cathedral in Pisa, and had been its administrator. But then he met St Bernard, who persuaded him to join the Cistercian

BIRTH NAME **Bernardo Paganelli di Montemagno**
BORN **Near Pisa, date unknown**
PREDECESSOR **Lucius II**
INSTALLED **18 February 1145**
DIED **8 July 1153**
SUCCESSOR **Anastasius IV**

order. In 1138 he entered Bernard's own monastery of Clairvaux, and in 1141 he became abbot of SS Vincent and Anastasius, the Cistercian house in Rome. It is not clear that he ever became a cardinal, but on the sudden death of his predecessor, Lucius II, he was immediately chosen as pope.

As pope, Eugenius III issued the very first crusading bull, in which he promised those who took part freedom from debt and also 'an indulgence', or forgiveness of their sins.

THE COMMUNE OF ROME

There was need for haste. The late pope had been forced to confront not just the sons of Roger II of Sicily, who were making incursions into papal territory, but, more problematically, the people of Rome themselves. In 1145 the Romans had established a commune, a form of republic, in the city, inspired by the radical monk Arnold of Brescia and headed by Giordano Pierleone, a member of one of Rome's most powerful clans. They managed to gain control of most of Rome, and of all the major churches. Pope Lucius had turned to the German king Conrad III, but he had only recently succeeded to the throne, and was in any case too insecure at home to concern himself with rebels in Rome. Lucius therefore took matters into his own hands. The militia was under the control of the commune, but the pope was able to muster a few troops and launched an attack on the Capitol, where the senate, the ruling council, was ensconced. In the course of the assault Lucius was hit by one of the heavy stones with which the senators were defending themselves. He was taken to St Gregory's monastery but died of his injuries soon afterwards.

With the city's churches in rebel hands, the new pope Eugenius III left Rome for Farfa, north of Rome, where he was consecrated, and then took up residence at Viterbo. This was a strategic spot, because it allowed papal forces to control supply routes from the north to the city. The commune had to sue, if not exactly for peace, at least for a compromise, which entailed the dismissal by the commune of the city prefect, Giordano Pierleone, and the acceptance of papal sovereignty. The accord did not last. The pope celebrated Christmas 1145 in Rome, but was back in Viterbo in January 1146. In the meantime, however, Eugenius had encountered Bishop Hugh of Jabala (in Syria) who had come to the papal court to report on the situation in the Holy Land, where Edessa (now Urfa in southeast Turkey) had fallen to the Muslims on Christmas Eve 1144. The pope also received a delegation of Armenian bishops under their primate, the Catholicos, who were complaining of the pressure that was being put upon them by the Byzantine emperor.

A CALL TO CRUSADE

These meetings prompted Eugenius to issue the very first crusading bull which, like all important papal documents, is called by its opening words, *Quantum predecessores*, 'How much our predecessors', that is, previous popes, 'laboured for the freedom of the Church in the East'. He went on to describe the fall of Edessa, the slaughter of the archbishop and his clergy as well as many other Christians, and the scattering of the relics of the saints. He called upon the nobles of Europe to go on crusade – and promised them freedom from harassment over debt at least while they were away, which may have proved a considerable attraction, as well as safety for their families. But he also granted them something new, an 'indulgence', which was to become in time a major part of Catholic devotion, and would help to bring about the Reformation in the 16th century. The church punished sinners, and so did God. Punishments that the church had imposed ('penances') it could of course commute into something else, such as going to the Holy Land. But now Eugenius seemed to be saying that the church could forgive not only the penance it had imposed itself, but through an indulgence the punishment placed by God upon a sinner (see box).

Louis VII of France, at his Christmas court, was immediately moved to announce that he was going on crusade, although it is not clear whether he had received a copy of the bull by then. Bernard of Clairvaux also received a copy from his former disciple, now pope, with a humble request for improvements. Bernard made some suggestions, and Eugenius reissued the bull on 1 March 1146. He also commissioned Bernard to preach the crusade. The bull had been addressed to the king of France, but Bernard went further and involved the German king. This was not entirely to Eugenius's liking because, still in exile from Rome, he needed German help to recover that city rather than to defend the Holy Land.

THE CHURCH IN ENGLAND AND IRELAND

Unable to settle in Rome, Eugenius went on his travels. He visited France, where he handed over the crusading banner to the French king at Saint Denis. He returned to Cîteaux, and held a synod at Rheims in March 1148 where reforms were agreed, essentially those that had been passed at the Lateran synod in 1139. There were no English bishops at the Rheims synod, because King Stephen had refused to let them attend. Eugenius thought about excommunicating the king, but instead gave his support to Henry I's daughter, the empress Matilda, then locked in civil war with Stephen. One unfortunate casualty of this conflict was William Fitzherbert, archbishop of York, who had been a chaplain to Stephen. He was opposed by the local Cistercians and by Bernard of Clairvaux, but had been supported by Lucius II. After Lucius's death the Cistercians returned to the attack, and this time the new pope Eugenius III backed them up. William was replaced by a Cistercian abbot, and retired to live as a monk at Winchester. But after the death of his replacement, which occurred at about the same time as the deaths of Bernard and Eugenius, he returned in triumph, only to die almost immediately afterwards, possibly by poison. He was canonized as St William of York in 1227.

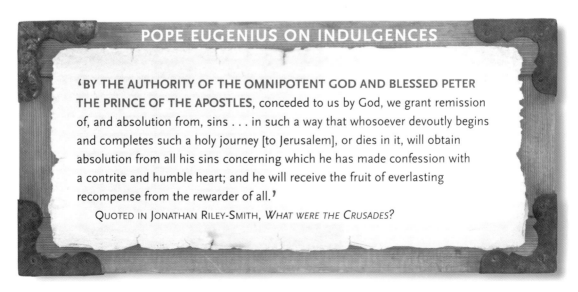

POPE EUGENIUS ON INDULGENCES

'BY THE AUTHORITY OF THE OMNIPOTENT GOD AND BLESSED PETER THE PRINCE OF THE APOSTLES, conceded to us by God, we grant remission of, and absolution from, sins . . . in such a way that whosoever devoutly begins and completes such a holy journey [to Jerusalem], or dies in it, will obtain absolution from all his sins concerning which he has made confession with a contrite and humble heart; and he will receive the fruit of everlasting recompense from the rewarder of all.'

QUOTED IN JONATHAN RILEY-SMITH, *WHAT WERE THE CRUSADES?*

Eugenius also involved himself in the affairs of the church in Ireland, which was divided up into four archdioceses, and with Scandinavia, to which he sent as legate the Englishman Nicholas Breakspear (later Pope Hadrian IV).

THE CRUSHING DEFEAT OF THE SECOND CRUSADE

Events seemed to be going well for the pope under the tutelage of Bernard of Clairvaux, who wrote for him a book of guidance, describing the ideal pontiff. But then in 1149 came news of the failure of the Second Crusade. It was not simply a failure, it was a débâcle, and kings Louis and Conrad returned home with nothing gained but many lives lost. The reputations of Eugenius and Bernard went into decline, while back in Rome the commune was reasserting itself, under the leadership of Arnold of Brescia. The papal court, unable to move back into the city, established itself at Albano, while the pope solicited support to recover the city. Roger of Sicily promised to help because he needed papal support against an alliance between the Germans and the Byzantines to attack Sicily. The attack on Rome failed, though the pope was shortly afterwards able to visit the city for a short time. Eugenius was wary of Roger: he did not want to be too dependent on a powerful neighbour to the south, and he also wanted free elections to bishoprics, which Roger was reluctant to grant but eventually conceded in July 1150.

> Louis VII, at his Christmas court, was immediately moved to announce that he was going on crusade.

German kings had been protectors of the papacy in the past. Now Eugenius turned to Conrad III, who agreed to come to Rome to be crowned emperor in autumn 1152. The pope's hand was forced, because the commune was also making approaches to Conrad, so Eugenius had to act. But Conrad never came. He died on 15 February 1152, to be succeeded by Frederick I Barbarossa. Frederick informed the pope of his election, but did not ask his approval: in his response Eugenius gave it anyway. Negotiations began between the pope and the German king. The commune therefore thought it politic to come to an understanding with Eugenius, who was able to return to Rome at the end of 1152.

At Constance, on 23 March 1153, a treaty was signed between pope and king. Eugenius undertook to crown Frederick emperor, while Frederick agreed not to enter into any treaties with either Sicily or the Roman commune without the prior agreement of the pope. Both undertook not to cede any part of Italy to the Byzantines, and each was to respect the other's sovereignty. But Eugenius died long before Frederick could visit Rome. And it was ironic that, after struggling to gain control of the city, he died outside of it, at Tivoli, in July 1153.

HADRIAN IV

s a young man Nicholas Breakspear tried to enter the Benedictine abbey of St Albans, but was refused. He had been educated there, and his father was already a monk at the abbey, but Nicholas was not allowed to become a novice. He subsequently travelled to France, where he continued his education, and eventually joined the canons regular of St Rufus at Avignon. He became prior of the monastery, then in about 1140 its abbot. His interpretation of the Rule proved too strict for the community, who complained to the pope about him. Nicholas therefore went to Rome in about 1145 and presented himself at the court of Pope Eugenius. Eugenius agreed to remove him from his abbacy, but kept him in Rome and in 1149 made him cardinal bishop of Albano. In 1152 he sent him to Scandinavia as papal legate.

Nicholas had found his niche: he proved to be the perfect civil servant. He arrived in Norway in July 1152, then spent the next six months on a fact-finding tour of the country. Early in 1153 he called a synod at Nidaros (modern Trondheim) which issued a constitution for the church in Norway, setting it on a sound financial footing and establishing Nidaros itself as the metropolitan see. Just six months later Nicholas set about doing the same thing for Sweden, calling a synod at Linköping. He set in train a reform of the Swedish church, but he was not able to establish a metropolitan see, although he laid the foundations for the future primacy of Uppsala. He also visited Denmark. And, again like the ideal civil servant, he introduced to Scandinavia Peter's Pence, a tax to be paid to the pope which had first been granted in the eighth century by the Anglo-Saxon king Offa of Mercia.

ANASTASIUS IV

By the time Nicholas returned to Rome in November 1154, Eugenius III had been succeeded by Pope Anastasius IV. Anastasius had been elected probably because he was Rome-born, and was therefore thought to be acceptable to the commune that controlled the city. The cardinal electors were proved right: in his short pontificate he managed the commune well, and succeeded in staying in the city, which neither Eugenius nor, as will be seen, Hadrian were able to do. When chosen Anastasius was already an old man. His pontificate lasted only a year and a half, and he died soon after Nicholas's return. The cardinals, impressed, it seems likely, by Nicholas's achievements in Scandinavia, elected him to succeed.

BIRTH NAME Nicholas Breakspear
BORN Abbot's Langley, Hertfordshire, c. 1100
PREDECESSOR Anastasius IV
INSTALLED 5 December 1154
DIED 7 September 1159
SUCCESSOR Alexander III

The only British-born pope Hadrian IV's accession caused riots in Rome. During his pontificate he was caught between the political schemes of Frederick Barbarossa and William of Sicily.

HADRIAN IV VERSUS THE ROMAN COMMUNE

The new pontiff was almost immediately challenged by the Roman commune. It had been happy enough with a Roman pope, but was discontented with the choice of an Englishman. There were riots, and an attempt was made to assassinate one of the cardinals. Hadrian reacted firmly, placing the city under an interdict, which meant the banning of all religious services. This was disastrous for Rome, which financially relied heavily upon the visits of pilgrims. The commune had to capitulate, and agreed to expel the chief agitator, Arnold of Brescia.

Pope Eugenius had agreed the treaty of Constance with the German king Frederick Barbarossa. Hadrian now had to renew it, for he was under pressure from Sicily. Roger II had died in February 1154, to be succeeded by his son William I, and William was now invading papal territory south of Rome. He was excommunicated for doing so, but the pope needed military assistance, and Barbarossa came to Hadrian's aid – though naturally with an agenda of his own. He wanted to be crowned as emperor by the pope, and he also wanted some places in northern Italy recognized as part of his territory: he had ambitions to restore the empire of Charlemagne. The Treaty of Constance was renewed in January 1155, and Hadrian and Frederick met at Sutri on 8 June. It was not an easy encounter. Frederick refused at first to perform the customary stirrup ceremony – that is to act as groom to the pope – but then agreed to do so. He also had Arnold of Brescia arrested and executed. Yet when the coronation took place in St Peter's on 18 June, the pope altered the ceremony to emphasize the submission of imperial power to papal.

It was a dangerous time to be in Rome. Frederick and the pope could enter only because Cardinal Octavian, a relative of Frederick, had previously secured it with military force. The Roman commune had not been informed of what was going to happen, and after the coronation its supporters rioted against the German soldiers in the city, then tried to imprison the pope. Hadrian and Frederick left the city together, but they fell out over Frederick's demands, and Barbarossa refused either to return to Rome to crush the commune, or to act against William of Sicily. Instead he went back to Germany, leaving Hadrian to cope as well as he could. But William was in a weak position. Some of his barons had risen in rebellion against him, and the Byzantines had opportunistically come to their aid. William agreed to crush the Roman commune and to make territorial concessions to the pope in return for his support. But then the tide turned in favour of William. He defeated the rebel barons and the Byzantines retreated. He besieged the papal city of Benevento, where the pope and the cardinals were residing. The cardinals, who had originally been against a deal with William, now changed their minds and a treaty was drawn up. By the Treaty of Benevento of June 1156 the pope recognized William as king not only of Sicily but of much territory in the south. In the south of Italy there were to be relatively free elections to ecclesiastical offices, in the spirit of the Gregorian reform (the king maintained a veto), though in

Sicily itself papal legates could come and go only with royal approval, and there were to be no appeals to the pope. William accepted that the pope was his feudal lord and agreed to pay an annual levy. In November 1156 Hadrian returned to Rome, much strengthened.

FRESH QUARRELS WITH THE EMPEROR

The Treaty of Benevento was seen quite differently by Frederick. It seemed to contradict the Treaty of Constance, according to which neither pope nor emperor were to make territorial concessions to the Normans in Sicily without the approval of the other. Benevento cut across Frederick's claims to territory in the south of Italy. In October 1157 two cardinal legates met Frederick at Besançon. They were sent by Hadrian to explain papal policy, and to complain about the arrest of Archbishop Eskil, whom Hadrian had made primate of Scandinavia. However, when the legates read out Hadrian's letter to the emperor, the German chancellor translated the Latin word '*beneficia*' ('benefits') in such a way as to suggest that it was the feudal term indicating that Frederick was a vassal of the pope. The emperor was furious and expelled the legates. A further letter from Hadrian, explaining that '*beneficia*' was to be interpreted as

THE BULL *LAUDABILITER*

THE BULL *LAUDABILITER* WAS ISSUED IN 1155 and addressed to King Henry II of England. The reference in the first line to the rights of the papacy over islands stems from the Donation of Constantine (see page 17).

'There is indeed no doubt, as thy Highness doth also acknowledge, that Ireland and all other islands which Christ the Sun of Righteousness has illumined, and which have received the doctrines of the Christian faith, belong to the jurisdiction of St Peter and of the holy Roman Church. Wherefore, so much the more willingly do we grant to them that the right faith and the seed grateful to God may be planted in them, the more we perceive, by examining more strictly our conscience, that this will be required of us. Thou hast signified to us, indeed, most beloved son in Christ, that thou dost desire to enter into the island of Ireland, in order to subject the people to the laws and to extirpate the vices that have there taken root, and that thou art willing to pay an annual pension to St Peter of one penny from every house, and to preserve the rights of the churches in that land inviolate and entire. We, therefore, seconding with the favour it deserves thy pious and laudable desire, and granting a benignant assent to thy petition, are well pleased that, for the enlargement of the bounds of the church. for the restraint of vice, for the correction of morals and the introduction of virtues, for the advancement of the Christian religion, thou shouldst enter that island, and carry out there the things that look to the honour of God and to its own salvation. And may the people of that land receive thee with honour, and venerate thee as their master; provided always that the rights of the churches remain inviolate and entire, and saving to St Peter and the holy Roman Church the annual pension of one penny from each house.'

QUOTED IN ERNEST F. HENDERSON, *SELECT HISTORICAL DOCUMENTS OF THE MIDDLE AGES*.

'benefits' and not as 'fiefs', patched up the quarrel for a time, but only for a time. In the summer of 1158 Frederick again marched into northern Italy, and at Roncaglia in November 1158 held a diet at which he claimed rights over the north, and even over Rome itself. He condemned the pope for having refused to approve the man he nominated to the archbishopric of Ravenna. Hadrian now proposed renewing the Treaty of Constance, but Frederick refused, proposing instead a form of board of arbitration to settle disputes – which Hadrian refused in turn. The emperor then began negotiations with the Roman commune.

A NEW PAPAL COURT

At this point Hadrian thought it politic to move south, closer to the Norman kingdom. He established his court at Anagni, southeast of Rome, where he made plans to establish an alliance of northern Italian cities against Frederick, promising to excommunicate the emperor unless he rescind the decisions of Roncaglia within 40 days. Before the 40 days were up, Hadrian had died.

The English writer John of Salisbury, later bishop of Chartres, was often in Rome, and knew Hadrian well. He was, he said, friendly and easy to talk to. Boso, whom Hadrian made a cardinal and sent as one of the legates on the disastrous mission to Frederick, liked him greatly. He was friendly and charitable, he said. Hadrian certainly was generous: despite the rebuffs he had suffered from the abbey at St Albans and the community at St Rufus in Avignon, he rewarded them both during his pontificate. He also encouraged the English king, Henry II, to take over Ireland. There is even a bull, *Laudabiliter*, which authorizes this act of aggression (see page 109). Its authenticity, however, is doubtful.

INNOCENT III

part from Hadrian's immediate successor, Alexander III (1159–81), and Innocent's immediate predecessor Celestine III (1191–8), the Roman pontiffs between Hadrian IV and Innocent III had short reigns. All were plagued by the same problems of an over-mighty German emperor and the kingdom of Sicily. In 1195 the emperor Henry VI captured the kingdom of Sicily for himself and the following year began an ultimately unsuccessful attempt to make the imperial title hereditary in his Hohenstaufen family. Henry's territorial gains left the papal states surrounded, and presented a whole new set of problems. Lotario de Conti, who was elected Pope Innocent III at the extraordinarily early age of 37, was the man to deal with them.

Lotario was born into the noble family of the Conti of Segni, which lies some 30 miles southeast of Rome. His mother was a Scotti, one of the ancient noble families of Rome itself, and traditional enemies of the Boboni, the family of Pope Celestine III. Lotario came to Rome to study, possibly in the monastery of Sant'Andrea, and then went to Paris, where one of his fellow students was the Englishman Stephen Langton, whom he was later to make archbishop of Canterbury. He returned to

Rome in 1186, and was ordained subdeacon by Pope Gregory VIII (1187), though he played no significant part in that pontificate. Four years later his uncle Pope Clement III (1187–91) made him cardinal deacon of SS Sergio and Bacco. Celestine III made little use of him because of the family feud, and instead he was able to put his considerable learning to good use by writing several books.

BIRTH NAME Lotario de Conti
BORN Gavagnano, near Segni, c. 1160 / 61
PREDECESSOR Celestine III
INSTALLED 22 February 1198
DIED 16 July 1216
SUCCESSOR Honorius III

On Celestine's death the cardinals met in the Lateran, but some, fearing for their safety, moved to what might be called a safe house, the fortified residence of the Frangipani family known as the Septizonium. Lotario, however, remained in the Lateran, and there he was swiftly elected pope. He was still a deacon, and was ordained priest on 21 February and consecrated bishop and enthroned as pope the following day.

He had immediate problems. First he had to secure Rome. He tried to do so by removing all those, including officials of the commune, who were more sympathetic to the empire than they were to the papacy. He did not entirely succeed, and after being insulted in the course of a procession on 7 April 1203 he had to withdraw to what is now Palestrina, to the east of Rome, for almost 12 months. By 1205, however, his writ ran relatively unchallenged in Rome itself. The empire, however, was a different matter.

THE GERMAN QUESTION

The problem was that there were two claimants to the imperial throne – three, if the infant Frederick II, king of Sicily, the son of the emperor Henry VI and Queen Constance, is included. Constance died in December 1198, leaving the pope as Frederick's guardian. The two main candidates for the kingship of Germany, and thus ultimately for the imperial title, were Henry's brother Philip of Swabia, who was elected in March 1199, and Otto of Brunswick, who was elected in opposition and was chosen the following June. Innocent tried at first to remain neutral, but inevitably this proved impossible because only he could bestow the imperial crown. It was his duty to decide, he said in his decree *Venerabilem* of 1202, on the basis of what would be best for the church. Innocent tended first to favour Philip, but then Philip launched an attack on Monte Cassino, so he switched to Otto, who promised to enlarge the papal states in Italy, and not to seize the personal property of German bishops when they died, as was hitherto the custom. However, when Otto invaded southern Italy and Sicily, the latter being saved only by the use of papal forces, Innocent restored his favours to Philip. To cement his relationship with Philip he set about arranging a marriage between one of Philip's daughters and a son of his brother Richard of Segni. But then in June 1208 Philip was assassinated, and it was Otto whom Innocent crowned emperor in Rome on 4 October 1209.

Otto proved to be an unsatisfactory ally. After his coronation as emperor he invaded southern Italy and Sicily. The pope released Otto's subjects from their oaths of loyalty, then in November 1210 excommunicated him and declared him deposed. Innocent now turned to the king of France, Philip Augustus. He also recognized as rightful king of Germany Frederick II, who was crowned in 1212 and who, in July the following year, issued the Golden Bull of Eger in

The most powerful of all medieval popes, Innocent III called for a crusade against the Cathar heretics of Languedoc. He gave himself the title of 'Vicar of Christ'.

which he promised fully to restore the papal states. Frederick's son Henry was crowned king of Sicily, and Frederick later undertook to allow Sicily independence of the empire, and agreed that it should be a vassal of the papacy. It seemed to Innocent, and it remained for the rest of his pontificate, an acceptable outcome.

KING JOHN OF ENGLAND

Innocent's problems with King John of England also had, at least from the pope's viewpoint, a satisfactory result. In 1207 there was a disputed election to the archbishopric of Canterbury. The pope as a consequence nominated the Lincolnshire-born Stephen Langton, whom he had created a cardinal priest in 1206. King John, however, was not prepared to accept Langton, and from 1208 to 1214 England was placed under a papal interdict. In 1213 John capitulated – declaring England and Ireland to be fiefs of the papacy – and the exiled Langton returned. But then Langton lent his support to the rebel barons who, in 1215, forced upon John the Magna Carta as a bill of their rights. Innocent was furious at what he regarded as a betrayal by his archbishop of one of the pope's vassals, and as an attack on the legitimate authority of a monarch. He suspended Langton from office and declared the Magna Carta worthless because it had been signed under duress. After Innocent's death Langton took up his post as archbishop once again. It was not just England and Sicily which became vassals of the papacy during Innocent's pontificate. So did Poland, Aragón and Portugal.

THE FOURTH CRUSADE

From the very beginning of his pontificate Innocent was eager to launch a new crusade. He announced that he was launching one in August 1198, and set a tax on ecclesiastical revenues to pay for it. He wrote to the Byzantine emperor Alexius III complaining about both the Greek church's failure to submit to papal authority and the emperor's failure to aid the crusader states, which were still precariously surviving. The Venetians were contracted to supply ships for the expedition, but when there turned out not to be enough money to pay for the transport, the crusaders agreed to attack Zara, a city on the Dalmatian coast, for the benefit of the Venetians, despite the fact that Innocent had forbidden them to attack other Christians. The crusaders arrived at Constantinople in July 1203, and went no further. They became caught up in a dynastic struggle in which Alexius was overthrown, and between July 1203 and 15 April 1204 the ancient city was pillaged by the Christian army.

A Greek chronicler wrote that 'Even the Muslims would have been more merciful.' A Western emperor, Baldwin of Flanders, replaced Alexius, and a Latin patriarch the Greek one. The pope was furious, but consoled himself with the thought that this might bring about reunion between the two branches of the church – which of course it did not. He was still eager to launch a crusade for the defence of the Holy Land, and set a new tax. A date was fixed for 1217, but by that time Innocent was dead, and it did not happen.

THE ALBIGENSIAN CRUSADE

He did, however, launch another form of crusade, one against the Albigensian (or Cathar) heretics in the south of France – they were so called from the city of Albi, taken to be the centre of the Albigensian faith. They had been many times condemned for their belief in the existence of two equal and opposed principles, the one of Good, the other of Evil, and there had been several preaching campaigns against them. In January 1208 Pierre de Castelnau, the papal legate, was assassinated by a servant of the count of Toulouse. Innocent responded by ordering the launch of a major military campaign against the Albigensians which deteriorated into a bloody war between the barons of the north of France and those of the south.

The Order of Preachers, better known as the Dominicans after their founder St Dominic Guzmán, were established to combat the Albigensians by preaching Catholicism. It was also at this time that the Order of Friars Minor, commonly named the Franciscans after Francis of Assisi, came into being. Both received their authority from Innocent, who was also concerned to reform the traditional orders, insisting in 1203 that they hold general chapters every three years.

> **It was not just England and Sicily which became vassals of the papacy during Innocent's pontificate. So did Poland, Aragón and Portugal.**

LATERAN IV ON HERETICS

'WE CONDEMN ALL HERETICS, WHATEVER NAMES THEY MAY GO UNDER. They have different faces indeed, but their tails are tied together inasmuch as they are alike in their pride. Let those who are condemned be handed over to the secular authorities present, or to their bailiffs for due punishment. Clerics are first to be degraded from their orders . . . Let secular authorities, whatever office they may be discharging, be advised and urged and if necessary compelled by ecclesiastical censure, if they wish to be reputed and held to be faithful, to take publicly an oath for the defence of the faith to the effect that they will seek, insofar as they can, to expel from the lands subject to their jurisdiction all heretics designated by the Church in good faith.'

QUOTED IN NORMAN P. TANNER, *DECREES OF THE ECUMENICAL COUNCILS.*

Note: It is important to understand while reading this quotation that the Church was unable to punish people by inflicting the death penalty, and that clerics were not allowed to be tried, or punished, by civil courts – hence they had first to be 'degraded'.

THE FOURTH LATERAN COUNCIL

These steps were all part of a much wider reform of the whole church, encapsulated in the Fourth Lateran Council which was summoned in April 1213, to meet in November 1215. All bishops of the Western Church were expected to attend, only one or two being left behind to attend to ecclesiastical matters in each province. They were even asked to submit suggestions for the agenda. When all had assembled, including abbots and lay representatives, it is thought that there were perhaps 1200 people present, 404 of them being bishops. This was for the most part, however, a Latin gathering, and dealt with issues of concern to the Western Church. But the issues it addressed were wide-ranging: heresy (see box, page 113), 'the pride of the Greeks towards the Latins', the behaviour and dress of clerics (no 'red or green clothes, long sleeves or shoes with embroidery or pointed toes'), schools (cathedrals and other large churches were expected to provide education, including for the poor), elections and appeals, and the calling of a new crusade. The council demanded that Jews and Muslims should be distinctive from Christians in their dress, and that Catholics should go to confession at least once a year. In short, it gave new power to the bishops of the church and in the century which followed led to reform across Europe.

Innocent left behind him a vast collection of letters and legislative acts. He was the most powerful of medieval popes, the vicar of Christ, as he regularly called himself – the term had already been used by Hadrian IV – rather than the vicar of Peter. The church of Rome was the mother of churches, and the mother church of all the Christian faithful. He believed he enjoyed the *plenitudo potestatis*, the fullness of power in all matters ecclesiastical. The temporal sovereign had his own sphere of authority, it is true, but it received this authority, Innocent preached, 'as the moon receives its light from the sun'.

Innocent was still a young man when he died. He was hurrying north, to settle a dispute between the port cities of Pisa and Genoa, so that the crusade fixed for the following year might be the better launched. En route he caught a fever and died on 16 July 1216. He was buried at Perugia. Towards the end of the 19th century his remains were reburied in the basilica of St John Lateran.

GREGORY IX

nnocent III had been very young when elected. Most popes, however, were chosen when they were in their fifties or sixties, or in some cases even older. They therefore tended to have fairly short pontificates. This in turn meant that the problems of one pontificate spilled over into the next and sometimes even further. The problems which Innocent had encountered with Frederick II, and his attempt to incorporate Sicily into the empire, thereby effectively surrounding Rome, had to be faced by his successor Honorius III during his – not particularly short – pontificate (1216–27), and by Gregory IX after that.

Ugolino dei Conti came from the same family as Innocent III, and was raised by him to the cardinalate in 1198. He was well educated, with numerous intellectual interests. Above all,

Pope Gregory IX with two Dominicans and a bishop – perhaps discussing his new compilation of church law which was known as the Liber Extra *and became a standard work for ecclesiastical lawyers.*

perhaps, he was noted for his devotion. He was particularly close to Francis of Assisi, and even for a time considered joining the Franciscans, but Francis dissuaded him. He took particular interest in the order founded by Francis's sister, now known as the Poor Clares, and drew up its rule. He was also a supporter of St Dominic, whom he seems to have met several times.

FREDERICK II AND THE PAPACY

In the election to succeed Honorius, which showed signs of being a fraught affair, the cardinals set up a committee to decide. Their first choice turned down the office; Ugolino was the second in line. He was immediately confronted by the problem of the emperor Frederick II who at his imperial coronation had undertaken to go on crusade, but had failed to do so. Soon after Gregory IX became pope Frederick gathered his troops at Brindisi, but then did not depart because he was ill. His sickness seems to have been real, not feigned, but an exasperated Gregory excommunicated him nonetheless. Frederick eventually embarked on crusade some nine months later, and the pope was mortified when the excommunicated emperor, with whom the prelates in the Holy Land were forbidden to do business, managed to negotiate the surrender of Jerusalem in March 1229.

After Frederick's return from crusade in 1230, relations improved, but later deteriorated again. In 1239 Gregory discovered that Frederick was writing to the cardinals, attempting to drive a wedge between them and himself. He issued a bull of excommunication and called a general council to be held at Easter 1241 in Rome. The emperor, however, took prisoner a number of prelates as they made their way to the council, and the meeting never took place – not at least in Gregory's pontificate: it would meet at Lyons in 1245 under Innocent IV. Meanwhile, the imperial army entered Rome in April 1241; Gregory died, still defiant, a few months later.

BIRTH NAME **Ugolino dei Conti de Segni**
BORN **Anagni, c. 1155**
PREDECESSOR **Honorius III**
INSTALLED **21 March 1227**
DIED **22 August 1241**
SUCCESSOR **Celestine IV**

THE INQUISITION

GREGORY IX IS OFTEN CREDITED – IF THAT IS THE WORD – WITH INVENTING THE INQUISITION. The real origin of the inquisition is to be found in Pope Lucius III's bull *Ad abolendam* ('For the abolition [of heresy]'), published in 1184. This called upon all bishops to set up an investigation – an inquisition – into heresy in their dioceses. If heresy were found, then they were to hand over the perpetrators to the secular authorities for punishment. Pope Gregory IX's refinement, about the year 1233, was to appoint special inquisitors, most of them either Franciscans or, particularly, Dominicans to undertake the investigations. They were not appointed for the church as a whole, but only in those places where heresy was known to exist and, importantly, where secular rulers would be prepared to support the suppression of heresy because inquisitors themselves had no coercive powers. Gregory's chief concern was the suppression of the Albigensians of Languedoc. Twenty years later Pope Innocent IV, in his bull *Ad extirpanda* ('For exterminating [heretics]'), permitted the use of torture, though there is no evidence that it was widely used. This medieval form of the inquisition had largely died out by the 15th century, but was revived in Rome in 1542 for use against Protestantism, especially in Italy. The Spanish Inquisition was something very different, but its story lies outside the limits of this book.

The expansion of Christian power

Such a story is typical of the medieval papacy, but Gregory's pontificate was importantly different in a number of ways. He was eager to see the restoration of Christian power in the Holy Land, but he was also committed to expanding Christianity into the still pagan areas of northern Europe. He sent the Teutonic Knights to the lands along the Baltic, and set the Dominicans on a preaching mission to attract recruits. He also approached the Dominicans, this time in the person of the Spanish scholar Raymond of Peñafort, to update the church's canon law. Raymond produced a new compilation of the law already in existence, editing it where need be, and adding new canons from Pope Gregory's own documents. It was known as the *Liber Extra*, and became the standard text for church lawyers. Gregory also restored the University of Paris, whose masters and pupils had been obliged to leave the city because of disturbances, and founded a new university at Toulouse.

The First Conclave

Gregory has a special place in papal history because it seems that it was he who invented the papal conclave. As he lay dying in the heat of a Roman summer, he is said to have recalled what a canon lawyer, an Englishman, had once suggested to him: that the way to achieve a swift decision about a new pope was to lock up ('*con clave*' comes from the Latin '*cum clavis*', meaning 'with a key') the cardinals until they had made up their minds. He instructed the senator of Rome, Matteo Rossi Orsini, to do just that. After Gregory's death he locked them into the Septizonium Palace, along with the late pope's coffin, until they had chosen a new pope. There were only 12 cardinals in all, two of whom had been seized by Frederick and were still held captive. They still took six weeks, living in very considerable discomfort: one cardinal complained that whenever he lay down to sleep a soldier prodded him with his spear. They chose a simple way out. They elected the extremely ill bishop of Sabina, who took the name Celestine IV. He died three weeks later, but by that time the cardinals were safely out of Rome.

GREGORY X

n Roman Catholic mythology the thirteenth is often referred to as 'the Greatest of the Centuries'. Certainly it had great saints — Francis and Dominic have already been mentioned, and there were many others. It saw a vast expansion of religious life — there were new orders of friars, and a growth of the more traditional monastic orders. It was the century in which the universities, then very much part of ecclesiastical rather than secular life, began to flourish across Europe. But it was also the period in which the crusaders were finally driven from the Holy Land, and in which the Teutonic Knights, sent to evangelize in northern Europe, crashed on the ice of Lake Peipus to an ignominious defeat at the hands of the (Christian) Alexander Nevsky, prince of Novgorod. And it was a time when the cardinals were so divided that it took them months, or, in the case of Gregory X, nearly three years, to choose a pope.

The popes of the 13th century had been much concerned with preventing the German Hohenstaufen kings, especially in the person of Frederick II, from ruling both the empire and Sicily. Gregory X's predecessor, Clement IV (1265–8) – whose own election had taken four months – had handed the crown of Sicily to Charles of Anjou, who had defeated Manfred, Frederick's bastard son. But the last of the Hohenstaufen line, Conradin, son of Conrad IV of Germany, now made a claim and marched on Rome, where he was well received. But Charles defeated him, too, and had him beheaded. Clement found himself faced with a new dynasty in Sicily which was not content to be restricted to Sicily, but also laid claim to lands north of Rome. This was the situation when Clement died in Viterbo – seat of the papacy from 1257 to 1281 – in November 1268, and which he bequeathed to his successor, the choice of

BIRTH NAME **Tebaldo Visconti**
BORN **Piacenza, 1210**
PREDECESSOR **Clement IV**
INSTALLED **27 March 1272**
DIED **10 January 1276**
SUCCESSOR **Innocent V**

UBI PERICULUM

THE BULL *UBI PERICULUM*, issued at the Council of Lyons of 1274, was designed
to prevent lengthy vacancies in the Holy See.

'Where there is greater danger, there must certainly be greater foresight. We learn from
the past how heavy are the losses sustained by the Roman church in a long vacancy, how
perilous it is; we see this all too clearly when we wisely consider the crises undergone . . .
With the approval of the sacred council, we decree that if the pope dies in a city where
he was residing with his curia, the cardinals present in that city are obliged to await the
absent cardinals, but for ten days only. When these days have passed, whether those
absent have arrived or not, all are to assemble in the palace where the pope lived. Each
is to be content with one servant only, clerical or lay, at choice. We allow however those
in evident need to have two, with the same choice. In this palace all are to live in
common in one room, with no partition or curtain. Apart from free entry to a private
room [the 'privy'], the conclave is to be completely locked, so that no one can enter or
leave. No one may have access to the cardinals or permission to talk secretly with them,
nor are they themselves to admit anyone to their presence, except those who, by consent
of all the cardinals present, might be summoned only for the business of the imminent
election. It is not lawful for anyone to send a messenger or a written message to the
cardinals or to any one of them. Whoever acts otherwise, sending a messenger or a
written message, or speaking secretly to one of the cardinals, is to incur automatic
excommunication. In the conclave some suitable window is to be left open through
which the necessary food may be served conveniently to the cardinals, but no entry
for anyone is to be possible through this way.'

whom proved particularly difficult and led to the longest ever vacancy of the See of Rome.
Some of the cardinals sided with the policy of Clement, backing the French connection, others
wanted to break with it. There were also family rivalries. In Viterbo the townspeople waited for
an announcement, but when none came they grew restive. They locked the cardinals into the
papal palace, cut down their rations and in desperation removed the roof to hasten them
to a decision.

The townspeople . . . locked the cardinals into the papal palace, cut down their rations and in desperation removed the roof to hasten a decision.

A CRUSADING NOBLEMAN

Their choice was unexpected.
Tebaldo Visconti was a nobleman
who had been in the service of
the papacy and for 20 years
archdeacon of Liège. He had been
invited by King Louis IX of France
to join him in a crusade, but when

Louis died in Tunisia he went to join
Edward, Prince of Wales (the future
Edward I of England). He arrived there
in mid-1271, and he was still in Acre on
2 October of that year when he learned he
had been elected pope a month earlier. He
returned to Europe, but did not arrive at
Viterbo until early February 1272. A month
later he was ordained priest, then went on
to Rome for his consecration as pope.

On leaving Acre he had promised
never to forget the Holy Land, and the
crusades were central to his policy as pope.
It was for that reason that he called the
Second Council of Lyons, which lasted
from 1 May to 17 July 1274. His was a
multifaceted approach. He wanted to
establish peace in Europe to allow its
princes to go on crusade; he needed to
organize papal finances; and he wanted to
reunite the Greek and the Latin churches.
The Byzantine emperors had regained
Constantinople from the Latins in 1261,
and Michael VIII Palaeologus wanted to
escape from the isolation into which he
had fallen. He had learned that Charles
of Anjou had plans to recapture
Constantinople and needed allies, while

Gregory X laid down the first rules for the conduct of conclaves for the elections of popes. This photograph from 1939 shows the white smoke which signals that a new pope has been chosen by the cardinals.

Tebaldo, then still in the Holy Land, had told Michael of his desire for reunion because it would advance the cause of the crusade. Michael was therefore invited to take part in the Council of Lyons, as long as he accepted the *Filioque* and the primacy of the church of Rome. He was willing to do so, and sent representatives to Lyons, where the reunification of the two churches was proclaimed on 6 July. That was the theory: in practice it never took place as the emperor could not carry his people with him.

A BID TO SPEED UP PAPAL ELECTIONS

But perhaps the decree of the council which had most long-lasting effect was *Ubi periculum maius* ('where there is greater danger . . .'). Undoubtedly prompted by the difficulties that had attended the election of Gregory, the council laid down rules for the conduct of subsequent conclaves, which were intended to speed them up (see box, page 118). They were not always followed and even when they were, they were not always effective, but nonetheless they laid the foundation for the modern method of selecting a pope.

After the closure of the council Gregory set off back to Italy, but caught a fever on the way and died at Arezzo, where he was buried. A man of great talent, he was revered as a saint soon after his death.

CELESTINE V

Thanks he conclave procedure which Gregory X introduced was employed with success for the election of his successor, Innocent V, and it was implemented again almost immediately, for Innocent was pope for only six months. At his death in Rome, the cardinals met in the Lateran in June 1276, with Charles of Anjou overseeing the proceedings. He implemented Gregory's rules strictly, cutting back on the cardinals' rations the longer they took to decide. The conclave lasted from the end of June into the second week of July, in a sweltering heat which laid low several of the electors.

The man they chose, Pope Hadrian V, just had time to announce that he was suspending the provisions of *Ubi periculum* because of the intolerable strain they had imposed upon the cardinals, before himself expiring at Viterbo in August. The next election, of John XXI, was relatively swift despite the suspension, but for the rest of the century voting dragged on for several months, except in the case of Pope Honorius IV in 1285 when the political situation required an immediate election.

When Nicholas IV (1288–92) died on 4 April 1292 the 12 cardinals met first in Rome, either in the Savelli Palace on the Aventine Hill, or in the monastery at Santa Maria sopra Minerva. Twice they had to abandon Rome because of the heat, and then in October 1293 they met in Perugia. There were political divisions, some cardinals favouring the alliance with the French king of Naples, Charles II of Anjou, some opposing it. But the more significant division was between two ancient Roman families, the Colonnas and the Orsinis. Charles was eager for a resolution because he needed a pope to confirm a treaty he had signed with the Spanish kingdom of Aragón. He himself suggested a shortlist of candidates, all of whom were rejected.

CHARLES AND THE HERMIT

On his way back to Naples Charles visited the grotto of San Onofrio in the Morrone, a remote mountain range, which was home to a hermit called Peter. Peter came of a peasant family and had originally entered a Benedictine monastery, but then became a hermit. About 1233 he was ordained priest in Rome, though he could scarcely read or write and knew little Latin. He was, however, a saintly man and a charismatic figure. After his ordination he returned to the hermitage of the Holy Spirit in a remote region of the Maiella mountains, where his reputation for holiness began to attract pilgrims. It also attracted others to join him, and he founded a brotherhood of hermits of which he became abbot. It was a relatively successful order, approved by

BIRTH NAME **Pietro del Morrone**
BORN **Molise, Sant' Angelo de Mimosano, *c.* 1210**
PREDECESSOR **Nicholas IV**
INSTALLED **29 August 1294**
ABDICATED **13 December 1294**
SUCCESSOR **Boniface VIII**

Gregory X and drawing inspiration from the most radical faction among the Franciscans. It gained endowments and acquired property, but Peter hankered after the solitary life and he retired to the hermitage of San Onofrio, where Charles visited him in 1293. Charles persuaded Peter to write to the cardinals, upbraiding them for leaving the church so long without a head. The contents of the letter were revealed to the electors on 5 July, and they immediately chose Peter himself – which well may have been Charles's intention.

Whether or not that was the case, after a momentary hesitation and pressure from Charles, who promptly went back to see him, Peter agreed. He was escorted to L'Aquila, a town in Charles's domain, which he entered sitting on an ass in imitation of Christ entering Jerusalem. He was consecrated there on 29 August 1294, and soon

A saintly and charismatic figure, Pietro del Morrone was pope for less than a year, abdicating when he realized he could not perform his role effectively. He was canonized less than 20 years after his death.

afterwards created 12 new cardinals – five of them French, thanks to the intervention of Charles. No doubt this was done in imitation of the 12 apostles, but it also had the effect, also intended, of diminishing the influence of the Roman nobility whose rivalries in recent conclaves had been the chief cause of delay in electing popes. He then re-enacted the rules for conclaves drawn up at the Council of Lyons, which he had himself attended, walking all the way and arriving rather late.

Incompetence and illness

As pope, Celestine was obliged by Charles to settle not in Rome but at the Castel Nuovo in Naples. He was very much under the influence of the king of Sicily, but that was not his chief problem. He had no experience of church government beyond managing his own congregation of hermits (who became known as Celestines after his papal title, and upon whom, as pope, he showered privileges). He was an old man, well over 80, and simply not competent to run the church, which he very quickly came to realize. He asked advice from the leading canon lawyer among the cardinals, Benedetto Caetani, and Caetani advised him, quite correctly, that it was possible for a pope to abdicate. He explained his reasons to the cardinals on 9 and 10 December 1294, and resigned on 13 December. He was ill, he said, administratively incompetent, and wished to return to his hermitage. Eleven days later Benedetto Caetani was elected Pope Boniface VIII after only three ballots.

Celestine once again became Peter de Morrone. He had said he wanted to return to his hermitage, and this he did, but he then went to his monastery of St John, in Piano, before, it seems, setting out for Greece. But he never reached his destination. On the orders of the new pope he was taken to Gargano, and then to Anagni, and was finally incarcerated by his irritated successor in Castel Fumone, where he died of an infection on 19 May 1296.

He was not forgotten. There was much argument about the validity of his abdication, and consequently whether his successor had been legally elected. His successor, Boniface VIII, was particularly unacceptable to the king of France, and it was Philip the Fair of France who orchestrated the campaign to have Peter canonized. He was recognized as a saint, under the name of Peter de Morrone, in 1313, less than two decades after his death (see page 130).

BONIFACE VIII

t the beginning of the 13th century Innocent III had claimed for the papacy enormous authority which he had largely been able to realize. It was an ideology to which most if not all the popes of the 1200s subscribed, and it reached its apogee – and also its nemesis – in the person of Boniface VIII.

Benedetto Caetani came from a minor aristocratic family of Anagni, where he became a canon. He served also as a canon in Todi, where he studied law, no doubt attracted to the city because an uncle of his was its bishop. He went on to study law at Spoleto, and at the best known of faculties of canon law, that of Bologna. He entered the papal service, assisting legates visiting France (1264) and England (1265–6) to collect taxes for a crusade. In 1281 he was made a cardinal deacon, and in 1291 a cardinal priest, being ordained in Orvieto. He was something of a papal trouble-shooter, settling conflicts in Paris between the religious orders and the diocesan clergy, and then in the Treaty of Tarascon of 1281 bringing an end to the tension between the houses of Aragon and Anjou. Meanwhile he was accumulating benefices which he used to enrich his family.

THE PAPACY RETURNS TO ROME

During the long vacancy which preceded the election of Peter Morrone as Celestine V, Benedetto managed to remain neutral between the competing houses of Colonna and Orsini, which no doubt helped him when he became a candidate in the election that followed Celestine's resignation. It was afterwards alleged that he had engineered the abdication, but there is no proof of this claim, only evidence that – when Celestine asked his advice about the possibility of abdication – he assured him that it was possible for a pope to resign. Benedetto's judgement was technically correct, although it is not clear that any earlier pontiff had ever resigned except under duress. After his election he moved the papal entourage back to Rome from Naples, where it had been based under Celestine V. He also purged the curial officials, installing his own men in place of those whom Charles II of Naples had imposed upon Celestine.

BIRTH NAME Benedetto Caetani
BORN Agnani, c. 1235
PREDECESSOR Celestine V
INSTALLED 23 January 1295
DIED 11 October 1303
SUCCESSOR Benedict XI

EXCERPTS FROM *UNAM SANCTAM*

THE BULL *UNAM SANCTAM*, issued on 18 November 1302, was a powerful statement of the supremacy of spiritual over temporal power.

'Urged by faith, we are obliged to believe and to maintain that the Church is one, holy, catholic, and also apostolic. We believe in her firmly and we confess with simplicity that outside of her there is neither salvation nor the remission of sins . . .'

'The one who denies that the temporal sword is in the power of Peter has not listened well to the word of the Lord commanding: 'Put up thy sword into thy scabbard' [Matthew 26:52]. Both, therefore, are in the power of the Church, that is to say, the spiritual and the material sword, but the former is to be administered for the Church but the latter by the Church; the former in the hands of the priest; the latter by the hands of kings and soldiers, but at the will and sufferance of the priest . . .'

'However, one sword ought to be subordinated to the other and temporal authority, subjected to spiritual power . . .'

'Furthermore, we declare, we proclaim, we define that it is absolutely necessary for salvation that every human creature be subject to the Roman Pontiff. '

RELATIONS WITH PHILIP OF FRANCE

Six months after his consecration Sicily was returned to Charles of Anjou by the terms of the Peace of Anagni of June 1295. But the Sicilians rebelled, and six months after that they offered the crown to Frederick of Aragon. Sicily had once been a fief of the papacy, and Boniface wanted to restore that feudal relationship, but he never succeeded in doing so, and shortly before his death had to recognize the independence of the island. His interventions in European politics, including his effort to maintain Scotland's independence from England, were for the most part similarly unsuccessful. He saw himself as Innocent III had seen himself, as the judge standing over monarchs, the arbiter of disputes between nations. The nations, however, were becoming increasingly aware of themselves, and their rulers were more and more concerned not, as a century earlier, to expand their boundaries, but to establish order within their realms.

England and France were then at war over the English king's fiefs of Guienne and Gascony. The kings of both countries needed money for the war, and they levied a tax on their citizens, including the clergy. The church had long claimed exemption from taxes levied by the temporal power, unless imposed with the consent of the papacy, which Philip the Fair (Philip IV) of France did not have and Boniface would not grant. Philip levied the taxes nonetheless, and the pope replied with the bull *Clericis laicos* in February 1296. Philip, furious at this challenge to his sovereignty, responded that nothing of value should leave the country –

He saw himself . . . as the judge standing over monarchs, the arbiter of disputes between nations.

THE PAPAL TIARA

TRADITIONALLY POPES WERE CROWNED WITH A HEADDRESS consisting of three 'crowns', one above the other around a helmet which might be shaped like a cone, or at other times bulbous. This form of crown still appears in the escutcheon of the Vatican, though Pope Benedict XVI (2005–) has replaced it, in his personal coat of arms, with a mitre, similar to the mitre worn by any bishop of the Western church. Pope Paul VI, at the end of the Vatican Council (1965) laid his triple crown on the altar of St Peter's, and it was afterwards given to the American Church's National Shrine, in Washington DC. No pope since Paul VI has been crowned, each choosing a much simpler ceremony. The history of the papal tiara, like that of the mitre itself, is unclear. From the early 10th century popes are represented as wearing a helmet with an ornamental band around it. In the first instance this may simply have been a circlet to hold the cap rigid, but it became decorated in the manner of a crown. Boniface VIII (1294–1303) is shown wearing a mitre with two bands around it, though it is probable that this style predated his pontificate. Within a decade or so of Boniface's death a third circlet had been added. It may be presumed that the circlets, or crowns, were added to symbolize papal plenitude of power, the *plenitudo potestatis*, but there is no agreement as to the meaning of the circlets.

including money – and expelled all foreign merchants. This was an enormous blow to the finances of the papacy, especially at a time when the pope was pursuing a vendetta against the Colonna family and needed all the money he could get. In February 1297 he approved an interpretation of *Clericis laicos* that allowed Philip to tax the clergy. As a further act of goodwill towards France he declared Philip's grandfather, the crusader Louis IX (1226–70), to be a saint.

CONFLICT WITH THE COLONNAS

The ancient Roman Colonna family felt itself under threat from the expansion of the estates of the Caetani family, funded by Boniface. In May 1297 a convoy of papal treasure being sent to Rome for further purchases of land was seized by Stephen Colonna, brother of Peter, the younger of two Colonna cardinals. When Boniface accused them of the theft, the cardinals undertook to return the money, but they would neither hand over Stephen nor surrender their castles as surety for good behaviour. The Colonnas were stripped of their benefices and excommunicated: in return they accused Boniface of being a tyrant. Furthermore, they alleged that the pope's election was invalid, a view long espoused by the radical branch of the Franciscans who had hoped for great things from the man they called 'the angel pope'. Boniface then went to war against the Colonnas, declaring his campaign a crusade, and that his crusaders would enjoy all the privileges which went with that title. They were forced to surrender their major stronghold, Palestrina, and the two Colonna cardinals made their way to France, where they joined forces with King Philip.

A HOLY YEAR

In 1300 Boniface VIII seemed to be in the ascendant. He conceived the notion of declaring that year, the turn of the century, a jubilee or holy year, with the idea of attracting more pilgrims to Rome with the promise of special indulgences. It was an enormous success. Pilgrims flocked to the city, and their offerings filled the papal coffers. Boniface was emboldened. He claimed he was now emperor as well as king, having refused to recognize the emperor-elect, Albert of Austria.

In the autumn of 1301 Boniface declared the town of Pamiers in southwestern France to be a diocese, and instituted a new bishop without reference to the king. Philip promptly had the bishop arrested, then, when the pope complained, charged the bishop with heresy. Boniface claimed that the king was trespassing once again on the

In 1303 Pope Boniface VIII was charged with sexual misconduct, simony and heresy on the orders of Philip IV of France .

freedom of the church, and reinstated his ban on the king collecting taxes from the clergy. He then summoned a synod of French bishops in Rome. It met on 18 November 1302, and heard the pope read out his bull *Unam sanctam*. This was an extravagant statement of papal claims, ending with the sentence that no one could be saved unless he or she submitted to the Roman pontiff (see box, page 123).

A CHARGE OF SEXUAL MISCONDUCT, SIMONY AND HERESY

Philip the Fair had a new, and more aggressive, advisor on religious affairs, Guillaume de Nogaret. Drawing upon a dossier prepared by the Colonnas, Nogaret publicly charged Boniface with usurping the papal office and with sexual misconduct, simony and heresy. He then set out for Italy. On 15 August 1303 Boniface responded with charges against Philip, saying that he was having a bull prepared to excommunicate the king, which would be published on 8 September. On 7 September Nogaret led an attack on Anagni in the hills southeast of Rome where the pope was residing. Perhaps his intention was simply to bring pressure on the pope, but his raiding party was joined by some Colonnas who were out to wreak havoc and exact vengeance. Boniface was manhandled, and the town was pillaged. The violence turned the townspeople against Nogaret's party, and Boniface was rescued. He returned to Rome, where he died on 11 October 1303.

Accounts of Boniface's pontificate inevitably focus on his clash with Philip the Fair. But he was a man of intelligence and learning, who founded a university in Rome, and had plans to found another, in Avignon. He published a book of canon law, reorganized the papal archives and library and patronized artists – although the number of statues of himself that he had commissioned was long after a matter of cynical comment.

*Denotes popes featured
within this section

OPPOSITE *The papal palace in
Avignon, where popes governed
from for more than 50 years
during the 14th century.*

POPES
AND
ANTIPOPES

The papacy in the 14th and 15th centuries

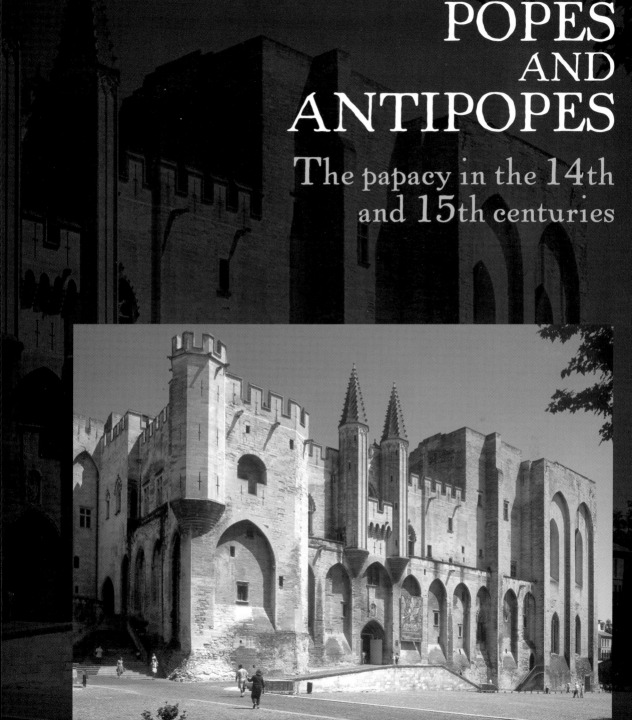

CLEMENT V

Any successor to Boniface VIII had to reconcile two seemingly incompatible positions: he needed to maintain the legitimacy of the election of Boniface, lest his own might be called into doubt; and he had to appease Boniface's great enemy, Philip the Fair of France. The learned and devout — he has been raised to the rank of 'blessed' — Benedict XI (1303–4), Clement V's immediate predecessor, is regarded as a weak pope, but on the whole he managed to achieve both these ends. He upheld Boniface's legitimacy, and then conceded to Philip what he had asked, the right to tax the clergy.

He also pardoned every Frenchman who had laid hands on Boniface at Anagni, with the exception of the ringleader, Guillaume de Nogaret. Nogaret and his Italian collaborators were summoned to appear before him, but Nogaret died before that could happen. The Colonnas did not get off so lightly. Benedict removed the sentence of excommunication against them, but restored neither lands nor titles. This was a mistaken tactic, because it annoyed the Colonnas' enemies, without winning over the Colonnas themselves.

A GASCON POPE

The issue of the Colonnas dogged the election of Benedict's successor. At the Council of the Lateran in 1179 a two-thirds majority had been laid down as a requisite for election to the papacy. It was this which had led to the frequently prolonged wrangles that plagued papal conclaves during the 13th century. At Perugia, where Benedict had died early in July 1304, the cardinals were almost equally divided between those who were against the French because of the attack on Boniface VIII at Anagni, and those seeking better relations with Philip of France, and a full rehabilitation of the Colonnas. When, after 11 months, they finally agreed on a candidate, Bertrand de Got won exactly two-thirds of the votes, becoming Pope Clement V.

Bertrand was born in Gascony, which was, at the time, a fiefdom of the English king. He studied at the priory of Deffez, near Agen, then at Orleans and finally at Bologna. He became a canon of Bordeaux and of Agen. His brother Beraud became archbishop of Lyons in 1289, and he was one of the 12 whom Celestine V made cardinals. Beraud employed his younger brother as a chaplain, and both brothers were used by their liege lord, King Edward I of England, on diplomatic missions. Bertrand, who became bishop of Comminges in 1295, was the English king's representative at the Estates General in Paris. In 1299 he

BIRTH NAME
Raymond Bertrand de Got
BORN Gascony, France, 1264
PREDECESSOR Benedict XI
INSTALLED 14 November 1305
DIED 20 April 1314
SUCCESSOR John XII

became archbishop of Bordeaux, and as such was one of the French bishops who attended Boniface VIII's synod of 1302. One of the aspects of papal policy had been to broker peace between England and France. This had not been successful, but Bertrand, subject to the English king, though a Frenchman, seemed well placed to do so. Moreover, unlike his brother, he had never been made a cardinal, so stood outside the conflicts that divided the papal electors.

PRESSURE FROM PHILIP IV

The first challenge facing the new pope was the conflict between England and France. This was an issue because it stood in the way of the launch of another crusade to recapture the Holy Places for Christendom. Clement therefore planned to be crowned at Vienne, where he hoped he might be able to broker a peace. However, he bowed to pressure from Philip – which was unremitting throughout his pontificate – and was crowned at Lyons in November 1305. This

A French pope who in order to gain the co-operation of the French king joined him in suppressing the order of the Knights Templar when, on 13 October 1307, all the Templars were arrested and tortured.

was technically not in France but part of the empire (it would come under the control of Philip in 1310). Shortly after his coronation Clement created ten new cardinals, of whom nine were French – and four of these were his nephews. The predominance of Frenchmen among the cardinals increased as the pontificate went on. The choice of Frenchmen for the college of cardinals may have represented Clement's own predilections, but it was also a sop to Philip, who was pressing for all those who had been involved on the attack on Boniface to be absolved of their crime. Clement was unwilling to do this, but he still wanted the king's co-operation, especially in a crusade. Philip's price was the suppression of the Knights Templars.

THE SUPPRESSION OF THE KNIGHTS TEMPLARS

The Templars were one of several military orders, part monks, part soldiers, who had been fighting either in the Holy Land, or to reconquer Spain from the Muslims, or to bring Christianity to Europe's northern regions. The Templars had become very powerful and, it was believed, very wealthy. One of the reasons for this power was their network of land holdings – or commanderies – all over Europe, between which their knights travelled, and which provided a useful means of moving money around. The Templars had in effect become international bankers. Perhaps it was to lay hands on their supposed riches that Philip wanted them suppressed, but in that case he was to be disappointed. His motives still remain uncertain: it may

His was a centralizing papacy, bringing control of benefices and of taxation increasingly to the papal court.

be that he wanted the military orders, not just the Templars, to be brought under his command. The Templars became particularly vulnerable, however, when a series of rumours began to spread of heretical, blasphemous and even obscene practices among the members of the order. Whether anyone even then believed these lurid stories is not important: they provided the grounds which Philip needed. On 13 October 1307 he had all Templars in France arrested, and confessions extracted under torture. These confessions were then passed on to Pope Clement, who was sufficiently alarmed by what he read to order the arrest of all Templars everywhere.

He was, however, very reluctant to suppress the order totally, as Philip wanted. The king kept up the pressure. He wanted the Templars suppressed and Boniface condemned, and threatened a general council of the church effectively to set, or so he hoped, the church against the papacy. When the issue was debated at the Council of Vienne (1311–12), the majority of delegates seemed not to share Philip's and Clement's hostility to the order, so it was in the end suppressed by papal decree. When the bull suppressing the Templars was read out on 3 April 1312 the council fathers sat in silence. Clement made a valiant effort at independence of the French crown: he did not hand over the Templar's property, but instead consigned it to the Knights Hospitallers (the Knights of Malta as they are now).

That, however, was the extent of his defiance. He rehabilitated the Colonna cardinals, absolved Nogaret of all blame for the attack at Anagni, and in the bull *Rex gloriae* praised Philip's zeal. The French king's vendetta against Boniface VIII went as far as wanting Celestine V to be canonized as a martyr who had died at Boniface's hands. At this the pope rebelled. He canonized Celestine as Saint Peter Morrone, during the course of the Council of Vienne, but refused to call him a martyr (that is, one who had died a violent death for the Catholic faith).

Plenitudo potestatis

There were other issues troubling Clement, quite apart from those of France. In 1305/6 he absolved Edward I of England from the vows he had taken before his barons and, when the archbishop of Canterbury criticized him for doing so, he suspended the archbishop from office, later reinstating him at the request of Edward II. In 1306 he excommunicated the Scottish king Robert the Bruce for murdering his rival John Comyn in church. In 1307 he settled the troublesome issue of the succession to the throne of Hungary.

When the German king Albert I was assassinated in 1308, Clement once again defied the French king. Philip wanted his brother Charles of Valois to succeed to the German crown, but Henry IV of Luxembourg was chosen instead, backed by Clement. Problems arose, however, when Henry went to Rome to be crowned. St Peter's was occupied by the army of Robert of Naples, so in June 1312 Henry was crowned Henry VII in the Lateran not by the pope, but by three cardinals. Henry then accused Robert of treason. Under pressure from Philip IV, the pope took Robert's part, insisting that his kingdom did not belong to the empire, but was held as a fief of the pope. He then declared Robert, after the early death of Henry in August 1313, to be imperial vicar in Italy. Robert, after all, belonged to the (French) house of Anjou.

THE CHARGES AGAINST THE TEMPLARS

THE CHARGES AGAINST THE TEMPLARS, ACCORDING TO THE ACTS OF THE COUNCIL OF VIENNE:

'It was against the Lord Jesus himself that they fell into the sin of impious apostasy, the abominable vice of idolatry, the deadly crime of the Sodomites, and various heresies ... There was even one of the Knights, a man of noble blood and no small reputation in the order, who testified secretly under oath in our presence, that at his reception the knight who received him suggested that he deny Christ, which he did, in the presence of certain other knights of the Temple; he furthermore spat on the cross held out to him by this knight who received him.'

QUOTED IN NORMAN P. TANNER, *DECREES OF THE ECUMENICAL COUNCILS.*

Clement did all this in virtue of the 'fullness of power', the *plenitudo potestatis*, to which pontiffs ever since Innocent III had laid claim. He laid out his ideas in a bull, *Pastoralis cura*, claiming that the pope was superior to the emperor, and therefore could declare Henry's charges against Robert of Naples as null and void.

Clement's was a centralizing papacy, bringing control of benefices and of taxation increasingly to the papal court. His administration was efficient, yet such was his generosity, especially to his relatives but to many others as well, including people and places in his native Gascony, that he left the papal treasury empty. Clement has been much criticized for his nepotism, but there were many positive aspects to his papacy. The Council of Vienne, in addition to condemning the Templars, launched a campaign of reform, particularly of the dress and behaviour of the clergy and of relations between the religious and the secular clergy. It showed, unusually, a concern for foreign missions. Another notable achievement of Clement's was the establishment of professorships of oriental languages, including Arabic, at Paris, Oxford, Bologna, Salamanca and 'wherever the papal curia happen to reside'.

CLEMENT MOVES TO AVIGNON

But where *was* the papal curia to reside? Rome was not under papal control, though a determined pope might have attempted to restore it, as Clement did in northeastern Italy when Venice claimed lordship of Ferrara. He sent papal forces, armed with crusader indulgences and commanded by a cardinal, to recapture it, which the cardinal did with, Venetian sources reported, extreme brutality. Yet Clement decided eventually to remain in what is now France. He settled at first in the Venaissin, the area around Avignon, which the papacy had purchased in 1229. Then in 1309 he went to Avignon itself, a city of the empire, and established himself in the Dominican house there. The church was to be governed from Avignon for well over half a century.

GREGORY XI

uring the period between the election of Clement V in 1305 and the election of Gregory XI in 1370 the popes resided at Avignon. This period is sometimes called, biblically, 'the Babylonian Captivity', with the suggestion that it was a disastrous period in the history of the papacy. This is unfair. Partly because of squabbles with the emperor, partly because of rebellion within Rome and the setting up of a commune, from the time of the investiture contest in the late 11th century successive bishops of Rome had lived more out of the city than within it. If the pope could not reside in Rome, then Avignon was a sensible choice.

For one thing, Avignon was relatively peaceful: there was no faction fighting among the noble families, no uprisings by the people. It was also conveniently situated on the River Rhône, an important waterway, especially for north–south travel. And the bridge across the Rhône, still remembered in song, was the route by which traffic going east or west traversed the river. The countryside around, the Venaissin, belonged to the papacy, and though Avignon itself belonged to the kingdom of Naples – itself a fiefdom of the papacy – in 1348 the city was purchased from Naples by Pope Clement VI (1342–52).

REFORM OF THE PAPAL REVENUES

Once he had bought the city, Clement VI set about extending the palace. The papal palace at Avignon, still the city's greatest tourist attraction, had been begun by Pope Benedict XII in 1335. It was very much more than just a residence. It became the centre of papal administration which, before the move to Avignon, had not always been located where the pope of the day was residing. A crucial aspect of the centralizing reforms set in train under the Avignon papacy was an improvement in the management of papal revenues. Clement V having had bequeathed 200,000 florins to friends and relatives, and another 300,000 to a nephew who was to lead 500 knights on a crusade, there were no more than 70,000 florins in the papal coffers. An unwelcome aspect of the Avignon papacy, as far as the rest of the church was concerned, was the regularity with which the popes, for a fee, and in return for taxes when they took up their see, 'provided' bishops to dioceses across Europe: four 'Statutes of Provisors' were enacted in 14th-century England to forbid the practice, three of them while the popes were at Avignon. They were not particularly effective.

BIRTH NAME Pierre Roger de Beaufort
BORN Château Maumont, near Limoges, 1329
PREDECESSOR Urban V
INSTALLED 5 January 1371
DIED 27 March 1378
SUCCESSOR Urban VI

St Catherine of Siena before Pope Gregory XI in 1376. In her letters to the pope she urged him to return to Rome, but he achieved this only briefly before new riots in the city forced him to leave.

A CEREMONIAL PAPACY

There was another aspect of the Avignon papacy that had a long-term effect. In Rome the election and consecration of popes had taken place in different churches of the city. The pope was a visible figure, and the liturgies over which he presided were attended not just by the papal household but by the clergy and people. This all changed in Avignon. Everything was gradually moved within the papal palace. The liturgy became a palace ceremonial, the pope became a king, removed from his people, rarely to be glimpsed except when he set off for his summer residence at Châteauneuf-du-Pape. Even his functionaries did not come and go. Just as the more important papal offices were moved inside the palace, so were those who ran them, along with the cardinals, the pope's college of advisors. The cardinals had become increasingly conscious of themselves as a group, and in the conclave of 1342 they laid down for the first time 'capitulations', or conditions, which were to be observed by whoever it was they elected. This implied that they had a right to control, to some degree, the activity of the pope – a claim which popes,

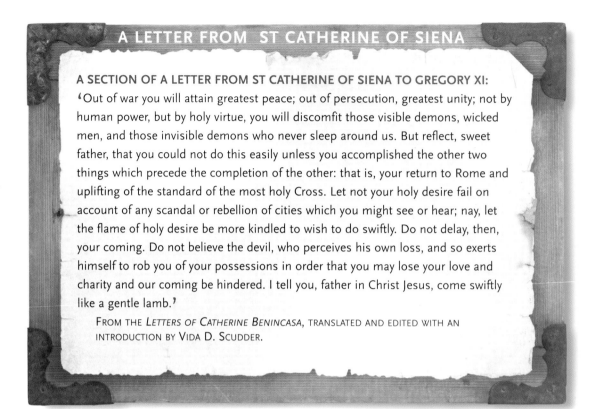

A LETTER FROM ST CATHERINE OF SIENA

A SECTION OF A LETTER FROM ST CATHERINE OF SIENA TO GREGORY XI:
'Out of war you will attain greatest peace; out of persecution, greatest unity; not by human power, but by holy virtue, you will discomfit those visible demons, wicked men, and those invisible demons who never sleep around us. But reflect, sweet father, that you could not do this easily unless you accomplished the other two things which precede the completion of the other: that is, your return to Rome and uplifting of the standard of the most holy Cross. Let not your holy desire fail on account of any scandal or rebellion of cities which you might see or hear; nay, let the flame of holy desire be more kindled to wish to do swiftly. Do not delay, then, your coming. Do not believe the devil, who perceives his own loss, and so exerts himself to rob you of your possessions in order that you may lose your love and charity and our coming be hindered. I tell you, father in Christ Jesus, come swiftly like a gentle lamb.'

FROM THE *LETTERS OF CATHERINE BENINCASA*, TRANSLATED AND EDITED WITH AN INTRODUCTION BY VIDA D. SCUDDER.

once elected, were reluctant to concede. One thing the cardinals wanted to ensure was that their number never rose above 20, and then to control entry into the college. They wanted to constitute themselves as a self-perpetuating oligarchy.

'WHERE THE POPE IS, THERE IS ROME'

Despite the relatively satisfactory running of the church from Avignon, no pope during this period ever forgot that he was technically bishop of Rome. When Clement VI declared another Jubilee Year in 1350, for example, he restored the Lateran for pilgrims. Papal enemies, particularly the emperor, Louis of Bavaria, who had been crowned in 1328 by the Roman people, argued that when the pope was not in Rome he lost that fullness of power to which the bishops of Rome laid claim. Naturally the Avignon popes rejected this. They responded that 'where the pope is, there is Rome' – and one wing of the papal palace at Avignon, built by Urban V (1362–70), was even called Rome. But it was clear that sooner or later the pontiffs would have to return to Rome. Urban V did indeed do so in 1367, but then returned to Avignon to die. He was succeeded by Pierre Roger de Beaufort as Gregory XI.

The nephew of Pope Clement VI, Pierre Roger was loaded with benefices from his childhood, and, by the time he became pope, he was archdeacon in at least 18 different places, and had been created a cardinal deacon by his uncle before he was 20. Clement sent him to study law in Perugia, and he earned a reputation for learning, as well as for holiness. Urban V had thought highly of him, and so indeed did his fellow cardinals – he was elected on only the second day of the conclave. He was, however, still only a deacon, and had to be ordained priest the day before he was consecrated.

Though from the outset Gregory was determined to return to Rome, for a time papal business kept him in Avignon. For one thing, he was eager for a crusade, and before that could happen peace – or at least a truce – had to be negotiated between England and France, then in the throes of the Hundred Years' War (1337–1453). Gregory also needed to settle disputes in Italy, where the Visconti in Milan were threatening papal territories in the north of the country. Gregory organized a league against them, led by Amadeus VI, count of Savoy. The Visconti were put under an interdict, and a crusade was declared against them, the pope promising the usual crusader indulgence to any soldier killed in battle. The Visconti were defeated, but the growing power of the papacy in northern Italy was beginning to worry the Tuscan states to the south.

> The pope became a king, removed from his people, rarely to be glimpsed except when he set off for his summer residence at Châteauneuf-du-Pape.

THE WAR OF THE EIGHT SAINTS

In 1375 Florence incited a rebellion in the papal states in central Italy. The ensuing conflict between a Florentine-led coalition of city-states and the papacy was known as the War of the Eight Saints (Florence's war council consisted of eight members). Gregory responded by placing the city under an interdict. Florentines were banished from Avignon and their goods confiscated. The pope dispatched a band of mercenaries (or *condottieri*) under Cardinal Robert of Geneva to quell the revolt. This he achieved with much brutality and with the aid, among others, of the English freebooter Sir John Hawkwood who not so long before had been besieging the pope at Avignon, but who switched allegiance to the papal coalition. Robert of Geneva was, notoriously, the commander of the papal troops who carried out a massacre of townspeople at Cesena, near Ravenna, in 1377.

Gregory had first set a date for returning to Rome in a consistory of his cardinals in February 1374. However, the troubles in Italy and continuing warfare between England and France had delayed his departure. In 1376 St Catherine of Siena visited the papal court, and this, together with her letters to him, may have strengthened his resolve. The papal court finally left Marseilles by ship for Rome on 2 October, arriving in the city on 17 January 1377. Gregory took up residence in the Vatican, rather than at the Lateran. It should have been a triumphant return, but as news of the massacres perpetrated by the troops under the command of Cardinal Robert reached Rome the populace turned against him, and for a time he had to retire to Anagni.

The last French pope died in March 1378, only a year or so after he had made his way back to his bishopric.

URBAN VI

o understand what happened at the death of Pope Gregory XI in 1378, it has to be remembered that the great majority of the cardinals were French – six, indeed, had even stayed behind at Avignon when Gregory moved the papal court back to Rome. This was the first conclave to have been held in Rome since the death of Pope Boniface VIII in 1303. The people of Rome were determined that the person elected would not be French, and move the curia back to Avignon. Obviously there was pride involved, but also economics: the presence of the curia brought visitors in large numbers, whether as pilgrims or on business. The 16 electors were warned of trouble just before the conclave began. The populace wanted a Roman pope, but failing that, at least one from Italy.

Rioting broke out the day the voting began. The almost unanimous choice was for Bartolomeo Prignano, then archbishop of Bari, and not himself a cardinal. But then the mob invaded the conclave. The terrified cardinals turned away any possible anger of the crowd by pretending that the votes had gone to an elderly Roman-born cardinal, Francesco de' Tebaldeschi, who died not long afterwards, rather than to Prignano. The mob melted away. The following day, 12 of the cardinals returned and confirmed their original choice.

The new pope, Urban VI, had enjoyed a distinguished career in papal service. He had been made successively archbishop of Acerenza (1363), and, from 1377, of Bari. He was an expert in canon law, and had worked in the curia in Avignon from 1368. When Gregory XI returned to Rome, Prignano had been put in charge of the chancery. He had observed the lifestyles of the cardinals at first hand, but he had not been one of them, which may help to explain his actions.

URBAN AND THE FRENCH CARDINALS

On his election in April 1378 Urban sent notice of it to the cardinals still at Avignon, and in customary fashion to the emperor Charles IV, and to other European monarchs. But he then succeeded in alienating the cardinals who had elected him by attempting a reform of their way of life. He criticized them for the number of their retainers, for absenteeism, for simony and for living a manner of life incompatible with the gospel. The cardinals, however, were not prepared to tolerate the changes he wanted to bring about. They announced that they wanted to return the curia to Avignon. If they tried to do so, Urban responded, then he would create so many new Italian members of the college that the French would be swamped. At the end of June the

BIRTH NAME **Bartolomeo Prignano**
BORN **Naples, c. 1320**
PREDECESSOR **Gregory XI**
INSTALLED **18 April 1378**
DIED **15 October 1389**
SUCCESSOR **Boniface IX**

French cardinals went off to Anagni to consider their strategy. Only the three Italians remained with Urban, and even they were uncertain whether to support him. When the French cardinals denounced Urban as an Antichrist, an apostate and a tyrant the Italians proposed calling a general council, but there was no eagerness to pursue such a route. On 9 August the French announced that they had deposed Urban. They then moved to Fondi where, on 20 September they elected Robert of Geneva, the cardinal who had been in command of the papal armies under Gregory XI when they had committed the massacre at Cesena. He took the name Clement VII. The case for deposing Urban was not so much that he was deranged – which is what they believed – but that they had been forced under the duress of the Roman populace to make a choice, and had not been free to choose the appropriate candidate.

Urban VI's harsh criticism of his cardinals led to the Great Western Schism, with two different popes vying for the support of European powers. Urban quarrelled with his army and his allies and it is possible he met his death by poisoning.

So now there were two popes, a situation that was not uncommon in papal history, except that this time the schism – 'the Great Western Schism' as it is known – developed into there being two, and then three, different papal lineages, as will be explained later. Meanwhile, both contenders for the title of pope tried to win support from the European states. France, not surprisingly, backed Clement, who in June 1379 moved back to Avignon. Also on the side of Clement were Burgundy, Savoy, Naples and Scotland – Scotland perhaps because England had opted for Urban, along with the empire, Hungary, Poland, Scandinavia and eventually Portugal. Portugal gave its allegiance to Urban partly because it was in alliance with England, partly because Castile, along with Navarre and Aragón, ultimately committed themselves to Clement.

But it was not just the 'great powers' that took sides. Universities, monasteries, cathedrals and individual bishops did likewise. If a bishop chose Urban his chapter of canons was prone to do the opposite. Some prelates tried to back both parties, in the hope of receiving benefices from both. Pilaeus de Prata, who was created cardinal by Urban along with 28 others of various nationalities on 17 September 1378, switched allegiance – or 'obedience' – to Avignon in 1387 after Urban had five cardinals executed for alleged conspiracy. He returned to the Roman obedience in 1391, after Urban's death: he was known in consequence of his wavering as 'cardinal three hats'. Catherine of Siena, on the other hand, remained loyal to Urban.

The 'Avignon obedience'

As Urban's creation of new cardinals indicates, most of the curia went over to his rival, and he had to establish one anew. He was in control of Rome, after capturing Castel Sant'Angelo from a garrison loyal to Clement, and defeating Clement's army in Italy at the Battle of Marino in April 1379. At this point Clement retired to Naples, and the protection of Queen Joanna of Naples. But he found that he was unpopular with the people, and in May he left for Avignon, settling an alternative curia there for the remainder of his (and his successors') pontificates, thus beginning the 'Avignon obedience'.

Urban, angry at the support which Queen Joanna had given to his rival, excommunicated her in 1380, replacing her as sovereign by Charles of Durazzo, whom he crowned the following year at a ceremony held in Rome. His wish to secure the kingdom of Naples for his own nephew led to a quarrel with Charles, who conspired against him with some of the cardinals, arguing that he was incapable of being pope. When Urban discovered the plot, he had six of the cardinals tortured and five of them put to death. Charles then besieged him at Nocera in 1385. Urban fled to Salerno and then to Genoa, where he stayed until 1386; from 1386 to 1387 he was in Lucca, and finally in Perugia until October 1388, when he returned to Rome after falling out with his mercenary army. But in Rome the populace turned against him. It is quite possible that he was poisoned.

THE GREAT SCHISM

If one looks at the official list of popes in the Vatican's *Annuario Pontificio*, the papal yearbook, it is clear that the Roman 'obedience' is regarded as providing the rightful pope. But that is only the more recent editions. Before 1947 the list was not so definite. There are a number of issues about the validity of the papacy of Pope Urban VI, not least the very point which the French cardinals made early on: that they had all acted under duress. The election was not free, therefore it was invalid. But the cardinals had chosen Bartolomeo Prignano before the mob burst in, and most of them returned the following day to confirm their original choice. The other question is whether or not Urban was fully in command of his faculties, whether he was mentally stable. His increasingly erratic behaviour could be cited in evidence for deposing him, it is true, but at the time Clement VII was chosen at Fondi there was probably insufficient evidence to prove his unstable mental state, apart from his over-brusque attempt to reform the luxurious lifestyles of the cardinals. In any case, what to do in the case of a mentally ill pope was, in the church's law, a grey area, to say the least.

Once the schism was a reality, however, the problem was how to resolve it, how to restore unity. The obvious answer was a council of the church, but it was also widely believed that only a pope could call a council, which in the circumstances was unlikely to happen. Popes were in any case wary of councils, especially at this time in history. The philosopher William of Ockham (*c.* 1285–*c.* 1348), so named after his English birthplace, had propounded the view that imperial authority came from God, and was not mediated through the pope but via the people. The emperor had a right, and a duty, to depose an heretical pontiff. This was a convenient theory for William to hold. He believed that Pope John XXII (1316–43) was acting heretically in his treatment of the radical group of Franciscans to which William himself belonged. Furthermore, this group was being supported by Emperor Louis of Bavaria.

An even more radical version of this theory was espoused by Marsiglio of Padua in his treatise *The Defender of the Peace* (1324). He denied that the pope had any authority over the emperor, rather the opposite, the church was subject to the state, and papal privileges stemmed not from his lineage as a successor to the apostle Peter, but from the Donation of Constantine. As has been seen, this was an eighth-century forgery, but Marsiglio did not know that. To him it was what it claimed to be, a grant of power in the West by an emperor just about to set off for the East.

'A CONGREGATION OF THE FAITHFUL'

These ideas were the foundation of the reform movement known as 'conciliarism', which fundamentally elevated a general council of the church to a higher position than the papacy. Quite obviously this was not a notion that found much acceptance among the various popes who ruled in the different 'obediences'. Those who held to this view talked about a 'congregation of the faithful', but membership of that congregation, in their minds, was not a gathering of all members of the church, but only of its office holders, whether in church or state. In other words, it was an oligarchy.

In any case, a council was not much use unless the two rival popes could be persuaded to resign. This was known to its advocates as 'the way of withdrawal': both popes were to resign or withdraw simultaneously. But neither pope of the different obediences was inclined to do so. The French decided to force the issue. In 1398 the king and the French church withdrew their support from the Avignon pope Benedict XIII. Benedict was besieged in the papal palace at Avignon for nearly five years before being able to escape.

The way of withdrawal failed to command much support outside France, and the sufferings Benedict XIII had undergone at the hands of the French won him support among waverers.

A peaceful cloister at San Giovanni in Laterano, Rome.

France responded by recognizing Benedict's authority once again, but only as long as he would try to negotiate a solution with his rival in Rome. In September 1404 Benedict XIII of Avignon sent representatives to talk to Boniface IX of Rome. Boniface died soon after Benedict's envoys arrived in Rome, and they were suspected of having a hand in his death, so Boniface's successor, Innocent VII, locked them up. Innocent, however, was pope for only a little over two years. He was succeeded by Angelo Correr, a Venetian, who took the name Gregory XII.

GREGORY XII'S SOLUTION

From the outset Gregory proclaimed that, to resolve the schism, he would be prepared to withdraw if Benedict did so. The two undertook to meet at Savona on 1 November 1407. Benedict turned up, but Gregory did not, and although emissaries were exchanged, those present came to the conclusion that if the two popes were working together, it was simply to put off the meeting. Gregory, who was 80 at the time of his election, had promised not only to work for the unification of the church, but also not to create any new cardinals. It was clear – especially after he had created more cardinals who were anti-French and anti-conciliarist – that he was insufficiently serious. Nine Roman cardinals defected from Gregory and took refuge in Pisa; six Avignon cardinals then did likewise. They together announced they were going to call a council for the spring of 1409. Alarmed that matters were slipping out of their control, the two popes announced rival councils. Benedict's met in Perpignan, and was relatively successful; Gregory's met in Cividale and was a fiasco. Gregory then fled to Rimini.

POPES OF THE THREE OBEDIENCES

Rome

Urban VI	Elected 8 April 1378	Died, Rome, 15 October 1389
Boniface IX	Elected 2 November 1389	Died, Rome, 1 October 1404
Innocent VII	Elected 17 October 1404	Died, Rome, 6 November 1406
Gregory XII	Elected 30 November 1406	Abdicated, 4 July 1415.
		Died, Recanati, 18 October 1417

Avignon

Clement VII	Elected at Fondi 20 September 1378	Died, Avignon, 16 September 1394
Benedict XIII	Elected at Avignon 28 September 1394	Died, Peñiscola, 27 November 1422

(Even after the resolution of the schism at Constance, Benedict XIII's supporters elected a successor in 1423, who took the title Clement VIII)

Pisa

Alexander V	Elected at Pisa 26 June 1409	Died, Bologna, 3 May 1410
John XXIII	Elected at Bologna 17 May 1410	Abdicated 29 May 1415
		Died, Florence, 22 November 1419

DEPOSITION

In Pisa, on 5 June 1409, both popes were found guilty of being schismatics, and declared deposed. On 26 June Cardinal Pietro Philarghi was elected as the Pisan pope, taking the name Alexander V. He lived for less than a year. He was succeeded, after an election in Bologna, by Baldassare Cossa, who had been made cardinal by Boniface IX, and had been sent as legate to Bologna by Gregory XII with instructions to bring the city back under papal control. He did so with extraordinary ruthlessness (he had been a pirate in his younger days) ravishing, it was said, 200 Bolognese ladies. He also made himself extremely rich in the process, and kept the Pisan obedience going largely out of his own funds.

Alexander V had undertaken to call another council to deal with church reform, but he died before it could happen. His successor, who took the title John XXIII, called a council for 1412, It began in 1413 but was suspended when few people turned up to attend it. Then Sigismund, the German king with aspirations to the imperial title, took a hand. He announced that there would be a general council, and it would meet in imperial territory, at Constance. Pope John had little alternative but to agree. It was to begin on 1 November 1414.

MARTIN V

he Council of Constance, called to resolve the Great Western Schism, was welcomed by almost everyone except those most intimately involved, the three rival pontiffs. John XXIII, who had been elected by a council, and who had undertaken to call another reforming council, was coerced into approving emperor-elect Sigismund's choice of Constance as a venue, and the gathering began its business in that city on 1 November 1414. Not that everyone arrived punctually. The numbers grew as time went on, but there was from the start a preponderance of Italians, which was unwelcome to those of other allegiances. It was therefore agreed that voting should be by 'nations', groupings of English, French, Germans and Italians. Spain, which at first remained loyal to the Aragonese Pope Benedict XIII, who was, indeed, the most capable of the three, was added later after Benedict had shown himself utterly unwilling to accept the council. As the only cardinal appointed before the outbreak of the schism, he vainly argued, he was the only one competent to elect a pope.

Sigismund had called the council, Pope John had been able to do no more than endorse it. While the emperor-elect was acceptable as an arbiter to Gregory XII and to Benedict XIII, most of the participants regarded John XXIII as the rightful pope. Gregory was prepared to do a deal with the council, and sent emissaries to negotiate the terms of his abdication, Benedict did not. Neither Gregory or Benedict would deal with John. It became clear that there would be no progress unless John seized the initiative and resigned first. He appeared to discuss terms, but on 21 March 1415 he fled, disguised as a groom, to Schaffhausen. If he had thought that any would rally to his cause he was mistaken. He was brought back ignominiously to Constance, and on 29 May was found guilty of simony, perjury and gross misconduct, all of which accusations were undoubtedly true, though it should be said in his defence that he lived out the rest of his life – in Florence, under the protection of the Medici – with admirable sobriety.

BIRTH NAME Odo Colonna
BORN Genazzano, near Rome 1368
PREDECESSOR Gregory XII
INSTALLED 21 November 1417
DIED 20 February 1431
SUCCESSOR Eugenius IV

CONCILIARISM TRIUMPHANT

A fortnight after John's flight the council approved the decree *Haec Sancta*, which proclaimed the superiority of council over pope (see box). This triumph of conciliarism was later entrenched by another decree, *Frequens*, which required any future pope to hold regular councils. The church was in need of reform, as well as in need of a pope, but there was insufficient time at Constance to legislate for all the reforms needed. The council condemned the teachings of the English theologian John Wyclif, and had the Bohemian heretic Jan Hus burnt at the stake on 6 July 1415, but otherwise those gathered at Constance were concerned with the issue of the papacy and papal revenues.

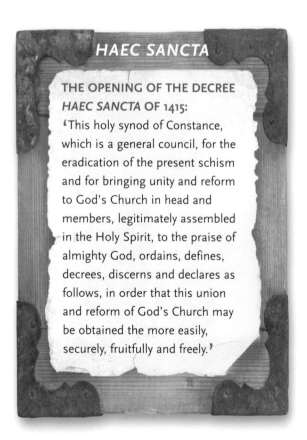

HAEC SANCTA

THE OPENING OF THE DECREE *HAEC SANCTA* OF 1415:

'This holy synod of Constance, which is a general council, for the eradication of the present schism and for bringing unity and reform to God's Church in head and members, legitimately assembled in the Holy Spirit, to the praise of almighty God, ordains, defines, decrees, discerns and declares as follows, in order that this union and reform of God's Church may be obtained the more easily, securely, fruitfully and freely.'

THE ELECTION OF MARTIN V

On 11 November 1417 the 23 cardinals of all three rival popes met together with 30 representatives of the five nations, six from each, and elected the first and only Colonna pope. Odo Colonna became Martin V: it was St Martin's feast day.

Odo was the second of seven children, and marked out for a clerical career. He studied at Perugia, and entered papal service under Urban VI. Pope Innocent VII appointed him cardinal deacon. In 1408 he abandoned Pope Gregory XII and threw in his lot with the cardinals who had gathered in Pisa. He took part in the conclave which elected Alexander V and then that which chose John XXIII. He continued to support John at Constance, even to the extent of accompanying him to Schaffhausen. Thereafter, however, he became a leading witness for the prosecution during John's trial and deposition. Two days after his election he was ordained priest, and was then consecrated bishop and crowned.

The council left him with a reform agenda, which he tried faithfully to follow. He set up a commission of cardinals, but when that failed to reach agreement he took matters into his own hands. He rebuilt the curia, using officials from both the Avignon and the Roman obediences; he produced a number of reforms of papal taxation; he negotiated agreements ('concordats') with the five nations, though, except in the case of England, the concordat was to last only five years; he announced his intention of calling another council, as *Frequens* required, at Pavia – which opened on 23 April 1423 (though because of an outbreak of the plague it had to be moved to Siena). There were few people present, and Martin dissolved it as soon as he could on the grounds of the sparse attendance, but his real reason was the hostility shown by the delegates to papal authority, something which he was determined to restore. He had a point: those hostile to the papacy could always use the threat of a general council to force its hand.

A humane man, Pope Martin V carried out many of the reforms called for in the Council of Constance which ended the Great Schism. The cardinals he appointed were also both distinguished and worthy individuals.

A MILITARY ENTERPRISE

One of the reforms requested of Martin was that he internationalize the papal curia. This was easily done. He had in any case to combine the curial officials from two different papacies. Those of Avignon had a reputation for efficiency, especially in the matter of collecting papal revenues. These revenues had been badly hit both by the Hundred Years' War, which had decimated receipts from France, but also by unrest in Italy, where by 1416 the mercenary warlord Braccio da Montone had established himself at the expense of the papal estates. First Martin did a deal with him, but only after he had ravaged his way across Italy and attacked the territory of Queen Joanna II of Naples – a fief of the papacy. Martin raised an army which defeated Braccio in early June 1423. He also struggled, ultimately successfully, to bring Bologna back within papal control. In all these military enterprises he was aided by his family, which not only helped him to feel more secure, but enriched itself in the process.

HUMANE REFORMER

Italy, in Martin's lifetime, was on the verge of the Renaissance. Martin was no humanist, though once back in Rome, which he did not reach until September 1420, he embarked on a programme of reconstruction of the

> The council left him with a reform agenda, which he tried faithfully to follow.

churches, the Lateran and St Peter's among them, and of decaying public buildings such as the Capitol and the Pantheon. If not a humanist, Martin was humane, revoking edicts against the Jews and insisting that no Jewish child might be baptized without parental consent before the age of 12. He supported the preaching of St Bernardino of Siena, who was controversially propagating devotion to the name of Jesus under the now familiar symbol IHS. He issued a constitution insisting on a reform of the lives of members of the papal curia, and his additions to the college of cardinals were distinguished, worthy individuals.

When he dissolved the council that had met first at Pavia, then Siena, he had announced that the next gathering would be in Basel in 1431. He died suddenly, of apoplexy, just after he had, albeit reluctantly, convened it.

EUGENIUS IV

nephew of Gregory XII, as a youth Gabriele Condulmaro had a reputation for piety, and with his cousin, Antonio Correr, and others he founded a congregation of Augustinian canons in Venice. In 1407 Gregory made him bishop of Siena, though he was well below the age required by church law, and the following year a cardinal priest, along with his cousin Antonio. As the two cousins were, as cardinals, creations as well as nephews of Pope Gregory, they remained aloof from the Council of Constance until Gregory abdicated, but at that point they joined in, supporting Sigismund rather to the annoyance of most other cardinals present. In the pontificate of Martin V (1417–31), Gabriele became governor of the March of Ancona and of Bologna.

Martin was exacting of his cardinals, and they resented it. In the conclave which followed his death they agreed a 'capitulation', or pact, that whoever was elected would give back much more control of the church, and of its revenues, to the college of cardinals. This Eugenius endorsed on becoming pope, but then largely ignored.

BIRTH NAME **Gabriele Condulmaro**
BORN **Venice, c. 1383**
PREDECESSOR **Martin V**
INSTALLED **11 March 1431**
DIED **23 February 1447**
SUCCESSOR **Nicholas V**

CONTROLLING THE COLONNAS

The major issue facing him, apart from the council which Martin had convoked to Basel, was that of the Colonnas. Under Martin they had flourished mightily; now they had to be brought under papal control, and forced to return to the papacy a great part of the lands with which Martin had enriched them. Naturally, they resented this. There was said to be a plot on their part to

Eugenius IV began the papal patronage of Renaissance artists. He brought Fra Angelico, Donatello and Pisanello to Rome, and restored many of its churches while also forbidding the destruction of the monuments of ancient Rome.

THE BULL OF UNION WITH THE COPTS

EXCERPT FROM THE BULL OF UNION WITH THE COPTS, issued by the Council of Ferrara–Florence, 4 February 1442:

'In less than three years our lord Jesus Christ by his indefatigable kindess, to the common and lasting joy of the whole of Christianity, has generously effected in this holy ecumenical synod the most salutary union of three great nations. Hence it has come about that nearly the whole of the East that adores the glorious name of Christ, and no small part of the North, after prolonged discord with the holy Roman Church, have come together in the same bond of faith and love. For first the Greeks and those subject to the four patriarchal sees, which cover many races, nations and tongues, then the Armenians, who are a race of many peoples, and today indeed the Jacobites, who are a great people in Egypt, have been united with the holy apostolic see.'

seize Castel Sant'Angelo. The plotters were arrested, but a peace with the Colonnas was patched up for the time being. In May 1434, however, there was an uprising in Rome. It was probably occasioned by the ravaging of papal territory beyond the city by the duke of Milan, Filippo Maria Visconti, abetted by the *condottiere* (or mercenary commander) Franceso Sforza. These troubles had wearied the landowners, many of whom lived in Rome. They complained to the pope, who sent his nephew, Cardinal Francesco Condulmaro, to deal with them. He was anything but receptive to their concerns, and, fanned by the Colonnas, they then broke out into open revolt. The pope feared for his safety. He took refuge for a while in a palace in Trastevere, but then escaped to Florence, where he arrived in June 1434. He fled in disguise, but was recognized nonetheless, and pelted by the crowd. He left the bishop of Recanati, Giovanni Vitelleschi, to cope with the rebels, which he quickly did, and then went on to attack and sack Palestrina, the stronghold of the Colonnas.

Meanwhile there was a council going on. It began in Basel on 23 July 1431. There were few prelates present, and Eugenius tried to dissolve it the following December, promising to call another 18 months later. The council fathers, remembering the decree at the Council of Constance (see page 142) which put council over pope, refused to bow to papal wishes. Nor would they listen to the emperor Sigismund, whom Eugenius crowned in Rome at the end of May 1433. Furthermore, most of Eugenius's cardinals sided with the council fathers, so the pope had to give way. Emboldened by their apparent victory over the pontiff, the council then moved to reduce papal taxation, and insisted on a reduction of the papal curia. However, as everyone recognized, the most significant issue before the council was the possibility of a reunion with the Greek Church. Thessalonika had fallen to the Turks in 1430, and the emperor John VIII Palaeologus was desperate for Western support.

A COUNCIL IN FERRARA

The problem was where to meet. The council fathers wanted the discussions to take place in Basel, or failing that, at Avignon or in Savoy; the pope wanted somewhere in Italy; the Greeks wanted Ancona. Eventually, however, the pope, who was still in Florence, moved to Bologna, then in September 1437 transferred the council to Ferrara, to which the Byzantine emperor came in March 1438, followed soon afterwards by the patriarch. The presence of these dignitaries and their extensive entourages in what seemed exotic dress stirred a great deal of excitement. After questions of protocol had been settled, discussions took place.

They lasted a year. In January 1438 the pope, citing the problems of plague but really for financial reasons, moved the meeting to Florence. The rump of the council meeting in Basel declared Eugenius deposed and elected an antipope, Count Amadeus VIII of Savoy, a devout layman who did not want the job, but who accepted it at the council's behest and took the name Felix V. He was the last ever antipope, and resigned the office as soon as he could, to be given the title of cardinal of Santa Sabina by Eugenius's successor. But that was a sideshow. At Florence a decree of reunion with the Greeks was published on 6 July 1439, and this was followed by similar decrees with the Armenians, Copts, the Syrian Churches and the Church of Cyprus. None of them lasted, but in the first flush of enthusiasm Eugenius committed himself to a war against the Turks. A papal fleet was despatched into Byzantine waters and a papal army, commanded by Cardinal Cesarini, who had been Eugenius's choice as president of the council, marched off into Bulgaria, where it was defeated in November 1444 at the Battle of Varna, Cesarini himself losing his life.

A REGRETFUL POPE

The papal court was still in Florence, where it was exposed as never before to the burgeoning Renaissance. One of the great humanists, the Greek Bessarion, who had come to Italy in the train of the Byzantines, stayed behind and in December 1439 was named a cardinal. Eugenius's difficulty in going back to the Vatican was that the papal states were being ravaged by the duke of Milan. When, however, the pope forged an alliance with Alfonso of Aragón, who had seized the kingdom of Naples, the Milanese, who would have been exposed to a powerful coalition against them, also came to an understanding with the pope and so he could return to the Vatican.

For much of his pontificate Eugenius seemed weak, but he had survived a hostile council and a reluctant antipope; he had brought in modest reforms of the lifestyle of the clergy. He restored churches in Rome, and brought there some of the great Renaissance artists such as Fra Angelico, Donatello and Pisanello. He also forbade destruction of the monuments of ancient, pagan Rome. He wrote his own epitaph. As he lay dying he is reported to have said that he regretted ever having left his monastery in Venice.

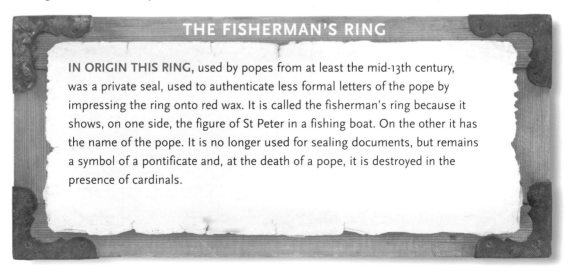

THE FISHERMAN'S RING

IN ORIGIN THIS RING, used by popes from at least the mid-13th century, was a private seal, used to authenticate less formal letters of the pope by impressing the ring onto red wax. It is called the fisherman's ring because it shows, on one side, the figure of St Peter in a fishing boat. On the other it has the name of the pope. It is no longer used for sealing documents, but remains a symbol of a pontificate and, at the death of a pope, it is destroyed in the presence of cardinals.

Nicholas V 1447–55	Marcellus II 1555
Callistus III 1455–58	Paul IV 1555–59
*Pius II 1458–64	*Pius IV 1560–65
Paul II 1464–71	*Pius V 1566–72
Sixtus IV 1471–84	Gregory XIII 1572–85
Innocent VIII 1484–92	*Sixtus V 1585–90
*Alexander VI 1492–1503	Urban VII 1590
Pius III 1503	Gregory XIV 1590–91
*Julius II 1503–13	Innocent IX 1591
Leo X 1513–21	Clement VIII 1592–1605
Hadrian VI 1522–23	Leo XI 1605
Clement VII 1523–34	Paul V 1605–21
Paul III 1534–49	Gregory XV 1621–23
Julius III 1550–55	*Urban VIII 1623–44

*Denotes popes featured within this section

OPPOSITE *The Council of Trent
(1545–63) in session.*

AUTHORITARIANS
AND
REVIVALISTS

The Renaissance and the
papacy renewed

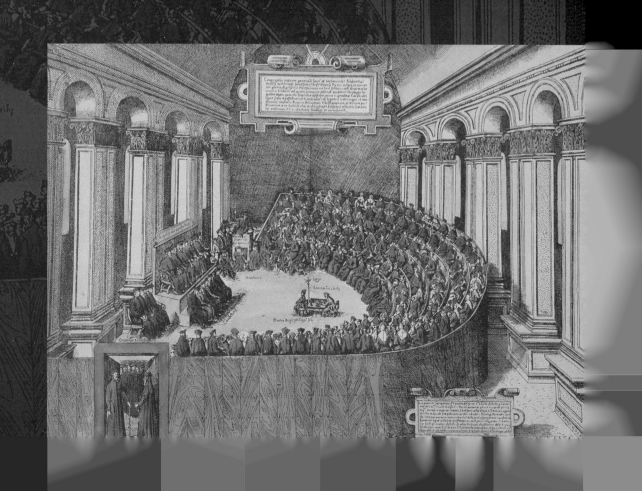

PIUS II

ope Nicholas V (1447–55), who succeeded Eugenius IV, is commonly regarded as the first of the Renaissance popes. He had grandiose plans for the redevelopment of Rome, and assembled a collection of some 1200 manuscripts, on account of which he has come to be regarded as the founder of the Vatican Library. But the pope who followed him, the forbidding Callistus III (1455–8), the first of the two Borgia pontiffs, was certainly no humanist. In Callistus's successor Pius II, however, humanists could reasonably believe they had at last a champion, though in the event he showed himself wary of them.

Enea Silvio Piccolomini's family was noble but poor and he studied at Siena and at Florence, where he was exposed to the full flowering of humanism. He embarked on a clerical career, and acted as an emissary first for Cardinal Capranica, then for Cardinal Niccolò Albergati, who sent him to the court of James I of Scotland. He attended the Council of Basel, where he distinguished himself by his oratory, and sided with Amadeus of Savoy when he was elected as Felix V by the rump of the council. Piccolomini then went to Frankfurt as an emissary of Felix, where he so impressed King Frederick III of Germany with his literary talents that he was made his poet laureate, and was offered a post in the imperial chancery. But in 1445, while in Germany, he withdrew his support for Felix and was reconciled with Eugenius. He had a serious illness, and decided to reform what had hitherto been a dissolute life in the course of which he had fathered several children, one of them in Scotland. He was ordained priest in Vienna in March 1446.

As his support for Felix illustrated, Piccolomini had been a conciliarist. He changed his mind, and persuaded King Frederick likewise to give his backing to Eugenius rather than to Felix. He later wrote a *Letter of Retraction* in which he explained his reasons for abandoning conciliarism. His change of heart stood him in good stead. Nicholas V made him bishop of Trieste and then, in 1449, archbishop of Siena. He was still being used on diplomatic missions both by Frederick and by Callistus, and at the close of successful negotiations on behalf of the pope with Alfonso V of Aragón and Naples, he was raised to the cardinalate.

BIRTH NAME Enea Silvio Piccolomini
BORN Corsignano, Siena,
    18 October 1405
PREDECESSOR Callistus III
INSTALLED 3 September 1458
DIED 14 August 1464
SUCCESSOR Paul II

THE ELECTION OF PICCOLOMINI

The conclave after the death of Callistus met on 13 August 1458. The obvious choice had been Piccolomini's former patron, Cardinal Capranica, but he died the day before the conclave opened. The two remaining candidates were Piccolomini of Siena and Guillaume d'Estouteville of Rouen. The

Pope Pius II at the port of Ancona from where Venetian galleys were supposed to leave for a crusade against the Turks in 1464. From the famous series of frescoes by Bernardino Pinturicchio in the cathedral at Siena (1502–5).

latter promptly started bribing the electors, while Piccolomini responded by haranguing them about the danger of choosing a Frenchman, with the possibility that he might move back to Avignon. Twelve votes were needed for election. When Piccolomini had won eleven, Cardinals Bessarion and d'Estouteville tried to prevent Prospero Colonna from voting, but failed, and Piccolomini won his two-thirds majority.

On his election his chief concern was to summon a crusade. Constantinople had fallen to the Turks in 1453 and the matter was pressing. But behind Pius's desire to launch another holy war was a wish both to re-establish the authority of the papacy and to unite the warring princes. So in October 1458 he issued a crusading bull, and called upon the European rulers to meet at Mantua on 1 June 1459. No one turned up apart from Francesco Sforza of Milan, but Pius went ahead and in January 1460 announced a crusade, imposing a tax to pay for it. He also wrote to the sultan, Mehmet, trying to persuade him of the truths of Christianity, and offering him the title of Byzantine emperor were he to convert – though it should be said there is some doubt about Pius's authorship of this letter.

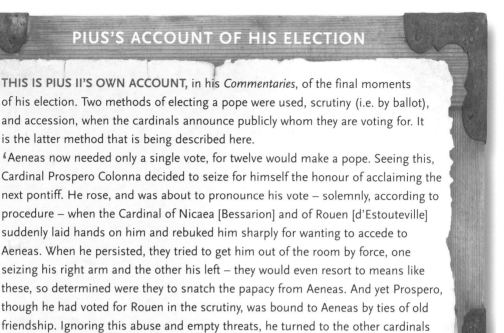

PIUS'S ACCOUNT OF HIS ELECTION

THIS IS PIUS II'S OWN ACCOUNT, in his *Commentaries*, of the final moments of his election. Two methods of electing a pope were used, scrutiny (i.e. by ballot), and accession, when the cardinals announce publicly whom they are voting for. It is the latter method that is being described here.

'Aeneas now needed only a single vote, for twelve would make a pope. Seeing this, Cardinal Prospero Colonna decided to seize for himself the honour of acclaiming the next pontiff. He rose, and was about to pronounce his vote – solemnly, according to procedure – when the Cardinal of Nicaea [Bessarion] and of Rouen [d'Estouteville] suddenly laid hands on him and rebuked him sharply for wanting to accede to Aeneas. When he persisted, they tried to get him out of the room by force, one seizing his right arm and the other his left – they would even resort to means like these, so determined were they to snatch the papacy from Aeneas. And yet Prospero, though he had voted for Rouen in the scrutiny, was bound to Aeneas by ties of old friendship. Ignoring this abuse and empty threats, he turned to the other cardinals and cried, "I too accede to the Cardinal of Siena and I make him Pope."'

FROM MARGARET MESERVE AND MARCELLO SIMONETTA, *PIUS II COMMENTARIES*, VOL I, BOOK 1 CHAPTER 36.

DISAPPOINTMENT AND DEATH

In 1462 a deposit of alum was found at Tolfa near Civitavecchia. A crystalline substance, it was used at the time in the fixing of dyes in textiles, and was a potential source of considerable income for the papacy. This, combined with some support from European monarchs, encouraged Pius to launch another crusade. To shame them into joining it he announced that he would lead it himself, and in June 1464 he took the cross in St Peter's, then set out for Ancona where the crusaders were to assemble. But the vessels which Venice had promised had not arrived and there were very few potential crusaders present. Pius was ill before he set out for Ancona, and it was there that he died. His heart was buried in the Italian port, but his body was taken back to Rome.

In Pius's lifetime he had written numerous books, including some volumes of autobiography. He also wrote history – the story of the Council of Basel and the life and times of the emperor Frederick III, for example – and, as a young man, before his conversion, two licentious novels. He canonized Catherine of Siena, both as an act of piety towards his former diocese, and because he admired her – one of the incidents in Pius's life depicted by Pinturicchio in his frescoes for the Piccolomini Library in Siena, established by Pius's nephew Francesco (Pope Pius III) in honour of his uncle. He defended Jews and black people. He used his position to reward his family, but not excessively so. In Rome he restored churches and repaired the city's walls, but he lavished most upon the Tuscan village in which he was born, Corsignano, and encouraged cardinals to build villas there. He renamed it Pienza, after himself.

ALEXANDER VI

n 1462 Pope Pius II wrote to Cardinal Rodrigo Borgia, 'We leave it to you to judge if it is becoming in one of your position to toy with girls, to pelt them with fruits … and, neglecting study, to spend the whole day in every kind of pleasure.' The pope had heard of a party Rodrigo had given in Siena where the ladies invited had been instructed to leave behind their husbands or brothers. He afterwards learned that reports of the party had been exaggerated and wrote again to apologize, but the details would not have been remarkable for a man who had nine children by sundry women, two of them when he was already pope. In the late 15th century the notion of a cardinal having children was unremarkable, but having a mistress while pope was unheard of.

Rodrigo was born near Valencia, in Spain, where his uncle, who later became Pope Callistus III (1455–8), was bishop. Callistus, though himself a pious and austere man, heaped benefices upon his sister's son, brought him to Rome and then sent him to study law at Bologna. He was created cardinal deacon in February 1456, and on 1 May that year vice-chancellor of the church, a highly lucrative position in which he remained until he became pope. In July 1471 he was made cardinal bishop of Albano, and dean of the college of cardinals. He still held a string of other benefices, making him, it was said, the second richest cardinal, outdone only by Guillaume d'Estouteville of Rouen. He was frequently used as a legate by successive popes, and was commissary general of the papal armies in Italy. No doubt all these posts brought him great wealth, but he also displayed considerable talent both as an administrator and as a diplomat. He was a possible candidate in the election of 1484, but decided against standing. As a Spaniard he was not greatly popular, but in 1492, when it became clear that it would be difficult for anyone else to command a two-thirds majority, votes shifted to him. It was obvious that, as pope, he would have to rid himself of many of the benefices he had accumulated. There could be rich pickings for his supporters. After his election he declared that he wanted to bring peace to Italy and war to the Turks, sentiments which found favour. His coronation was a grand affair, too grand even for him: he twice fainted in the heat of the Roman summer.

BIRTH NAME **Rodrigo Borja**
BORN **Játiva, near Valencia, 1 January 1431**
PREDECESSOR **Innocent VIII**
INSTALLED **26 August 1492**
DIED **18 August 1503**
SUCCESSOR **Pius III**

THE BORGIA FAMILY

Alexander VI lost no time in advancing his family. His first group of cardinals was on the whole impressively international, but it included Cesare, his son by Rosa Vanozza dei Catanei, and Alessandro Farnese, the brother of Giulia Farnese, who was Rodrigo's mistress at the time of

The infamous Borgia pope, Alexander VI, as portrayed by Bernardino Pinturicchio in the Borgia apartments in the Vatican. Notorious for his debauchery and nepotism, Alexander was believed by some to have met his death by poisoning.

his election. He married his daughter Lucrezia, also a child of Rosa's, to Giovanni Sforza, lord of Pesaro, in an attempt to link Milan to the papacy, and frustrate the ambitions on the city of Charles VIII of France – Charles also wanted an alliance with Milan to help him lay hands on the kingdom of Naples. Charles was advised by Alexander's great enemy, Cardinal Giuliano della Rovere, who had fled to France no doubt fearing for his life. The pope put together a Holy League of the emperor, Venice and Milan, the ostensible purpose of which was to attack the Turks, but whose real purpose was to oppose the French.

AN ALLIANCE WITH FRANCE

In the summer of 1497 Alexander was thrown off course by the assassination of his son Juan, duke of Gandia, who was in charge of the papal armies. This occasioned a (temporary) change of heart. He resolved to reform the church, and set up a commission of cardinals to make proposals. But he soon lost interest, and only a few of the reforms they suggested were ever initiated. Shortly afterwards Lucrezia's Sforza marriage was annulled, and she married instead Alfonso, son of the king of Naples. Alfonso was attacked on the steps of St Peter's in July 1500, and died some time later despite the care with which Lucrezia looked after him. He was in all likelihood strangled by one of Cesare's men – Cesare may very well have organized the original assassination attempt – because papal policy was again changing. Cesare, who had given up his cardinalate, had married the sister of the king of Navarre in 1499 and was close to the king of France, who had made him duke of Valentinois. The alliance with the new French king, Louis XII, owed something to the fact that the pope had annulled Louis' marriage to allow him to wed Anne of Brittany. As part of the package, Cesare helped France to recover Milan, while the French helped Cesare to take the Romagna and convert it into a duchy, which the family hoped would survive under Borgia control even after the death of Alexander. The French king also undertook to help the pope bring the great Roman families to heel. So powerful now were the Borgias that they could seize Colonna lands and put Orsinis in prison. However, the d'Estes of Ferrara were another matter, hence Lucrezia's third and last marriage, to the heir to the duchy of Ferrara. She seems to have proved a dutiful and, at the end of her days, a strikingly devout duchess.

The Borgia pope was something of a patron of the arts ... employing Pinturicchio to decorate the papal apartments.

THE DEATH OF ALEXANDER VI

THE FOLLOWING ACCOUNT WAS WRITTEN BY JOHANN BURCHARD, ALEXANDER VI'S MASTER OF CEREMONIES:

'When I saw the corpse again, its face had changed to the colour of mulberry or the blackest cloth and it was covered with blue-black spots. The nose was swollen, the mouth distended where the tongue was doubled over, and the lips seemed to fill everything. The appearance of the face then was far more horrifying than anything that had ever been seen or reported before. Later, after five o'clock, the body was carried to the Chapel of Santa Maria della Febbre and placed in its coffin next to the wall in a corner by the altar. Six labourers or porters, making blasphemous jokes about the pope or in contempt of his corpse, together with two master carpenters, performed this task. The carpenters had made the coffin too narrow and short, and so they placed the pope's mitre at his side, rolled his body up in an old carpet, and pummelled and pushed it into the coffin with their fists. No wax tapers or lights were used, and no priests or any other persons attended to his body.'

JOHANN BURCHARD, *AT THE COURT OF THE BORGIA.*

A PATRON OF THE ARTS

But then, in his own way, Alexander VI was also devout. He had a particular piety towards the Virgin Mary and was at first in favour of Girolamo Savonarola's call for reform in the church. But the fiery Dominican preacher went too far in supporting Charles VIII when he invaded Italy, and in attacking the papacy itself. Savonarola also made himself extremely unpopular with the rulers of Florence, where he lived. The pope tried to silence him, but when that failed, had him hanged and burned as a heretic. Alexander was active against heretics elsewhere in Europe. He was also active against the Turks, and was having some success until Venice signed a treaty with the Turks in 1502. The Borgia pope was something of a patron of the arts. He employed Pinturicchio to decorate the papal apartments, still known as the Borgia apartments, in the Vatican. He added the splendid ceiling to the basilica of Santa Maria Maggiore, which was decorated with some of the first gold to be brought back from the Indies. He built the University of Rome, La Sapienza, and had a new road built from Castel Sant'Angelo to St Peter's in time for the Holy Year of 1500. And in 1493 he published the bull *Inter caetera*, which granted to the Catholic kings of Spain and Portugal all the lands they might discover in the Indies, laying down a line of division which proved too favourable to Spain and had to be revised the following year in the Treaty of Tordesillas. He also made provision for missionaries to be sent to these new territories.

In August 1503 the pope fell ill after a dinner at which Cesare was present. The rumour was that Cesare had poisoned him – though that is highly unlikely, especially because Cesare himself was taken ill – or that he had been poisoned by accidentally taking poison intended for another guest. The rumours of poison were given credence by the state of his corpse (see box), but it is far more likely that both he and Cesare were struck down by fever in the sultry heat of the Roman summer. Only the younger man survived.

JULIUS II

t the death of Alexander VI in 1503 the cardinals in conclave feared the intervention of Cesare Borgia and swiftly elected someone who had been considered in earlier conclaves, was untrammelled by allegiance to the major parties among the cardinals, and was so old that he was not expected to live long. They were perhaps not expecting quite such a short pontificate: Pius III died only ten days after his coronation. The next conclave was even shorter. It lasted a single day, and by dint of generous bribes Giuliano della Rovere achieved his ambition and became Pope Julius II.

He had been educated by Franciscans in Perugia, and chose a clerical, rather than a commercial, career. But then his uncle Francesco, who had been minister general of the Franciscans, became Pope Sixtus IV (1471–84), and the fortunes of Giuliano, who had been born into a poor family, suddenly improved. In the year of Sixtus's election he became bishop of Carpentras, and cardinal priest of San Pietro in Vinculi, and a few years later cardinal bishop of Sant Sabina. He was endowed with a string of further benefices, including that of Avignon in 1474, which the following year was raised to the rank of an archbishopric.

BIRTH NAME Giuliano della Rovere
BORN Albisola, near Savona,
5 December 1443
PREDECESSOR Pius III
INSTALLED 18 November 1503
DIED 21 February 1513
SUCCESSOR Leo X

During the pontificates of both Sixtus and his successor Innocent VIII (1484–92), Cardinal della Rovere proved himself a highly accomplished political negotiator, but after the election of his arch-enemy Rodrigo Borgia in 1492, Giuliano fled to France. He accompanied Charles VIII of France when, during the pontificate of Alexander VI, he invaded Naples, capturing Rome en route – the attempt to depose Alexander ended in failure – and then retired back to France.

A WARRIOR POPE

Julius's policy was to enhance the standing of the papacy by recovering the papal states, parts of which Alexander had generously bestowed on his family, and by beautifying Rome. He was interested equally in the arts and in the art of war. He frequently led his troops personally, clad in full armour, and in January 1511 at the siege of Mirandola he drew his sword and was the first to cross through a breach in the walls. He had at first been in league with the French, but ignored the claims of Louis XII of France to the crown of Naples, which turned Louis against him, especially after he had attacked Ferrara, France's main ally in Italy. Louis invaded Italy, and his troops defeated the papal army under Cardinal Giovanni de' Medici. The future Leo X, Julius's successor, was taken prisoner, but managed to escape. He let Julius know that the French, although technically victors at Ravenna (April 1512), had suffered such heavy losses that their army had been seriously weakened. With the aid of Swiss mercenaries Julius drove France out of Italy, and as a thank-offering to Giovanni de' Medici helped him recover Florence, which had risen against his family. So strengthened were the papal states at the end of Julius's pontificate that he might reasonably be called their second founder.

REBUILDING ST PETER'S

The papal states – with the exception of the Vatican City, the smallest state in the world, – have now entirely disappeared. But tourists still visit in their hundreds of thousands the much more lasting achievement of Pope Julius II – the new St Peter's. At the beginning of the 16th century

A contemporary chalk drawing of Julius II by Raphael in preparation for painting his portrait. Pope Julius was interested equally in the arts and the art of war. It was Julius who commissioned Michelangelo to paint the Sistine Chapel.

the much embellished Constantinian Basilica was still standing, but only just. Julius determined to replace it, a task which took more than a century. He called the architect Bramante to Rome to design the new building in a style utterly different from the traditional Roman one based upon classical models. It is quite possible that the pope thought of the new basilica simply as a setting for his own memorial, which he wanted to place above the tomb of St Peter. Julius had been much impressed by a Pietà he had seen, and brought its sculptor, Michelangelo, to Rome to design his own tomb. Although several parts of the vast memorial to Pope Julius survive, only the statue of

THE LIFESTYLE OF CARDINALS

DURING THE FIFTH LATERAN COUNCIL (1512–17) a decree of reform was enacted on 5 May 1514 which had the following to say about the lifestyle of cardinals:
'Their house and establishment, table and furniture, should not attract blame by display or splendour or superfluous equipment or in any other way, so as to avoid any fostering of sin or excess, but, as is right, let them deserve to be called mirrors of moderation and frugality. Therefore, let them find satisfaction in what contributes to priestly modesty; let them act with kindness and respect, both in public and in private, towards prelates and other distinguished persons who come to the Roman curia; let them undertake with with grace and generosity the business committed to them by our self [i.e. Leo X] and our successors.'
QUOTED IN NORMAN P. TANNER *DECREES OF THE ECUMENICAL COUNCILS.*

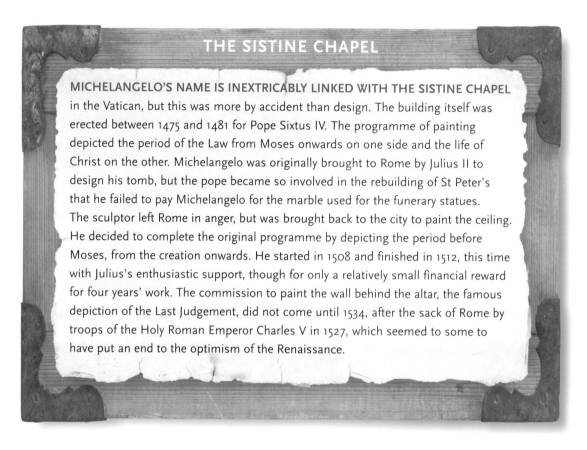

THE SISTINE CHAPEL

MICHELANGELO'S NAME IS INEXTRICABLY LINKED WITH THE SISTINE CHAPEL
in the Vatican, but this was more by accident than design. The building itself was
erected between 1475 and 1481 for Pope Sixtus IV. The programme of painting
depicted the period of the Law from Moses onwards on one side and the life of
Christ on the other. Michelangelo was originally brought to Rome by Julius II to
design his tomb, but the pope became so involved in the rebuilding of St Peter's
that he failed to pay Michelangelo for the marble used for the funerary statues.
The sculptor left Rome in anger, but was brought back to the city to paint the ceiling.
He decided to complete the original programme by depicting the period before
Moses, from the creation onwards. He started in 1508 and finished in 1512, this time
with Julius's enthusiastic support, though for only a relatively small financial reward
for four years' work. The commission to paint the wall behind the altar, the famous
depiction of the Last Judgement, did not come until 1534, after the sack of Rome by
troops of the Holy Roman Emperor Charles V in 1527, which seemed to some to
have put an end to the optimism of the Renaissance.

Moses remains in Rome, in the church which had been Giuliano della Rovere's titular church as
cardinal priest, San Pietro in Vincoli, a church which he restored. The tomb was never completed,
for Michelangelo was set by the pope to various other tasks, most importantly the painting of the
Sistine Chapel, built for Julius's uncle Sixtus IV (see box).

THE FIFTH COUNCIL OF THE LATERAN

In 1511, after Bologna had fallen to the French, a number of cardinals rebelled against Julius
and went over to the French side. They may well have been alarmed at the fate of the governor
of Bologna, Cardinal Alidosi, who was put to death by Julius's nephew, the duke of Urbino, for
allowing Bologna to fall into French hands. The rebels called a council in Pisa, which met in
October 1511 and declared Julius deposed. The pope, who had little interest in church reform,
felt he had to respond and called his own Council of the Lateran, the fifth of that name, which
sat from 1512 to 1517. It thus began in Julius's time, achieving little, and continued into the
pontificate of his successor, Leo X, who had even less interest in reform.

AN ILL-ADVISED DECISION

Julius's pontificate left a lasting effect on the church, and not just through his remarkable artistic
programme. In order to pay for the new St Peter's he effectively allowed the sale of indulgences,
the abuse of which lay at the origins of the Protestant Reformation. And he allowed King Henry
VIII of England to marry Catherine of Aragón, his brother's widow. It was Henry's later
allegation, that the marriage was unlawful, because Julius had no right to grant Henry a dispensation to wed Catherine, that precipitated the English Reformation.

PIUS IV

ian Angelo de' Medici was no relation of the famous Medicis of Florence, though he rather liked to claim it. His family was not wealthy, and in his early years, during his studies at Pavia and then Bologna, he had to struggle to pay his way. In 1527, two years after completing his doctorate in law, he entered papal service. He rose to become archbishop of Ragusa in December 1545, at which point he became a priest and bishop, and was made a cardinal in 1549. His private life was not blameless – he had three illegitimate children – but he was not given to the luxury which commonly surrounded the life of a cardinal. His tastes were simple, whether in food or ceremonial. He was deemed politically astute, but was generally friendly and a great walker.

He was not, however, an easy choice for the electors to make. The pontificate of Paul IV (1555–9) had been problematic. Though personally austere and dedicated to reform of the church, Paul had practised nepotism on a grand scale, not least in the advancement of Carlo Carafa, who had become a cardinal, and who had led Paul into a war with Spain that was both unnecessary and disastrous. He also harboured such a distaste for Protestant reform that he refused to call the Council of Trent (see box, page 161) back into session, and wanted instead to establish a reform commission under total papal control. What that might have meant was to be seen in the extensive list of books which, he decreed, Catholics were forbidden to read (the *Index Librorum Prohibitorum* – List of Forbidden Books), commonly known simply as the Index (see box, page 162), and his treatment of Jews who, he believed, were allied to Protestantism and had to be confined to ghettoes and made to wear distinctive dress.

So in the four-month conclave which followed his death in 1559, the factions had to deal with the fall-out from his pontificate. The balance of power was held by the Carafas, two of whom were cardinals, because the other electors were divided between supporters of the emperor Ferdinand I and Philip II of Spain, both of whom had succeeded to their titles on the abdication of Emperor Charles V – an abdication which Paul IV had refused to countenance, because he had not been asked to approve it. The electors drew up a capitulation, to which all agreed, that whoever was chosen would call the Council of Trent back into session.

The Carafas had much to fear. After the election of Pius IV, Cardinal Carlo Carafa and Giovanni Carafa, whom the

BIRTH NAME **Gian Angelo de' Medici**
BORN **Milan, 31 March 1499**
PREDECESSOR **Paul IV**
INSTALLED **6 January 1560**
DIED **9 December 1565**
SUCCESSOR **Pius V**

Pope Pius IV oversaw the final period of the Council of Trent (1562–3) and made sure of its satisfactory outcome.

late pope had made duke of Palino, were arrested and put on trial along with several others of their entourages. Carlo and Giovanni were executed for having started the war against Spain and for sundry other crimes – including the assassination of Giovanni's wife. The measures against the Jews were eased, as were the operations of the Inquisition, and a revision of the Index was set in motion.

CHARLES BORROMEO

Pius, too, indulged in nepotism, promptly making his nephew Charles Borromeo a cardinal and a week later archbishop of Milan, as well as giving him in the course of time sundry other appointments. But Borromeo was an outstanding archbishop – he has since been declared a saint – and from 1565 until his death in 1584 proved himself the model of a Tridentine bishop. Even before Borromeo's departure from Rome he had reformed his lifestyle, and for a time considered becoming a monk.

THE RECALL OF THE COUNCIL OF TRENT

In 1562 Pope Pius recalled the Council of Trent as the electors had wanted (see box, page 161). He did so despite the opposition of the emperor Ferdinand I, who still hoped, as Charles V had done, that the Protestants in his dominions would be won over by a council, though one of a different sort to Trent. The pope gave the presidency of the council to Cardinal Giovanni Morone, whom his predecessor had imprisoned in Castel Sant'Angelo on the trumped-up charge of heresy. Morone presided over it with great skill, and to a large extent was personally responsible for the satisfactory outcome.

On one issue the pope bowed to the pressure of Ferdinand. Protestants had condemned the Catholic practice of receiving the Eucharist in the form of bread alone, the communion wafer. It had been a major aspect of their liturgy that the chalice, likewise, was handed to the laity. Pius agreed to concede this in imperial territory, though not elsewhere. He did not, however, grant Ferdinand's other demand, that Catholic clergy, like Protestant ones, should be allowed to marry. Philip of Spain was opposed to such a move, so Pius put it on hold.

CATECHISM OF THE COUNCIL OF TRENT

The council ended formally on 4 December 1563. The papal bull confirming the decrees, *Benedictus Deus*, was published on 30 June 1564. This bull encompassed all three periods of the council, making it clear that it was one event, though it had taken place over an extended period

THE COUNCIL OF TRENT

POPE CLEMENT VII (1523–34) HAD BEEN PRESSURED BY EMPEROR CHARLES V to call a council which would both reform the church and deal with the divisions within it caused by the rebellion of Martin Luther. It was eventually summoned not by Clement but by Pope Paul III (1534–49). He had wanted it to meet in Mantua, but when that location proved unacceptable to both Charles and the then French king Francis I, he suggested Vicenza. That, too, was unsatisfactory. Charles's patience was running out. He threatened to call a synod of the church in Germany, over which the pope would certainly have had no say, so a compromise was agreed upon. Moreover, Pius was alarmed because Lutheranism appeared to be making progress in Italy itself. The council, it was decided, was to meet in Trent (modern Trento) in northern Italy, a city which lay just within the empire, but was nonetheless in Italy, and not so far from Rome that it would have been entirely outside the control of the papacy. It was announced by the bull *Laetare Jerusalem* – 'Rejoice, Jerusalem' – published on 19 November 1544. The pope proposed that the council meet on 15 March the following year. In the event it started on 13 December 1545. According to the bull, the Council of Trent was to heal division in the church, establish peace among Christians so that a crusade might be launched against the Turks, and reform the church, the churchmen and the church's administration.

They were no doubt noble aims, but there was little likelihood they would be met. Though Protestant reformers were invited, they did not come to the opening session and though, as will be seen, a crusading alliance was put together under Pius's IV's successor, Pius V, it had little lasting effect. But Trent managed to lay down Catholic positions on theological matters in dispute, and to set in train a major reform of the life of the church, a reform so thorough that commentators looking back at the history of Catholicism from the late 16th to the mid-20th century speak of 'the Tridentine Church' – 'Tridentine' being the adjective derived from Trent.

Though it was in many ways a success, the council had a chequered history. Paul III did not give up hope of moving the gathering to more congenial territory, and transferred it to Bologna on the grounds that there was plague in Trent, but the imperial representatives refused to budge. Then for a time Protestant representatives turned up, but they wanted everything that had been discussed before their belated arrival reconsidered, and refused to deal directly with papal representatives. Then the military success of the Protestant princes sent German bishops hurrying home, so the session which the Protestants attended was brought to a sudden close.

There were three periods of the council. The first, under Pope Paul III, lasted from 1545 to 1548; the second, under Julius III, from 1551 to 1552; and the final period, under Pope Pius IV, from 1562 to 1563.

THE INDEX

THE BANNING OF BOOKS WITHIN CHRISTIANITY HAS A HISTORY ALMOST AS LONG AS THAT OF CHRISTIANITY ITSELF. In the 16th century, however, the invention of printing and the development of Protestantism made it more important to have a list of books judged heretical or immoral. The first such lists were not papal at all, but produced in Holland, Venice and Paris. The Index produced under Pope Paul IV was judged to be too restrictive, and was almost immediately revised, to be published in 1564 under Pius IV. It was this edition which became the basis for all subsequent editions until a complete revision was undertaken under Pope Leo XIII in 1897. A special Congregation was given responsibility for it, the Congregation of the Index, which survived until 1917. The Index itself was effectively abolished under Pope Paul VI in 1966. The purpose of the Index was to alert Catholics to, and ban them from reading, books judged harmful to faith and morals. Hence it listed the writings of a good many philosophers, such as Descartes, Hume and Kant, essayists such as Addison and Diderot, as well as novelists such as Alexandre Dumas, both father and son, André Gide and Émile Zola. Even Graham Greene, often regarded as a Catholic novelist, was for a time included.

of time. There remained the matter of interpreting the decrees: the pope kept that technically to himself, though he handed its administration over to a committee of cardinals, later to become The Congregation of the Council.

Pius also set about drawing up a Catechism of the Council of Trent to make its deliberations better known, and revoked all privileges which might have contradicted the spirit of the council. He also began a revision of the mass book, the missal and the prayers said by the clergy each day, known as the breviary. And as a practical step in implementing the reforms, the pope ordered all bishops to take up residence in their dioceses. He also founded the Roman seminary for the education of the clergy, and handed it over to the Jesuits to run.

On the other hand Pius IV was not a very satisfactory administrator of the papal states, a failure which ultimately led to an attempt on his life. His care of Rome itself was rather better. He built the Porta Pia and the Porta del Popolo. He restored an aqueduct, and commissioned Michelangelo to restore the church of Santa Maria degli Angeli. He also called to Rome Paolo Manuzio, son of the famous Venetian printer, Aldus Manucius, to establish a printing press in the city to print the revised texts for which the council had called. And in the Vatican gardens he had an exquisite small house built, the Casina, which is still commonly known by his name, the Villa Pia.

PIUS V

he Council of Trent initiated a period of revitalized Catholicism in response to the Protestant Reformation. It is a period which is often called the Counter Reformation. This is a much-discussed and disputed term, partly at least because it makes it sound as though the new spirit in Catholicism — expressed in baroque architecture, polyphonic music, a deepened spirituality and missionary activity on a scale never before seen, not just in the Americas but also in the Far East, most dramatically in India and China — was simply a response to the challenge of Protestantism. But it could equally be argued that the purified faith and the devotion of the protagonists of the Counter Reformation were inspired by the same spirit which gave rise to the Reformation. Be that as it may, many see the Counter Reformation embodied in the person of Michele Ghislieri.

Ghislieri was christened Antonio. He came from a farming family, and worked in his childhood as a shepherd, but the family was wealthy enough to send him to a school run by Dominicans, whom he joined at the age of 14, taking Michele as his name in religion. He was a very capable young man. He studied at Bologna and taught at Pavia. He then became inquisitor at Bergamo and Como where his zeal in this position brought him to the attention of Cardinal Giampietro Carafa, the future Pope Paul IV (1555–9), named Inquisitor General when the tribunal of the Inquisition was restored in 1542. He was appointed commissary general of the Inquisition in Rome in 1551. Ghislieri then became a bishop, a cardinal the following year and Inquisitor General in 1558. Unfortunately for the new cardinal, after the death of his patron he fell into relative disgrace because of his association with the Carafa family. He then gave himself over wholeheartedly to the reform of his diocese, which so impressed the reformers among the cardinals that he was elected pope with their support, though only after a conclave lasting three weeks.

THE BATTLE OF LEPANTO

One of his first acts was to rehabilitate the Carafa family, no doubt a principled action, but one which promptly alienated Spain whose help he needed if he was, as he eagerly wished, to launch yet another crusade against the Turks. However, when the Turks, after burning down the Arsenal in Venice and capturing Cyprus, seemed about to dominate the Adriatic and possibly the whole of the Mediterranean, Spain, Venice and the papacy succeeded in putting together a fleet. It was under the command of Don John of Austria, the illegitimate son of the

BIRTH NAME Antonio Ghislieri

BORN Boscomarengo, near Alessandria, 17 July 1504

PREDECESSOR Pius IV

INSTALLED 17 January 1566

DIED 1 May 1572

SUCCESSOR Gregory XIII

A portrait of Pope Pius V by Pulzone. His greatest concerns were the reform of the church and the removal of heresy. One of his actions was to issue a bull against Elizabeth I of England, whom he regarded as a usurper – thereby freeing her Catholic subjects from their allegiance to her.

emperor Charles V, and therefore a half-brother of Philip II of Spain, and it defeated the rather larger Turkish navy at Lepanto in the Gulf of Corinth on 7 October 1571. It is sometimes said that this victory – which the pope marked with a new feast day, that of Our Lady of the Rosary – had no significant consequences. Certainly it did not hold up the Turkish advance into Europe, but it possibly prevented Turkish forces commanding the Mediterranean.

HOSTILITY TO ELIZABETH I

But Pius V's greatest concern was always the reform of the church, and the extirpation of heresy. To the latter end he reinvigorated the Inquisition and even as pope attended its meetings. He started a special committee (a 'Congregation') of cardinals to oversee the Index, and financially assisted the French Catholics in their military action against the Protestant Huguenots. He was deeply hostile to Elizabeth I of England, whom he regarded as a usurper and, in the bull *Regnans in Excelsis* of 25 February 1570, declared her deposed, freeing English Catholics from their allegiance to her (see box, page 165). This was a major mistake. It made little or no difference to Elizabeth, but it turned all English Catholics into potential traitors, thus giving the government grounds for persecution, in so far as they needed them. But it also angered the emperor and the kings of France and Spain. If the pope could try to do this with one legitimate monarch, he might attempt to do so with others, calling upon powers that had not been in use since the Middle Ages. The situation was not helped by Pius's reissue of the bull *In coena Domini* ('On the Lord's Supper', i.e. on Maundy Thursday, when it was to be read out) which reiterated papal privileges and the censures, reserved to the papacy for absolution, for infringing them. The kings of Spain, France and Portugal opposed the bull. Pius's hostility to Protestants was also an irritant to the emperor, who had many Protestants in his dominions.

Pius was personally extremely austere. He continued to wear, even as pope, the plain white habit of a Dominican under his pontifical robes. He had little time for the arts, and tried to rid Rome of the remnants of pagan culture, though it was Pius IV (1560–5) and Paul V (1605–21), rather than Pius V, who had fig leaves placed on the naked torsos of statuary and breeches painted onto figures in Michelangelo's *Last Judgement*. The pope tried to drive debauchery out of Rome, and made Jews live in ghettoes in an attempt to coerce them into becoming Christians. He attempted to enforce the decrees of the Council of Trent throughout the Christian world, with varied success, publishing the Catechism of the Council of Trent, begun under his predecessor, as well as revised versions of the breviary, which appeared in 1568, and the missal, or mass book, which came out in 1570. In recognition of the austerity of his life, and for his commitment to the revitalizing of Catholicism in accord with the teachings of Trent, he was declared a saint in 1712.

AN EXCERPT FROM THE BULL *REGNANS IN EXCELSIS*, 25 FEBRUARY 1570, ADDRESSED TO THE ENGLISH:

'Therefore, resting upon the authority of Him whose pleasure it was to place us (though unequal to such a burden) upon this supreme justice-seat, we do out of the fullness of our apostolic power declare the foresaid Elizabeth to be a heretic and favourer of heretics, and her adherents in the matters aforesaid to have incurred the sentence of excommunication and to be cut off from the unity of the body of Christ.

And moreover (we declare) her to be deprived of her pretended title to the aforesaid crown and of all lordship, dignity and privilege whatsoever.

And also (declare) the nobles, subjects and people of the said realm and all others who have in any way sworn oaths to her, to be forever absolved from such an oath and from any duty arising from lordship. fealty and obedience; and we do, by authority of these present, so absolve them and so deprive the same Elizabeth of her pretended title to the crown and all other the above said matters. We charge and command all and singular the nobles, subjects, peoples and others afore said that they do not dare obey her orders, mandates and laws. Those who shall act to the contrary we include in the like sentence of excommunication.'

SIXTUS V

ith the Council of Trent legislating for the reform of church discipline and restating the faith of Catholics, and with the revised texts of liturgical books being published, what remained was a reform of the central administration of the church. This was undertaken by Sixtus V, whose reorganization of the papal curia laid down a pattern which can still be observed today.

Felice Peretti was born to poor parents, peasant farmers, and he spent his childhood looking after pigs. He began his education in the charge of an uncle who was a Franciscan, and in 1533 he himself joined the order at Montalto, keeping his own name rather than taking a new one. He studied at Fermo, Ferrara and Bologna, displaying great

BIRTH NAME **Felice Peretti**
BORN **Grottammare, March of Ancona, 13 December 1520**
PREDECESSOR **Gregory XIII**
INSTALLED **1 May 1585**
DIED **27 August 1590**
SUCCESSOR **Urban VII**

intellectual ability, so much so that he went on to teach canon law and metaphysics in Rimini and Siena. He came to the attention of the Cardinal Protector of the Franciscans, Rodolfo Pio de Carpi, who brought him to Rome to deliver a series of Lenten sermons which got him into trouble with the Inquisition. He was cleared of all charges of being unorthodox, but his brush with the Inquisition brought him into contact with Cardinal Michele Ghislieri, the Inquisitor General. Peretti then became inquisitor in Venice, where he proved to be too severe and was recalled, but was reappointed by Pius IV (1560–5). Under Pius V he flourished, being made vicar general of his order and then bishop of Sant'Agata dei Goti in the kingdom of Naples. In 1570 he became a cardinal. Under Pius V's successor, Gregory XIII (1572–85), his star faded as he had crossed with Gregory when the two were members of a four-man tribunal in Spain to judge the orthodoxy of the archbishop of Toledo, Bartolomé Carranza de Miranda. (All four members of the tribunal went on to become popes.) He spent the years of Gregory's pontificate in his Roman palace on the Esquiline preparing an edition of the writings of St Ambrose.

A FRANCISCAN LIFESTYLE

The conclave which followed Gregory XIII's death was brief, lasting from 21 to 24 April 1585. It was notable for the large number of absences. Of the 60 cardinals, only 42 were present, and in particular, only 14 of the 30 cardinals created by Peretti's old enemy, the late pope, turned up. Peretti took the name Sixtus in honour of Sixtus IV (1471–84), who had also been a Franciscan. The religious orders – the Jesuits apart – were to flourish under Sixtus's papacy, especially the Franciscans. He himself remained very much a Franciscan in his personal life, which no doubt

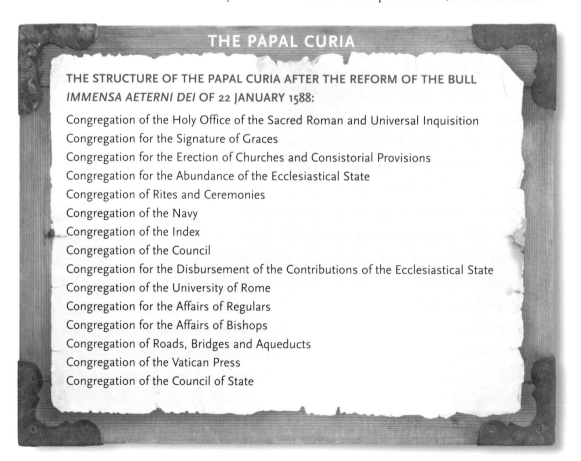

THE PAPAL CURIA

THE STRUCTURE OF THE PAPAL CURIA AFTER THE REFORM OF THE BULL *IMMENSA AETERNI DEI* OF 22 JANUARY 1588:

Congregation of the Holy Office of the Sacred Roman and Universal Inquisition
Congregation for the Signature of Graces
Congregation for the Erection of Churches and Consistorial Provisions
Congregation for the Abundance of the Ecclesiastical State
Congregation of Rites and Ceremonies
Congregation of the Navy
Congregation of the Index
Congregation of the Council
Congregation for the Disbursement of the Contributions of the Ecclesiastical State
Congregation of the University of Rome
Congregation for the Affairs of Regulars
Congregation for the Affairs of Bishops
Congregation of Roads, Bridges and Aqueducts
Congregation of the Vatican Press
Congregation of the Council of State

helped to replenish the papal treasury, relocated to Castel Sant'Angelo, but he was also in general financially acute. He raised taxes in the papal states, and attempted to improve agriculture and the wool and silk industry (his favourite architect, Domenico Fontana, had the curious idea of turning the Colosseum into a factory for treating wool). These improvements were much helped by his restoring order in the papal states through the simple but effective process of executing great numbers of brigands, and punishing their abettors.

A HEALTHY TREASURY

The result of all these reforms was a very healthy treasury, making the pope one of the richest princes in Europe, but it was all part of a broader strategy to centralize power in the papacy. One of the ways he did this, and the one for which Sixtus is most remembered, was the establishment in the bull *Immensa aeterni Dei* of 22 January 1588 of 15 permanent congregations of cardinals (see box, page 166) to oversee the governance of the church. This not only streamlined the administration,

Sixtus V took over the reform of the central administration of the church. His reorganization of the papal curia laid down a pattern which can still be observed today.

but also effectively broke the power of the cardinals who in the past, meeting together in consistories, had vied with the pope of the day in running the church. In future cardinals would meet only rarely, and then on formal occasions, with the business of the church being handled by small groups of them and their officials. Sixtus reinstituted the rule that all bishops should visit the curia to report on the state of their dioceses. He divided them up into four groups, depending on the convenience of such visits. Those closest to Rome had to come every three years, those furthest away every ten – and they could be suspended from office if they did not do so. From now on, the pope was to be an absolute monarch.

NEW BUILDINGS FOR ROME

The same centralization can be seen in Sixtus's town planning for Rome. He built new streets to meet the demands not of commerce but of religion, linking churches rather than businesses. He also acquired, and began to build, the Quirinal Palace, now the residence of the president of Italy. He built a new aqueduct, the Acqua Felice, named after himself, and a new hall, the Sistine Hall, for the Vatican Library, and began the Vatican publishing house.

With a full treasury he could help causes close to his heart. He promised Philip II of Spain a subsidy for his invasion of England in 1588, but when the Armada failed he refused to pay the money he had promised. He did, on the other hand, support Philip against the Protestant Henry of Navarre, at least until it became clear that Henry might become (as he did) king of France and convert to Catholicism in the process. As part of his battle against Protestantism he promoted a new edition of the Vulgate, the Latin version of the Scriptures (see page 20), and, becoming impatient with its slow progress, took a hand in it himself. His edition, however, was so full of errors that it had to be withdrawn.

He limited the number of cardinals to 70, a number not exceeded until the mid-20th century. In one so concerned for the good of the church it is odd that the very first cardinal he created, a fortnight after his election, was his great-nephew Alessandro Damasceni Peretti, then aged only 14.

URBAN VIII

 ope Julius II, at the beginning of the 16th century, had embarked on the project of rebuilding St Peter's. It was Pope Urban VIII who finally consecrated it, on 18 November 1626. Maffeo Barberini was born into a successful family of merchants, dealing in silks from the East, the fifth of six children. His father died when he was still young, and he was taken under the wing of Francesco Barberini, an uncle who was already in the papal curia. He was educated first with the Jesuits in Florence, then at their Roman College, and finally at the University of Pisa. The year that he graduated from Pisa, 1589, he entered papal service, his uncle having purchased a post for him.

His subsequent rise owed much to his uncle, then to the patronage of Pope Clement VIII (1592–1605), also from Florence, who made him an archbishop in October 1604 and soon afterwards sent him to Paris as nuncio, or ambassador. He was made a cardinal in 1606. Two years later he became bishop of Spoleto, a post he resigned in 1617 when he became head of the curial office, the Signatura of Justice.

Maffeo never forgot how indebted he was to the Barberini family. He made his brother (who would have much preferred to stay in his Capuchin friary at San Gimignano) and two nephews cardinals, one of the nephews, Francesco, playing a particularly significant role in his pontificate as a political advisor to the pope. He also enriched many other members of his wider family, making his elder brother a duke and placing him in charge of the papal forces.

BIRTH NAME **Maffeo Vincenzo Barberini**
BORN **Florence, April 1568**
PREDECESSOR **Gregory XV**
INSTALLED **29 September 1623**
DIED **29 July 1644**
SUCCESSOR **Innocent X**

The Thirty Years' War

Urban VIII's pontificate coincided with the Thirty Years' War (1618–48). From his time in Paris, where he received the red hat at the hands of King Henry IV – he was sympathetic to France and antipathetic to Spain, though he tried as much as he could to appear neutral in the conflict between the powers. This bias was bolstered by his fear of Habsburg domination in Italy, which he was determined to avoid. His Francophile leanings were strained, however, when Cardinal Richelieu sided with Swedish and German Protestants against the emperor Ferdinand II, forcing on Ferdinand a peace favourable to Protestants. When the Swedish king Gustavus Adolphus was killed in battle at Lützen in November 1632, Urban ordered masses of thanksgiving to be said across Rome.

His concern may have been the triumph of Catholicism against Protestantism, but more practically he was determined in his foreign policy to defend the papal states. He fortified many of the cities, including Rome itself. A wall was built around the Vatican, and Castel Sant'Angelo was provided with cannon made from metal taken from the Pantheon. He was able to annex the duchy of Urbino, which meant that the papal states cut a swathe right across the centre of Italy, with Habsburg territory to the south of it. He also tried to annex the duchy of Castro, a small enclave to the northwest of Rome, but this ended in defeat for the papal army, and an empty treasury.

The condemnation of Galileo

There is much to remember Urban by: it was he, for instance, who gave cardinals the right to the title of 'Eminence'; more substantially, it was he who purchased and built the palace at Castel Gandolfo as the papal summer residence. But he is unfortunately perhaps most often remembered as the pope who condemned Galileo Galilei. This last story is not quite as straightforward as it is sometimes presented. There was an issue over the interpretation of Scripture, because the Bible presents the earth as still and the sun moving around it. The contrary theory – that the earth moves round the sun – had been presented in the 16th century by Nicholas Copernicus but, after correction at the insistence of the Congregation of the Index, as a hypothesis only. Galileo had espoused the Copernican system, but in 1616 he was warned against further defending the Copernican view. In 1632, however, he published *Dialogue on Two Great World Systems* which was promptly banned (the ban lasted until 1822), partly because of its advocacy of the heliocentric system, but also in part because it appeared to contain a studied insult to Pope Urban who, as Cardinal Barberini, had been one of Galileo's friends. He was condemned by the Inquisition to indefinite imprisonment, but this was effectively commuted to house arrest. Galileo spent the remainder of his days at Siena, then Florence, then at Arcetri where he continued his researches.

It also fell to Pope Urban to condemn the teachings of Cornelius Jansen, the bishop of Ypres, contained in a book called the *Augustinus*, a study of St Augustine of Hippo. Jansen's views, which gave rise to a movement known as Jansenism, appeared to its Jesuit accusers to deny free will, and to be pessimistic about the possibility of salvation. It also inculcated, they argued, an extreme moral rigorism. This debate dragged on for a century, and their opposition to Jansenism contributed to the growing hostility to Jesuits, especially in 18th-century France.

A cultured pope

It is a pity that Urban is so often associated with these condemnations. He was a vigorous protagonist of missions, establishing a college in Rome, the Collegium Urbanum, still existing,

GALILEO ON INTERPRETING SCRIPTURE

GALILEO GALILEI ON INTERPRETING SCRIPTURE, FROM A LETTER TO THE GRAND DUCHESS CHRISTINA OF TUSCANY, 1615:

'In discussions of physical problems we ought to begin not from the authority of scriptural passages but from sense experiences and necessary demonstrations; for the holy Bible and the phenomena of nature proceed alike from the divine Word, the former as the dictate of the Holy Ghost and the latter as the observant executrix of God's commands.

It is necessary for the Bible, in order to be accommodated to the understanding of every man, to speak many things which appear to differ from the absolute truth so far as the bare meaning of the words is concerned. But Nature, on the other hand, is inexorable and immutable; she never transgresses the laws imposed upon her, or cares a whit whether her abstruse reasons and methods of operation are understandable to men. For that reason it appears that nothing physical which sense experience sets before our eyes, or which necessary demonstrations prove to us, ought to be called in question (much less condemned) upon the testimony of biblical passages which may have some different meaning beneath their words. For the Bible is not chained in every expression to conditions as strict as those which govern all physical effects.'

to train clergy from missionary territory. He gave new life to the Congregation for the Propagation of the Faith, ('*de Propaganda Fide*'), founded shortly before he became pope, and established a multilingual printing press to produce material for mission territory in the East, and in eastern Europe.

He was also a cultured man, and from the time that he settled in Rome had surrounded himself with artists, including Poussin, Velasquez, Claude Lorrain and Van Dyck, and with scholars, and had created one of the best libraries in Rome, later to be incorporated in the Vatican Library. He commissioned Gian Lorenzo Bernini to complete St Peter's, and he and Borromini built the Barberini Palace, as well as that of *Propaganda Fide*. The Barberini symbol is a bee, and the fountain of the bees, as well as the fountain of the Tritons, is to be found, designed by Bernini, in front of the Palazzo Barberini. It is in a tomb designed by Bernini that Urban VIII was finally buried in St Peter's. Yet despite all Urban had done to beautify the city, he died despised by its inhabitants for the heavy taxation he had laid upon them in his last years.

> He ... surrounded himself with artists, including Poussin, Velasquez, Claude Lorrain and Van Dyck.

OPPOSITE *The famous baroque monument of Pope Urban VIII in St Peter's by Gian Lorenzo Bernini. He also commissioned Bernini to complete St Peter's.*

*Denotes popes featured within this section

OPPOSITE *St Peter's Square
and Basilica in Rome.*

1644–2007

TRADITIONALISTS
AND
ECUMENISTS

The papacy, science and
the secular state

BENEDICT XIV

T he popes of the late 17th and 18th centuries faced many similar problems. The papal states were no longer of great significance in European politics. Their army, which consisted of some 50,000 men in the 17th century, by the French Revolution – when the papacy, as will be seen, was dragged back on the stage of European politics – had shrunk to 3,000, a tenth of whom were officers, and whose task was one of policing the states of the pope rather than defending them against aggression. Even so, the great powers still struggled through their cardinals to control the election to the papacy. The conclave of 1740 was the longest of the modern church, taking six months and 255 ballots before finally electing Cardinal Lambertini – who almost until the last had been an unconsidered candidate – as Pope Benedict XIV.

Lambertini came from a noble family, but one which was certainly not wealthy. He came to Rome aged 11, to study at the Collegio Clementino, and eventually at the University of Rome, La Sapienza, where he took a doctorate in theology and canon law. He then remained in Rome until 1727, when he was appointed archbishop of Ancona. From 1720 he was secretary to the Congregation of the Council, but he was better known for his work in the Congregation of Rites, where he became the Promoter of the Faith – the Devil's Advocate in canonization processes, whose task it was to find flaws in the case for a person's canonization. He wrote the most important book on the work of the Congregation, a three-volume study, which is still essential for anyone serious about the procedures surrounding saint-making in the Catholic Church. Published in Bologna, where he was archbishop from 1731, it broke new ground by being based on solid historical research. He also wrote a book on diocesan synods, and the need for them, which did not find favour with the censors, and therefore appeared only after he had become pope. As archbishop in Bologna he was well-loved, and very hands-on, but always ready to receive visitors, among them English Protestants on their Grand Tour of Europe, such as the poet Thomas Gray and the writer and collector Horace Walpole. Others of his flock he would meet as he strolled the streets each morning after breakfast. After he had become pope, Walpole wrote in praise of him, but Benedict was not impressed. Popes, he remarked, are like the statues on the top of St Peter's, better seen at a distance.

BIRTH NAME **Prospero Lambertini**
BORN **Bologna, 31 March 1675**
PREDECESSOR **Clement XII**
INSTALLED **21 August 1740**
DIED **3 May 1758**
SUCCESSOR **Clement XIII**

A RELUCTANT POPE

Lambertini loved Bologna, and for more than a decade after his election remained its archbishop. He was a reluctant pope. He only accepted, he said, because he did not want to oppose God's will, appear ungracious to those who voted for him, or to drag the conclave on for any longer – two cardinals having already died in the course of it. In fact four died during the vacancy, but two of those had not entered the conclave.

As Pope Benedict XIV, he was a realist in international affairs. He entered upon concordats with a number of countries. Some thought he had gone too far in conceding control over the appointment of bishops to the sovereigns of Spain and Portugal, for example, but he was possibly right in believing that had he not done so there was a risk that they might, as Henry VIII of England had done, establish a national church, independent of Rome. That was particularly true in Prussia. In 1742 Frederick II had conquered Catholic Silesia, annexing it to his Protestant Prussia. Benedict cultivated good relations

A pope during the Age of Enlightenment, Benedict XIV restarted the practice of sending encyclical letters to all the bishops in the world.

with him, even conceding the use of the title of king which his predecessor had refused to do. An agreement was reached on the tricky issues of marriage and of benefices. The Prussian king became the first non-Catholic to send a permanent representative to the papal court, and Benedict's approach was hailed as a model of enlightened tolerance. His sureness of touch briefly deserted him over the question of the Austrian succession: he neglected to recognize the hereditary right of Maria Theresa, and then delayed his recognition of her husband, Francis I, as the emperor. As a consequence the papal states were invaded, and the papacy lost Parma and Piacenza. In the aftermath Benedict cut the papacy's military expenditure in an effort to reduce its debt. He took practical steps to improve manufacturing, agriculture and commerce in the papal states, modernizing the administration and attempting to create a free market – except in Rome itself.

A MAN OF THE ENLIGHTENMENT

Although a man of the Enlightenment – even Voltaire dedicated a book to him, perhaps rather tongue-in-cheek – Benedict was in many ways a traditionalist. He put Voltaire on the Index, along with Montesquieu's *Spirit of the Laws* and other works (see box, page 162), but he declared that authors so treated should have the right to defend themselves, something that did not in practice happen until Pope Paul VI repeated the directive when reforming the Holy Office in

1965. He instructed Polish bishops to act against anti-Semitism in their own country, but did not do the same for the papal states. His was the pontificate in which research was started into the Christian antiquities of Rome, such as the catacombs. This he encouraged, opening a new museum for such antiquities attached at first to the Vatican Library. Benedict built up an impressive library of his own, which he bequeathed not to the Vatican but to his beloved Bologna, where he expanded the university with new chairs of science and medicine, and an Institute of Sciences.

> The Prussian king became the first non-Catholic to send a permanent representative to the papal court, and Benedict's approach was hailed as a model of enlightened tolerance.

JESUITS AND JANSENISTS

There were two matters that had occupied popes for a half century and more upon which Benedict acted decisively. Both involved the Jesuits. The first concerned the doctrine of Jansenism (see page 169), which the Jesuits bitterly opposed. This was a difficult matter for the papacy, because it was associated with Gallicanism (see box), at least in people's minds if not in theory. The question at issue was the bull *Unigenitus* of 1713, which condemned 101 Jansenist propositions. There was uncertainty as to whether these propositions really represented Jansenism or not, but the French crown had demanded acceptance of them. Jansenists, backed by the Parlement of Paris, found ways round this, but some were refused the sacraments even when

GALLICANISM

IN 1682 A GATHERING OF THE FRENCH CLERGY, called together by King Louis XIV, approved the Four Articles of the Gallican Church, claiming that at least from the time of the clash between Philip the Fair and Pope Boniface VIII, the church in France had been largely independent of the Roman Church. The Articles stated:

1 The Pope has no power in secular matters, and kings cannot be subject to them on such issues. The Pope has no authority to release citizens from their oaths of allegiance to a king.

2 A general council is superior to the Pope.

3 In France, papal authoriy is limited by the customs and traditions of the French Church.

4 Even in matters of faith, a papal decision is not binding unless it has the consent of the whole Church.

Similar movements to Gallicanism, though obviously under different names, were to be found in the 18th century in Germany, Austria and Italy.

ENCYCLICALS

THE TERM 'ENCYCLICAL' MEANS 'CIRCULAR LETTER' and is used generally of letters sent by the pope to all bishops who are in communion with Rome. On rare occasions, however, an encyclical can be addressed to a smaller group of bishops, such as those of one country, as was the case for example with Pope Pius XI's encyclical against Nazism of 21 March 1937. Most encyclicals are published in Latin, though some, such as *Mit brennender Sorge*, have been in the language of the nation to which they are addressed. Like papal bulls, they are named by their opening words. Encyclicals are less formal documents than bulls and although bishops in the early church communicated with each other by letter, the form of encyclical as it currently exists dates only from the time of Pope Benedict XIV (1740–58).

dying. Benedict upheld the constitution of one of his predecessors, but insisted that no one should be refused the sacraments unless they were determined openly to flout papal teaching. Jansenism did not then go away, but it became much less of a problem in France.

The other question in which the Jesuits were entangled was that of the 'Chinese rites'. Jesuit missionaries in China, and also in India, had developed the Roman liturgy in such a way as to accommodate it to the customs of the region. Other missionaries, Dominican and especially Franciscan, were scandalized and complained to Rome. These rites had largely been banned in the mid-17th century, but the missionaries had managed to circumvent the prohibition, and complaints continued to come to Rome. Benedict laid down that all missionaries had to take an oath to observe the ban – but his directive was phrased in such a way as to leave open the possibility of liturgical developments on the missions in India, if not in China.

ENCYCLICAL LETTERS

Benedict's concern was above all with the internal workings of the church. He restarted the practice, long in abeyance, of encyclical letters, sent out from Rome to all the bishops in the world (see box), and he instituted a Congregation in Rome to advise on episcopal appointments. But one of his last acts was to bow to the wishes of the Marquis de Pombal, the chief minister of Portugal, and permit the archbishop of Lisbon to investigate, and if necessary to reform, the Society of Jesus, the Jesuits, a decision which led in 1773 to the suppression of the Society.

PIUS VII

ope Pius VII's predecessor, Pius VI (1775–99), had been elected bishop of Rome because it was thought by the pro-Jesuit faction among the cardinals that he might mitigate the Brief of Suppression, issued by Clement XIV (1769–74), while he had assured the anti-Jesuit faction that he would do no such thing. He was a handsome, and highly cultured man, and much had been hoped from his pontificate, but it was overtaken by events in Paris, as the French Revolution grew increasingly radical. The French government had no great interest in the church, or in the fate of the clergy, but that lack of concern was not shared by Napoleon Bonaparte as his armies marched south through Italy. He believed religion to be a vital moral force within society, something to be harnessed rather than suppressed.

At the Peace of Tolentino of February 1797 the pope was forced to cede to France large swathes of the papal states: the ancient papal enclave of Avignon and of the surrounding Venaissin district were definitively made over to France. But still the French kept coming, arriving outside the walls of Rome on 9 February 1798. General Berthier expected his presence to give rise to riots against papal governance, but no such uprising occurred. Instead, when there was a rebellion, it was against the invaders, in the course of which General Duphot was killed. Berthier then proceeded to occupy the city, declare Pius VI deposed and Rome a republic. Pius was then bundled out of the city, ending his days across the Alps in Valence, where he was buried in the common cemetery. As he lay dying, the pope urged that the conclave to elect his successor should be held in the dominion of a Catholic ruler, and, in the event of there being an 'anti-conclave' organized by France), that it should be the one attended by the most cardinals. It was decided that it would meet in Venice. This was technically within the dominions of the Austrian emperor, but still on Italian soil.

There were 35 cardinals in the monastery of San Giorgio Maggiore, in the Venetian lagoon, on 1 December 1799, one of them being the bishop of Frascati, the cardinal duke of York, and the last representative of the Stuart line. There were those who were eager for some kind of reconciliation with France, and there were those who most definitely were not, the latter group having the backing of the emperor and the claimant to the French throne, the future Louis XIII. It was the secretary of the council, Ercole Consalvi, who suggested Cardinal Barnaba Chiaramonti, known as

BIRTH NAME **Barnaba Chiaramonti**
BORN **Cesena, 14 August 1742**
PREDECESSOR **Pius VI**
INSTALLED **21 March 1800**
DIED **20 August 1823**
SUCCESSOR **Leo XII**

pious, intelligent and open to new ideas –
which last, many of the cardinals certainly
were not. Chiaramonti did not want to
accept the office, but agreed because what
he called 'the widowhood of the Church'
had already gone on too long. He took the
name Pius in honour of his predecessor,
to whom he was distantly related.

A PHILOSOPHER
AND THEOLOGIAN

Both had been born in Cesena. Barnaba
had attended the Benedictine monastery
in the town for his education, and in
August 1758 he became a professed monk
there, taking the name Gregorio. He
studied at Padua, then at San Anselmo
in Rome, soon after which he was sent
to teach in Parma. His subjects were
philosophy and theology. For the latter
he used the new critical editions of the
Fathers of the Church, for the former he
drew upon John Locke and other modern
writers, who proved to be rather too up-
to-date when he was brought back to
Rome to teach at San Anselmo. Thanks to

Pius VII, painted by Jacques Louis David in 1805. Intelligent and open to new ideas, his papacy was clouded by the Napoleonic Wars.

Pope Pius VI he became bishop of Tivoli in December 1782, and in February 1785 bishop of
Imola, and a cardinal. He remained at Imola for 15 years, a model bishop, concerned for the
spiritual welfare of his flock, but also for its temporal well-being. When the French army
arrived he tried to prevent conflict between the two sides, and in a remarkable sermon for
Christmas Day 1797 he insisted that Catholicism was compatible with democracy (see box,
page 180) – he, in fact, had not been entirely comfortable in Imola, part of the papal states,
as a spiritual leader in a clerically-run state.

Chiaramonti was crowned in Venice, in the monastery of San Giorgio, because the Austrian
emperor, irritated that none of his favoured candidates had been elected, refused permission for
the ceremony to take place in the patriarchal basilica of San Marco. The emperor wanted the new
pope to visit him in Vienna, but Pius refused and made his way to Rome. He arrived in what was
still an occupied city, though Neapolitan troops had by this time replaced the French, on 3 July
1800. Consalvi, now the papal secretary of state, or chief minister, began to put the papal state
back together again, persuading Naples and Austria to withdraw. There followed in the pope's
dominions a whole series of reforms of the monetary system, of trade and industry, of taxation,
and even permitting the employment of lay people – the nobility, naturally – in some of the
posts of responsibility. This last somewhat backfired, because the nobility were angered at being
allowed to progress so far and no further in the papal administration. A special military unit, the
Noble Guard, was established as a sop for them in 1801.

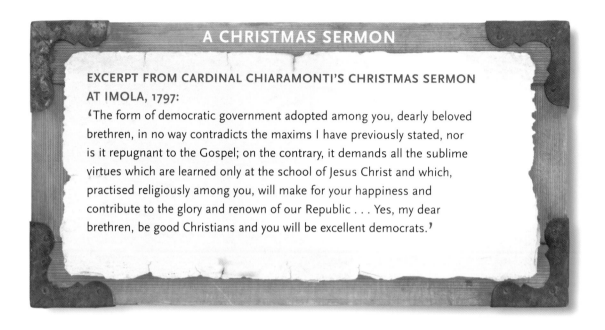

A CONCORDAT WITH NAPOLEON

Consalvi then negotiated a series of concordats, including one with Napoleon. The concordat with France, signed in July 1801, made a large number of concessions to the French state, but they were ones which Pius could live with, especially as, in effect, they abolished Gallicanism by acknowledging papal authority. But when it was promulgated as law in France, in April 1802, Napoleon unilaterally attached to it what were known as the 'Organic Articles' which brought Gallicanism back. The pope protested, but in vain. When he was asked to crown Napoleon as emperor in a ceremony in Notre Dame, Paris, on 2 December 1804, he agreed to go despite advice of sundry cardinals to the contrary because he believed – wrongly – that he might be able to change Napoleon's mind.

A FURTHER OCCUPATION OF ROME

Napoleon's armies continued their victorious advance, conquering the Austrian, Russian and Prussian armies. His ambition was to control the whole of Europe and as the papal states stood in the way of this, he progressively annexed them. He also took Naples, putting first his brother Joseph, then his brother-in-law Murat on the throne. The other state which stood in his way was England, and the French emperor instituted a continental blockade of English shipping, which Pius simply refused to join. Rome was again occupied, the papal forces incorporated in the French army, and Pius VII and his secretary of state, now Cardinal Pacca because Consalvi had been forced by the French to resign, imprisoned in the Quirinal Palace. The pope then resorted to the only weapon open to him: he excommunicated Napoleon, who promptly ordered the pope to be imprisoned. He was seized in the Quirinal on 6 July 1809,

> The sufferings of the pope, and the dignified way in which he had borne them, won for the papacy a new respect.

arriving at Savona on 17 August. All the cardinals were then summoned to Paris, and the Vatican archives shipped there – not all of them returned. In June 1812 Pius was taken off to Fontainebleau, to be near to Paris and there, after a personal visit by Napoleon, Pius agreed to a new concordat which conceded to the emperor everything he wanted. But then Cardinals Consalvi and Pacca were allowed to join Pius, and, bolstered by their presence, the pope proceeded to reject the concordat which he had just signed.

By then, however, Napoleon had launched himself upon his Russian campaign. He returned much weakened. He sent the pope back to Savona, and then finally released him in March 1814. Pius was back in Rome on 24 May to a tumultuous reception. But by then Napoleon had been defeated, Louis XVIII was on the throne of France, and the deposed emperor's mother and other relatives were in exile. They went to Rome, where the pope generously received them. When Napoleon escaped from imprisonment on Elba the pope had briefly to flee Rome again, taking refuge in Genoa, but at the Congress of Vienna, thanks to the diplomatic skills of Consalvi, the papal states, with the exception of Avignon, were restored to him.

A MODERNIZING POPE

Pius VII made a great effort to return the church to the situation before the Napoleonic Wars, but in a rather more modern guise. One of his first acts was to bring back the Jesuits, some of whom had managed to survive the long years of suppression, despite opposition to the move. He entered a new concordat with France, and with Bavaria and the kingdom of the Two Sicilies, and even agreed concordats with Protestant Prussia and Orthodox Russia. In the papal states he hoped to modernize the administration and judicial system, and made some improvements, but there were too many around him who simply wanted a restitution of the old ways for him to make fundamental changes. But those who lived in the papal states had experienced a different form of government imposed by the French. They were not readily going to settle back under clerical rule.

That apart, the sufferings of the pope, and the dignified way in which he had borne them, won for the papacy a new respect around Europe, in Protestant as well as in Catholic lands.

PIUS IX

T he major problem facing the popes who succeeded Pius VII was that of the papal states. It sharpened as Italy grew increasingly conscious of itself as a nation, and who better to unite the nation — still at this point a group of diverse states, including the papal ones — than the pope. In Cardinal Mastai-Ferretti, bishop of Imola, the progressive cardinals in the conclave of 1846 believed they had found just the man. He was elected on the fourth ballot.

The Mastai-Ferrettis belonged to the provincial nobility – Giovanni's father was a count. They were fairly well-off, traditional, and quite devout. Giovanni studied in Volterra, where he suffered from epilepsy. The disease remained with him a number of years, and as a consequence he was refused admission to the Noble Guard. It was also a bar to entering the priesthood, but he was granted a dispensation, and began his ordination training at the Jesuits' Roman College. His theological studies were somewhat perfunctory, and he decided against becoming a Jesuit himself, or pursuing an academic career. He thought of himself as a pastor, and devoted himself to the care of a Roman orphanage. He then found himself on a diplomatic visit to Chile, seemingly under the impression that it was a missionary journey. When he returned to Rome he went back to charitable work, running a hospice. In 1831 he was made bishop of Spoleto,

and in 1832 bishop of Imola, regarded as a difficult diocese because of its strong anticlericalism. In 1840 he became a cardinal. During all this time he came to be considered something of a liberal, partly because he tried to moderate the more extreme politics of Pope Gregory XVI (1831–46), and partly because he was a known sympathizer with nationalist aspirations in Italy.

THE 'YEAR OF REVOLUTIONS'

His election was followed by a number of initiatives concerning the status of religious orders, and a programme of reforms in the papal states. A month after he was elected he proclaimed an amnesty for political prisoners, which was greeted with great enthusiasm. On 14 March 1848, the 'Year of Revolutions', he granted a new

A deeply conservative pope, Pius IX saw the papal states annexed to the new secular kingdom of Italy. This photograph dates from c. 1869.

constitution to the papal states. There were anti-Austrian uprisings in Milan and Venice, and the king of Sardinia declared war on Austria with the intention of driving it out of Italy. The papal army advanced to the frontiers of the state but, uncertain that he could control his generals, and faced with protests from Austria, Pius had to make his position clear. What was not clear was where his own sympathies lay – they were quite possibly with the nationalists, but the speech as he delivered it, probably corrected by his secretary of state, Cardinal Antonelli, declared that as pastor of the universal

BIRTH NAME Giovanni Maria Mastai-Ferretti
BORN Senigallia, near Ancona, 12 May 1792
PREDECESSOR Gregory XVI
INSTALLED 21 June 1846
DIED 7 February 1878
SUCCESSOR Leo XIII

church he could not make war on other Catholics. The Italians were not prepared for a neutral pope. His very capable prime minister, Pellegrino Rossi, was assassinated in the parliament building in November 1848, and Pius himself fled to Gaeta in the kingdom of Naples. From there the pope appealed to the Catholic powers. The French sent an army which suppressed the nascent Roman Republic, and Pius re-entered Rome in April 1850. For the next 20 years the pope, having withdrawn all the concessions he had made to a more liberal regime, ruled the papal states with French protection.

THE KINGDOM OF ITALY

From 1859 the papal states began to disappear into what was proclaimed on 18 March 1861 as the kingdom of Italy. Rome, still protected by the French, was to be the new capital. The pope was to give up temporal power, but was otherwise to enjoy full liberty. Neither the pope nor his advisors trusted the new government. They believed that only temporal power guaranteed the papacy freedom of action, and they were aware, too, that the government of Italy was a secularizing one. The pope's response was the *Syllabus of Errors*, published in 1864. It condemned in 80 propositions a series of errors of the day, as they appeared to the pope. The condemnations were largely drawn from other documents, and perhaps should be read in context, but the impact of their publication was

During all this time he came to be considered something of a liberal.

to reinforce the notion of a conservative and intransigent pope. His decision to forbid Catholics to take part in Italian politics in the *Ne expedit* ('It is not fitting') decree of 1868 was further evidence for this view.

What lay behind the pope's attitude was a conviction that the ideal society was a Roman Catholic state, a Christian commonwealth, governed by Christian law, with the Catholic Church as the state religion. It was in an effort to promote this ideal that he called the First Vatican Council, which began on 8 December 1869. It was adjourned at the end of October 1870, never to meet again, because the French troops, required elsewhere during the Franco-Prussian War, had been withdrawn and, on 20 September, the Italian army had entered Rome.

Originally the pope had declared that the papal forces were to surrender at the first cannon shot, but on the eve of the attack, and at the urgings of the papal commander, he had altered his instructions, with the result that some 50 soldiers died. Resistance was of course futile. The last remnant of the papal states had been annexed to the kingdom of Italy.

The Italian government then carried out what it had promised. In The Law of Guarantees, passed in May 1871, the pope was promised full liberty of action and the tenure of the Vatican and other buildings in Rome, but Pius refused to accept that the papal states had gone for ever. He remained for the rest of his life, as did his successors for the next half century, 'the prisoner of the Vatican'. His self-imposed confinement won him tremendous sympathy throughout the Catholic world, and vast pilgrimages were organized to demonstrate solidarity with the pontiff. Moreover, the decrees of the Vatican Council had bolstered his standing, declaring his primacy over the whole church, and proclaiming him to be infallible when teaching a doctrine of faith or morals to be held by the whole church. In fact the decree on infallibility was carefully worded, but the nuances were generally overlooked so that the papacy came to be regarded as something of an oracle, and revered as such.

> He remained for the rest of his life, as did his successors for the next half century, 'the prisoner of the Vatican'.

The pope had displayed some of his new – though at the time yet to be proclaimed – authority when, in 1854, he declared that Mary, the mother of Christ, had alone of all human beings been conceived without the stain of original sin on her soul, the much misunderstood dogma of the Immaculate Conception.

The longest-ever pontificate

Pius IX's was a centralizing papacy, abetted by the improvements in transport which made it much easier for bishops to come to Rome. And they, losing their authority in their home countries because of the increasingly secular nature of other states, needed the papacy. Pius created a large number of dioceses in mission lands, and restored the hierarchy of Holland and of England, as well as the Latin patriarchate in Jerusalem.

The devotion which Catholics around the world were to offer him was not shared by the people of Rome. He was buried, after the longest pontificate in the history of papacy, in St Peter's, but in July 1881, when his body was moved to the basilica of San Lorenzo fuori Le Mura, a mob tried to seize his coffin and throw it into the Tiber.

LEO XIII

The papacy of Pope Pius IX had been, and remains, the longest pontificate in history. Rather oddly it was followed by the next longest, at least until the years of the papacy of Leo XIII were exceeded — just — by those of John Paul II (1978–2005). Perhaps it had not been meant to be like that. Leo XIII was hardly known in Rome before his election, certainly not to the cardinal electors. But he was the recently appointed *camerlengo*, or chamberlain, of the college of cardinals, and it had fallen to him to organize the conclave. He did this, apparently, with impressive efficiency, and was chosen on only the third ballot. But his administrative skills may not have been the chief reason. There is a tendency after long pontificates to look for short ones. Giacchino Vincenzo Pecci was nearly 68 at his election, not a great age, but he was thought to be in ill-health. In fact he lived to the age of 93.

He was born in a town near Anagni, south of Rome, into a well-known family. He studied in Viterbo, at the Jesuits' Roman College (he had an older brother, Giuseppe, who joined the Jesuits in 1824 but left in 1848, only to rejoin again in 1887, three years before his death, by which time Pope Leo had made him a cardinal), and then in the Academy for Noble Ecclesiastics. He joined the papal service, and was quickly given charge first of Benevento, then of Perugia. It was a far from easy time in the papal states, but Pecci succeeded well enough, and came to understand the aspirations for a more liberal regime. His diplomatic flair then secured him a posting to Brussels as papal nuncio, or ambassador, where once again he was highly successful, at least at first, but problems over education led the king of the Belgians, with whom he had hitherto enjoyed a good relationship, to ask for his recall.

From then on, until his election, he was bishop of Perugia, being made a cardinal in 1853. He had been close to Gregory XV (1831–46), but was not popular with Pius IX's powerful secretary of state, Cardinal Antonelli. It was only after Antonelli's death that he was made *camerlengo*. In Perugia he modernized the seminary and in particular encouraged the study of Thomas Aquinas, the 13th-century Dominican theologian whom as pope he was to commend to the whole church.

A CLASH WITH BISMARCK

During his time in Brussels Pecci had made short visits to Cologne, Paris and London, and had come to know at first hand some of the issues facing modern industrialized

BIRTH NAME
Giacchino Vincenzo Pecci
BORN Carpineto, 2 March 1810
PREDECESSOR Pius IX
INSTALLED 3 March 1878
DIED 20 July 1903
SUCCESSOR Pius X

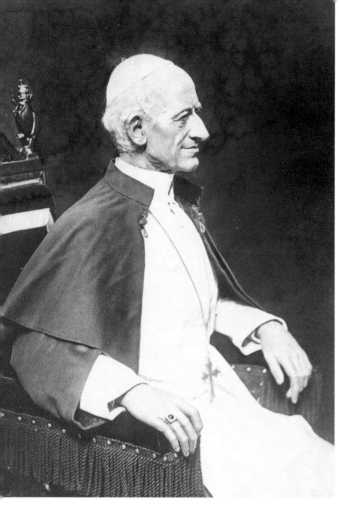
Leo XIII battled with the issues of democracy, secularism and communication with the Protestant churches.

societies. He had a realistic view of what might be achieved by diplomacy, and was prepared to do deals with states and meet them halfway. The clash with Bismarck's Germany, occasioned partly by the unification of Germany (1871) and the alliance of formerly Catholic states in what seemed a heavily Protestant federation, and partly by the apparently new status of the papacy defined by the Vatican Council (the *Kulturkampf*), he managed to bring to an end. He dispatched diplomatic representatives to such nations as would receive them. He hoped to include Britain within this circle, and did not support Irish rebels against the Westminster government. Even though the British government did not reciprocate as he wished, he continued to show an interest in Britain: he made cardinals of both the theologian John Henry Newman and the archbishop of Westminster, Henry Edward Manning, and he instituted a study of the validity (in Catholic eyes) of the ordination of Anglican clergy. This was, however, to end with the rejection of Anglican orders, possibly through the machinations of the then archbishop of Westminster, Cardinal Vaughan, who was opposed to any accommodation with Anglicanism.

A DIFFICULT RELATIONSHIP WITH THE UNITED STATES

Leo's relationship with the United States was fraught. It started well, but deteriorated because of what the pope saw, or was led to believe he saw, as an accommodation between the American Catholic Church and American society that was incompatible with Catholicism. In particular he criticized the notion of the separation of church and state, and the growing relations of the Catholic Church in the United States with the Protestant churches. These concerns found expression in 1899 in an encyclical which condemned the heresy he called 'Americanism', though he did not name any of the possible heretics. A later encyclical expressed his reservations about democracy.

Clearly the major issue for the pope was the situation in Italy, and his relations, or non-relations, with the Italian government. He tried to win states over to the papal point of view, but without much success. Although the *Kulturkampf* had ended on the whole to the church's advantage, Bismarck remained hostile to the papacy. Germany strengthened Italy by renewing the Triple Alliance of Germany, Austria and Italy. Being isolated in Europe, Leo was advised by his secretary of state, Cardinal Rampolla, to attempt better relations with the distinctly secular government of France. At Leo's request, Cardinal Lavigerie proposed a toast to the French Third Republic at a formal dinner. French royalists were outraged, while the gesture did not win the

French regime's sympathy for the papacy. This may sound like a list of foreign policy failures, but at least the papacy had been put back into the international arena.

DEVOTION TO MARY

Leo was a devout man, and wrote nine encyclical letters on devotion to Mary. He was deeply concerned by issues within the church. As has been seen, he encouraged the study of St Thomas, and commissioned a definitive edition of his writings, still being published, which is named after him – 'the Leonine edition'. He opened up the Vatican archives to researchers, and when cardinals complained that scholars might reveal uncomfortable facts he responded that the church has nothing to fear from the truth. He set up a biblical commission to foster the study of scripture, though it rapidly came to play a very conservative role, especially in the pontificate of his successor, Pius X (1903–14). He was active in encouraging missionary activity. He was interested in the churches of the East, and published an encyclical about them. He also published an encyclical inviting the Orthodox and Protestant churches to reunite with Rome.

'OF NEW THINGS'

But his best remembered encyclical is on an altogether different topic. In 1891 he published *Rerum Novarum*, which literally means 'Of new things', the Latin way of saying 'revolution'. Pope Leo had lived through many forms of revolution, but here he was writing particularly of the impact of industry on the workers. The encyclical has been called, somewhat romantically 'the working man's charter' (see box). It was in reality nothing of the kind. It is a complex document with many strands, not least a nostalgia for the Middle Ages, or at least the time before the

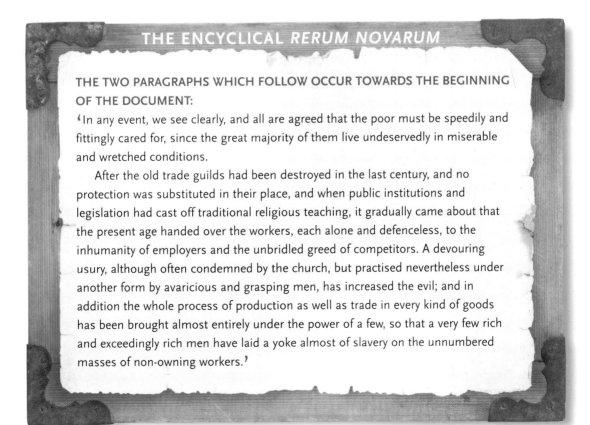

THE ENCYCLICAL *RERUM NOVARUM*

THE TWO PARAGRAPHS WHICH FOLLOW OCCUR TOWARDS THE BEGINNING OF THE DOCUMENT:

'In any event, we see clearly, and all are agreed that the poor must be speedily and fittingly cared for, since the great majority of them live undeservedly in miserable and wretched conditions.

After the old trade guilds had been destroyed in the last century, and no protection was substituted in their place, and when public institutions and legislation had cast off traditional religious teaching, it gradually came about that the present age handed over the workers, each alone and defenceless, to the inhumanity of employers and the unbridled greed of competitors. A devouring usury, although often condemned by the church, but practised nevertheless under another form by avaricious and grasping men, has increased the evil; and in addition the whole process of production as well as trade in every kind of goods has been brought almost entirely under the power of a few, so that a very few rich and exceedingly rich men have laid a yoke almost of slavery on the unnumbered masses of non-owning workers.'

unification of Italy, when Italy was a rural society rather than the industrial one it was becoming in the north of the country. But the encyclical insists upon the obligation of the state to intervene to protect the rights of workers (a fairly revolutionary notion, coming from a sovereign), and upon the right of workers to associate in what Leo called 'guilds', but others called trades unions. The encyclical condemns socialism outright, but nevertheless one English translation of the text appeared with the papal coat of arms on the cover and a hammer and sickle replacing the crossed keys of St Peter.

PIUS XII

Popes are, by definition, bishops of Rome, yet when Cardinal Pacelli was elected on only the third ballot (though not quite unanimously) he was the first pope for more than two centuries to have been a priest of the diocese of Rome, and the first pope for almost two centuries who had served his predecessor as cardinal secretary of state.

His family had long served the papacy. Eugenio's brother Francesco played an important part in the negotiations with the kingdom of Italy which led to the signing of the Lateran Pacts and the establishment of the Vatican City as the residence of the pontiff in the world's smallest sovereign state. Eugenio had studied at a state secondary school, but then attended the Gregorian University and a number of other Roman institutions, including the University of Rome. He was particularly interested in canon law, not surprisingly given his family's tradition as lawyers. When Pope Pius X (1903–14) decided that a code of canon law should replace the amorphous collection which constituted the 'corpus' of canon law, he was put on the commission which undertook the task under the direction of Enrico Gasparri who later, as cardinal secretary of state, was responsible on the papal side for the Lateran accords. Pacelli then, under the patronage of Gasparri, entered the Vatican department of Extraordinary Ecclesiastical Affairs, the pope's foreign ministry. Though he had been teaching canon law at the Academy for Noble Ecclesiastics (and had been offered a similar post at the Catholic University of America in Washington DC), he now became a diplomat rather than an academic.

BIRTH NAME Eugenio Maria Giuseppe Giovanni Pacelli
BORN Rome, 2 March 1876
PREDECESSOR Pius XI
INSTALLED 12 March 1939
DIED 9 October 1958
SUCCESSOR John XXIII

NEUTRALITY IN WAR

During the First World War he was close to Pope Benedict XV (1914–22), helping to work out the Vatican's neutral stance, and promoting its efforts at peacemaking. It was in that context that he was appointed nuncio in Bavaria – the only such post in German territory – and was made an archbishop. Though his efforts at peacemaking in Germany came to nothing, after the war the papacy was able to establish diplomatic relations with

Germany itself, and Archbishop Pacelli was accredited to Berlin. From that vantage point he followed the Holy See's vain efforts to come to some sort of an understanding with the USSR. In 1929 he was made a cardinal, and came back to Rome as secretary of state in succession to Gasparri. He used his time as secretary of state to travel widely, including a visit to the United States in 1936.

He was a diplomat through and through. He hoped to resolve issues by diplomatic means, by exchanges of notes or where necessary through concordats, or treaties. He signed one with Austria in June 1933 and the following month with Nazi Germany. He had no great hopes of the latter, and the initiative had come from Germany itself so it was difficult to refuse, but he had constantly to complain about Nazi infringement of its provisions. The Vatican was concerned about Nazism, and the archbishop of Vienna was summoned to Rome to explain why the Austrian bishops had welcomed the German annexation of Austria

Pius XII was a consummate diplomat who tried to keep the Vatican out of politics, but his stance towards the Nazis during the Second World War has been the subject of much controversy.

(the Anschluss). In March 1937 the encyclical *Mit brennender Sorge* ('With burning anxiety') was smuggled into Germany and read out at mass. Originally drafted by the archbishop of Munich, its language, critical of Nazism, had been considerably sharpened by Pacelli himself.

SILENCE ON THE HOLOCAUST

Given this stance it is strange that an encyclical which Pope Pius XI (1922–39) had instructed to be drawn up on 'The Unity of the Human Race', which was an attack on Nazi persecution of the Jews, remained unpublished when Pacelli succeeded Pius XI after the latter's death just before the outbreak of the Second World War. Pius XII's stance during the war, his 'silence' on the atrocities committed against the Jews by the Nazi regime, has been the subject of vast debate. The Vatican certainly knew what was happening, and Pius XII protested publicly at least twice, but only in somewhat general terms which the pope's critics complain were not explicit enough – though the Hitler regime recognized them for what they were. In order to resolve the debate the Vatican published a 12-volume collection of documents from its archives covering the war, but critics believe it to be selective, in that it only provides material favourable to the Vatican. A commission of Catholic and Jewish scholars was appointed, with access to the archives, but this broke up in disarray for undisclosed reasons. According to the criteria laid down by

> Pius XII's 'silence' on the atrocities committed … by the Nazi regime, has been the subject of vast debate.

Pope John Paul II (1978–2005), the Vatican's papers covering the pontificate of Pius XII should become available on the death of Pope Benedict XVI, but that may not solve the controversy. It is an argument less about fact than about judgement.

When the war was perceived as inevitable, the Vatican's policy was to attempt to keep Italy out of it. The Vatican tried to remain neutral between the warring parties in order, if at all possible, to mediate. It proved impossible to do so, however, because the relations between the Vatican and the nations at war were not good, except with the USA (the US president sent a personal representative, Myron Taylor, to the Vatican in 1939) and to some extent with Britain whose diplomatic representative, D'Arcy Osborne, found himself from the time Italy entered the war a guest of the Holy See, and a perceptive chronicler of its doings. To protest, Pius seems to have believed, would not only have compromised the Vatican's neutrality but given rise to even worse atrocities. Some commentators claim that the pope gave help in secret to Jews seeking refuge, and certainly many Jews were hidden in Catholic institutions in Italy, but evidence that this was in any sense directed by the pope is hard to come by.

EXCERPTS FROM *HUMANI GENERIS*

5 If anyone examines the state of affairs outside the Christian fold, he will easily discover the principle trends that not a few learned men are following. Some imprudently and indiscreetly hold that evolution, which has not been fully proved even in the domain of natural sciences, explains the origin of all things, and audaciously support the monistic and pantheistic opinion that the world is in continual evolution. Communists gladly subscribe to this opinion so that, when the souls of men have been deprived of every idea of a personal God, they may the more efficaciously defend and propagate their dialectical materialism.

6 Such fictitious tenets of evolution which repudiate all that is absolute, firm and immutable, have paved the way for the new erroneous philosophy which, rivalling idealism, immanentism and pragmatism, has assumed the name of existentialism, since it concerns itself only with existence of individual things and neglects all consideration of their immutable essences.

37 When, however, there is question of another conjectural opinion, namely polygenism, the children of the Church by no means enjoy such liberty. For the faithful cannot embrace that opinion which maintains that either after Adam there existed on this earth true men who did not take their origin through natural generation from him as from the first parent of all, or that Adam represents a certain number of first parents. Now it is in no way apparent how such an opinion can be reconciled with that which the sources of revealed truth and the documents of the Teaching Authority of the Church propose with regard to original sin, which proceeds from a sin actually committed by an individual Adam and which, through generation, is passed on to all and is in everyone as his own.

AN OPPONENT OF COMMUNISM

Some writers have suggested that Pius XII, possibly because of his experience in Germany in the 1920s, was more concerned about the dangers of communism to the church than about Nazism. After the war he showed himself to be an implacable opponent of communism. The Holy See battled vigorously in favour of the Christian Democrat Party in Italy to keep communism out, and in 1949 communists were excommunicated. Western Europe remained free of communist governments, and the pope welcomed the growing signs of European integration as a bulwark against the spread of communism. The Treaty of Rome (1957) was hailed as 'the most important and significant political event in the history of the Eternal City'.

Pius XII's was a very political papacy, perhaps inevitably given world events, but the pope was deeply concerned about the moral issues of the age, speaking out about them time and again. He also wrote a number of encyclicals of considerable theological importance, not least *Divino afflante Spiritu* of September 1943, encouraging the study of Scripture, still in the doldrums in Catholic circles after the heavy-handed suppression of the use of modern scholarship by the Biblical Commission in the first decade of the century. Without that encyclical it is unlikely that the flourishing of Catholic theological scholarship, which reached a high point at the Second Vatican Council soon after Pius's death, could ever have happened. In his last years, however, he seems to have been alarmed by modern developments in theology, and in *Humani generis* of August 1950 warned theologians, and especially those in France (though the encyclical named no one) that they were going too far (see box, page 190).

JOHN XXIII

here could hardly be a greater contrast between Pius XII and his successor, the first thin and austere, gazing over the photographer's shoulder as if seeing visions, the second small, roly-poly, looking straight into the lens and smiling. Perhaps he was chosen to be as different as possible from his predecessor, though more likely he was elected as a transitional pope. Pius XII had created few cardinals, and there were only 51 present at the conclave, a small number for papal elections of the 20th century, and not a broad electoral base. It took 11 ballots to elect John.

Roncalli came from a peasant family, the third of 12 children. He first went to the village school, then to the seminary at Bergamo where he won a scholarship to study at the Apollinare Institute in Rome in 1901. While in Rome he had to break off his studies to undertake military service in the infantry – he rose to the rank of sergeant. He graduated as a doctor of theology in 1904, the year he was ordained priest. His first post was as secretary to the radical bishop of Bergamo, Giacomo Radini-Tedeschi, to whom he was much devoted, and lectured in church history at the diocesan seminary. Radini-Tedeschi died in August 1914, in the early days of the First World War, and Roncalli was conscripted, first as a medical orderly and then as a military chaplain. At the end of the war he returned to the seminary, but in 1921 he was summoned to Rome, to take charge of collecting funds for the missions. During this time he started work on the life of St

Charles Borromeo, the great 16th-century archbishop of Milan (see page 160). His researches took him to the Ambrosian Library where he encountered the librarian, Achille Ratti, who shortly afterwards became Pius XI (1922–39). It was Pius XI who sent him as a diplomat first to Bulgaria, then to Greece and Turkey. These were lonely years. There were few Catholics for him to minister to, and the church was not open to contacts with other faiths, or even to other Christian denominations, such as Orthodoxy. But he came to know these far better than any of his predecessors had been able to, and to appreciate how Eurocentric Roman Catholicism was, despite its wide missionary activity. And in Greece he was able to save many from Nazism.

NUNCIO IN PARIS

After the liberation of France in 1944 Roncalli was posted as nuncio to Paris. This was a problematic appointment. His predecessor had been removed because General de Gaulle had thought him too sympathetic to the Vichy government of Marshal Pétain. Moreover, de Gaulle wanted the removal of a good many of the French bishops whom he believed had collaborated with the regime of occupied France. Roncalli handled this with a grace that delighted both Rome and Paris. He also had the problem of dealing with Pius's encyclical *Humani generis*, which was aimed particularly at the French protagonists of what was called 'the new theology'. Another difficulty was the issue of worker priests, clergy who entered factories to work alongside others on the production lines. Rome did not like them, and the experiment came to an end, but Archbishop Roncalli had been encouraging. He was also the Holy See's observer at the meetings of UNESCO.

BIRTH NAME
Angelo Giuseppe Roncalli
BORN Sotto il Monte, near Bergamo, 25 November 1881
PREDECESSOR Pius XII
INSTALLED 4 November 1958
DIED 3 June 1963
SUCCESSOR John Paul II

He was named a cardinal on 12 June 1958, and three days later he was made patriarch of Venice. It was the first full-time pastoral post he had been given since he was a military chaplain almost 30 years before. He found the role of diocesan bishop fulfilling, and he was greatly loved, but he still had time to complete his work on Charles Borromeo. The fifth and final volume appeared shortly before he set off for Rome for the conclave of 1958. He was not wholly surprised to be elected, but he surprised the electors by his choice of name. It had been his father's name, but there had already been a John XXIII, deposed in 1415, who may or may not have been an antipope. The new Pope John XXIII indicated that he was, by his choice of the title, not making any judgement about the legal status of his earlier namesake.

A WISH FOR OPENNESS

One of his first acts was to create new cardinals. Among them was the archbishop of Milan, Giovanni Battista Montini, who would have been the natural successor to Pius XII, but Pope Pius had neglected to make him a cardinal, and the electors were not prepared to break a 500-year tradition of appointing cardinals, though they had considered breaking another 400-year old one by choosing Cardinal Agagianian who was an Armenian, not an Italian, and had been born in

An informal photograph of Pope John XXIII taken at the papal summer palace of Castel Gandolfo in 1961. Pope John strove for greater openness within the papal curia and mediated in the Cuban missile crisis of 1962.

what was then the Soviet Union. Cardinal Montini was swiftly to succeed Pope John as Pope Paul VI (1963–78). John then set about doing the rounds of his Roman diocese, visiting parishes, hospitals and prisons. He called what turned out to be a not very satisfactory synod of the Rome diocese. He announced a revision of the Code of Canon Law, and set up a commission to oversee it, and started a reform of the papal curia, that would result in a greater openness within it between the pope and the officials. He did not always get his way. The secretariat of state, for example, steadfastly refused the pope's wishes that the minutes of the meeting between himself and the daughter and son-in-law of Nikita Khruschev should be published. This encounter, which took place in March 1963, was also vigorously opposed by one of the most powerful of the curial officials, Cardinal Ottaviani, head of the Holy Office. It had come about because the pope had mediated in the Cuban missile crisis of October 1962. Both sides, President John F. Kennedy in the USA and Khruschev in the USSR, were grateful for the part he played, and especially

> Pope John had made it clear ... that there was to be dialogue, even with communists.

Khruschev. At Christmas the Soviet newspaper *Pravda* published the papal address. There was still a long way to go, but Pope John had made it clear, and insisted on it in his encyclical *Pacem in terris* (see box), that there was to be dialogue, even with communists.

'TO ALL THOSE OF GOOD WILL'

But there was also to be dialogue within the church. To the great astonishment and distress of most of his curia he announced there was to be another council of the church. The Second Vatican Council opened in October 1962, and closed, after the pope's death, in December 1965. The pope declared in his opening address that the purpose of the gathering was to update – the term used became familiar, *aggiornamento* – the church's teaching in the language of the present. He did not lay down an agenda, but left that to the bishops of the church, and to the preparatory commissions. There was a great deal of conflict between the conservative and the more liberal minded, with Cardinal Ottaviani as perhaps the leader of the former and Cardinal Bea, the Jesuit head of the newly established Secretariat for Christian Unity, of the latter. The

EXCERPTS FROM *PACEM IN TERRIS*

158 It is always perfectly justifiable to distinguish between error as such and the person who falls into error – even in the case of men who err regarding the truth or are led astray as a result of their inadequate knowledge, in matters either of religion or of the highest ethical standards. A man who has fallen into error does not cease to be a man. He never forfeits his personal dignity; and that is something that must always be taken into account. Besides, there exists in man's very nature an undying capacity to break through the barriers of error and seek the road to truth. God, in His great providence, is ever present with His aid. Today, maybe, a man lacks faith and turns aside into error; tomorrow, perhaps, illumined by God's light, he may indeed embrace the truth.

Catholics who, in order to achieve some external good, collaborate with unbelievers or with those who through error lack the fullness of faith in Christ, may possibly provide the occasion or even the incentive for their conversion to the truth.

159 Again it is perfectly legitimate to make a clear distinction between a false philosophy of the nature, origin and purpose of men and the world, and economic, social, cultural, and political undertakings, even when such undertakings draw their origin and inspiration from that philosophy. True, the philosophic formula does not change once it has been set down in precise terms, but the undertakings clearly cannot avoid being influenced to a certain extent by the changing conditions in which they have to operate. Besides, who can deny the possible existence of good and commendable elements in these undertakings, elements which do indeed conform to the dictates of right reason, and are an expression of man's lawful aspirations?

council did not condemn heresies, but published documents which on some major issues – such as relations with those of other faiths, the role of the laity in the church, or the responsibility of all Roman Catholic bishops collectively (the word used was 'collegially') for the governance of the church – thoroughly re-oriented Catholic theology, and had a profound impact on other churches as well.

His final encyclical, *Pacem in terris*, 'Peace on Earth', was published less than two months before his death. Even in his last days he broke with tradition. Encyclicals were letters addressed to the bishops of the Catholic Church. This one, on war and the arms race, was addressed to the whole world, 'To all those of good will'.

JOHN PAUL II

The Second Vatican Council, begun under John XXIII, continued under Pope Paul VI (1963–78). To demonstrate that he was heir to the programme of reform of the church that they had begun, Paul VI's successor, Albino Luciani, the patriarch of Venice, took both their names as John Paul I. But he died suddenly, after only a month as pope, to be succeeded by a Pole, the first non-Italian to be elected since 1522.

Karol Wojtyla was born less than two years after Poland had come back into existence as a result of the settlement at the end of the First World War. The centre of Polish culture during the years of occupation was Cracow, and after his childhood in Wadowice it was to Cracow's Jagellonian University – the name itself recalled a high point in Polish history – that Wojtyla went in 1938. But before that, while still at school, he had several times taken part in plays put on by a history teacher at a neighbouring girls' school. In all he took part in ten, always playing the leading role.

In the summer of 1939 Wojtyla undertook his military training in what was known as the Academic Legion. Very shortly afterwards Germany invaded, and his country was once again occupied and partitioned. Poland disappeared from the map after only two decades of existence. His friend who had directed plays in Wadowice came to Cracow, and Wojtyla, who was now working at the Solvay chemical factory – at first in a quarry attached to the plant – once more took up acting. After the death of his father in 1942 he was able to enter a secret seminary in the archiepiscopal palace in Cracow. He was ordained shortly after the war, in November 1946, and then went to Rome, where he completed his doctorate, on the concept of faith in St John of the Cross, in June 1948.

BIRTH NAME Karol Wojtyla
BORN Wadowice, Poland, 18 May 1920
PREDECESSOR John Paul I
INSTALLED 22 October 1978
DIED 2 April 2005
SUCCESSOR Benedict XVI

John Paul II: a visionary pope who sought spiritual unity in Europe and who travelled throughout the world far more than any of his predecessors.

POLAND UNDER COMMUNISM

When he returned from Italy he came back to a country under the control of the communist party and dominated by Russia. Though the church in Poland enjoyed a measure of freedom that Christianity in other Eastern bloc countries was denied, it was nonetheless an extremely difficult time. The Catholic University of Lublin survived, however, and Wojtyla was sent there to undertake another doctorate, this time in philosophy, more particularly in ethics. He became extremely interested in the philosophic style known as phenomenology, and eventually published a major work, *The Acting Person*.

After his philosophy doctorate he taught at Lublin, commuting there by train from Cracow, where he worked in a parish. He was an excellent lecturer, and established a firm rapport with the university students whom he served as chaplain. The fact that he was an outstanding sportsman – skiing, canoeing and football were his particular passions – no doubt helped. He was on a canoeing and camping trip with his students when he heard that he was to be made assistant bishop of Cracow. It was from what seem to have been remarkably frank exchanges with these young people, together with a friendship with an eminent woman psychiatrist in Cracow, that he learned intimate details about sexual relations upon which he developed his theories on the relationship between the sexes and sexual ethics, which he wrote about in *Love and Responsibility*.

HUMANAE VITAE

Paul VI turned to him before writing the encyclical *Humanae vitae*, which condemned artificial means of birth control. The publication of *Humanae vitae* in July 1968 caused an uproar, not least because the commission which Pope Paul had set up to discuss the issue had produced a majority report approving of artificial contraception. The pope chose to go with the minority, and his ban was widely ignored. Never in modern times had a clear papal teaching been so openly rejected. It was a challenge to the pope's authority. By now Wojtyla had become archbishop of Cracow (December 1963) and a cardinal (June 1967).

A VISION OF EUROPE

It is clear that, from the start, Pope John Paul II had a vision, and it is difficult not to think that it was based on the almost messianic expectations of the Polish Romantic literature to which he had been so devoted as a student. In December 1980 he proclaimed Cyril and Methodius, the apostles of the Slavs to whom he later dedicated an encyclical, as co-patrons of Europe, alongside Saint Benedict. In Santiago de Compostela, on the westernmost fringe of Europe, in November 1982 he presided at a 'European Act' or event, attended by academics, clerics, members of European organizations and other members of the intelligentsia from all over the continent. He told them to rediscover their Christian past and the spiritual unity of Europe. A year later, speaking in Vienna on the 300th anniversary of the raising by a Pole of the Turkish siege of that city, the pope emphasized the European dimension of Vienna as the former capital of the Austro-Hungarian empire and now close to the borders of the Eastern bloc. The true Europe, he insisted, was a continent which included the communist East as well as the capitalist West.

On 8 October 1988 he visited various European institutions in Strasbourg, including the European Parliament, and warned members against too narrow a notion of what constituted Europe. 'Other nations could certainly join those which are represented here today,' he said. 'My wish as supreme pastor of the universal church, someone who has come from Eastern Europe and who knows the aspirations of the Slav peoples, that other "lung" of our common European

THE ASSASSINATION ATTEMPT

AT 5.17 P.M. ON 13 MAY 1981, AS JOHN PAUL II WAS BEING DRIVEN IN THE POPEMOBILE ACROSS ST PETER'S SQUARE, HE WAS SHOT. Two others were wounded in the shooting, though not seriously. A Turk, Mehmet Ali Ağca, was arrested while the pope was being rushed to Rome's Gemelli Hospital. He was put on trial on 20 July, and found guilty. There was never any doubt about his guilt, but the real question was, and remains, why did he do it? He had, some time before, claimed in a letter to a newspaper that he was going to kill the pope during John Paul's visit to Turkey in November 1979, but it has always been assumed that he could not have been acting alone. Suspicion fell particularly on the Bulgarians, especially as he admitted he acquired his gun in Bulgaria. And if the Bulgarians had been involved (there were some unexplained happenings at the Bulgarian embassy in Rome at the time of the shooting), then it is unlikely they were acting without the approval of the Soviet Union's KGB. Since the fall of communism in Eastern Europe and the disintegration of the USSR, much archival material has become available. This reveals the extent to which the Soviet government, and the communist government in Poland, were alarmed by the election of the Polish pope, but there is absolutely no evidence that the KGB plotted to assassinate him. John Paul II, meanwhile, was in hospital for just three weeks. Three years later, on 13 May 1984, he visited the shrine of Our Lady at Fatima in Portugal (it was on her feast that that he was shot), and gave to the shrine the bullet which had lodged in his body. It has since been set in the crown of precious stones on the statue of the Virgin.

motherland, my wish is that Europe . . . might one day extend to the dimensions it has been given by geography and still more by history.'

In 1988 Karol Wojtyla's hopes for a united Europe including the Slavic countries seemed a very distant dream. Speaking after his retirement as papal secretary of state, or prime minister, Cardinal Casaroli commented that the Vatican had not foreseen the dramatic collapse of the Soviet bloc (for Pope John Paul's explanation of the fall of communism, see box, page 199). Pope John Paul is commonly said to have significantly contributed to this collapse. It is undoubtedly true that had he not had the courage to return to Poland the year following his election, the independent trade union Solidarity would probably not have flourished under the oppression which it suffered from successive Polish administrations.

Travelling and saint-making

There were many distinctive, not to say idiosyncratic, features of John Paul II's quarter of a century in office. No pope travelled as much, and his journeyings included visits to Islamic countries. Wherever he went he preached human rights, even to dictators, several of whom – in Chile, Paraguay and Haiti – did not long survive his visit. And no pope canonized as many saints – more than all his predecessors put together from the time of the establishment of the Congregation of Rites towards the end of the 16th century. In many instances, the two things, the saint-making and the travels, came together. He was bringing the authority of the papacy which, with some reason, he believed to be under threat, from the centre in Rome to the periphery of the church. But papal power is never more vividly displayed than when proclaiming someone to be a saint worthy of veneration by the whole church. Here was an act, restricted since the 13th century to the papacy, where the ordinary, to use the technical term, universal jurisdiction of the bishop of Rome as defined at the First Vatican Council was most clearly on display. It was in other words an exercise of his primacy and, if some commentators on the theology of canonization are to be believed, an exercise also of papal infallibility.

As his secretary once remarked, had he not been subjected to the assassination attempt on 13 May 1981 (see box, page 199), he might have lived much longer – or at least, his last years might not have been so blighted by Parkinson's disease and other debilitating conditions. But his was still the second longest pontificate in papal history. He stamped his mark on the church, especially through the actions of the Congregation for the Doctrine of the Faith under the man who was to become his successor, Cardinal Joseph Ratzinger, afterwards Benedict XVI (2005–). This most political of popes disapproved of clerical involvement in politics, and condemned the Liberation Theology movement in Latin America both because it seemed to be political, and because he believed it had too readily embraced Marxism. But many other theologians who appeared to step out of the traditional Catholic line felt the weight of the Congregation for the Doctrine of the Faith, once the Holy Inquisition, upon them.

When he was elected, Pope John Paul had a fairly clear-cut agenda. One item was the establishment of religious freedom in eastern Europe, and the reuniting of what he called 'the two lungs'. But the collapse of communism did not bring with it quite the benefits that he had hoped for, as the Eastern bloc countries in general, and Poland in particular, eagerly embraced the materialism of the West. He was even moved, in his latter years, to find virtues in Marxism. He had been born on the borders of Greek-rite Catholicism in the Ukraine and he hoped in his pontificate to have brought the Orthodox and Catholic churches closer together. They ended as further apart, though that was hardly the fault of Papa Wojtyla.

CENTESIMUS ANNUS

EXCERPT FROM CENTESIMUS ANNUS – 'THE HUNDREDTH YEAR' – PUBLISHED ON 1 MAY 1991 TO MARK THE CENTENARY OF RERUM NOVARUM:

23 Among the many factors involved in the fall of oppressive regimes, some deserve special mention. Certainly, the decisive factor which gave rise to the changes was the violation of the rights of workers. It cannot be forgotten that the fundamental crisis of systems claiming to express the rule and indeed the dictatorship of the working class began with the great upheavals which took place in Poland in the name of Solidarity. It was the throngs of working people which foreswore the ideology which presumed to speak in their name. On the basis of a hard, lived experience of work and of oppression, it was they who recovered and, in a sense, rediscovered the content and principles of the church's social doctrine.

Also worthy of emphasis is the fact that the fall of this kind of 'bloc' or empire was accomplished almost everywhere by means of peaceful protest, using only the weapons of truth and justice ...

24 The second factor in the crisis was certainly the inefficiency of the economic system, which is not to be considered simply as a technical problem, but rather a consequence of the violation of the human rights to private initiative, to ownership of property and to freedom in the economic sector. To this must be added the cultural and national dimension: it is not possible to understand man on the basis of economics alone, nor to define him simply on the basis of class membership. Man is understood in a more complete way when he is situated within the sphere of culture through his language, history, and the position he takes towards the fundamental events of life, such as birth, love, work and death. At the heart of every culture lies the attitude man takes to the greatest mystery: the mystery of God. Different cultures are basically different ways of facing the question of the meaning of personal existence. When this question is eliminated, the culture and moral life of nations are corrupted. For this reason the struggle to defend work was sponta-neously linked to the struggle for culture and for national rights.

But the true cause of the new developments was the spiritual void brought about by atheism, which deprived the younger generations of a sense of direction and in many cases led them, in the irrepressible search for personal identity and for the meaning of life, to rediscover the religious roots of their national cultures, and to rediscover the person of Christ himself as the existentially adequate response to the desire in every human heart for goodness, truth and life. This search was supported by the witness of those who, in difficult circumstances and under persecution, remained faithful to God. Marxism had promised to uproot the need for God from the human heart, but the results have shown that it is not possible to succeed in this without throwing the heart into turmoil.

Chronological list of popes

Those names in bold in the table below are featured in this book. The term 'Installation' is used rather than consecration, coronation or enthronement because at various times there were different forms of a pope taking office, and indeed different ways of timing the beginning of a pontificate. Those dates marked with an asterisk (*) indicate an abdication, sometimes a voluntary act, but most times not.

Name	Election	Installation	Death or Abdication
Peter			**c. 67**
Linus	c. 67		c. 76
Cletus (Anacletus)	c. 80		c. 91
Clement I	c. 91		c. 101
Evaristus	c. 101		c. 107
Alexander I	c. 108		c. 115 or 118
Sixtus I	c. 115 or 118		c. 125
Telesphorus	c. 125		c. 136
Hyginus	c. 136		c. 140
Pius I	c. 140		c. 155
Anicetus	c. 155		c. 166
Soter	c. 166		c. 174
Eletherius	c. 174		189
Victor I	189		199
Zephyrinus	199		217
Callistus I	217		222
Urban I	222		230
Pontian	21 July 230		28 September 235*
Anterus	21 November 235		3 January 236
Fabian		10 January 236	20 January 250
Cornelius	January 250	March 251	June 253
Lucius I		26 June 253	5 March 254
Stephen I	12 March 254		2 August 257
Sixtus II	September 257		6 August 258
Dionysius	22 July 260		26 December 268
Felix I		3 January 269	30 December 274
Eutychian	4 January 275		7 December 283
Caius	17 December 283		22 April 296
Marcellinus	296		24 October 304
Marcellus I	May/June 308		January 309
Eusebius	18 April 309 or 310		August/ September 309 or 310
Miltiades	2 July 311/312		10/11 January 314
Sylvester I	31 January 314		31 December 335
Mark	18 January 336		7 October 336
Julius I	16 February 337		12 April 352
Liberius	17 May 352		24 September 366
Damasus I		**1 October 366**	**11 December 384**
Siricius	**December 384**		**26 November 399**
Anastasius I	26 November 399		14 or 19 December 401
Innocent I	**21 December 401**		**12 March 417**
Zosimus		18 March 417	26 December 418
Boniface I	28 December 418	29 December 418	4 September 422
Celestine I		10 September 422	28 July 432
Sixtus III		31 July 432	10 August 440
Leo I		**29 September 440**	**10 November 461**

Name	Election	Installation	Death or Abdication
Hilarus	19 November 461		29 February 468
Simplicius	3 March 468		10 March 483
Felix III[i]	13 March 483		1 March 492
Gelasius I	**1 March 492**		**21 November 496**
Anastasius II	24 November 496		19 November 498
Symmachus	**22 November 498**		**19 July 514**
Hormisdas	20 July 514		6 August 523
John I	13 August 523		18 May 526
Felix IV	12 July 526		22 September 530
Boniface II	22 September 530		17 October 532
John II	2 January 533		8 May 535
Agapitus I	13 May 535		23 April 536
Silverius	June 536		25 March 537*
Vigilius	**29 March 537**		**7 June 555**
Pelagius I		16 April 556	3 March 561
John III	17 July 561		13 July 574
Benedict I		2 June 575	30 July 579
Pelagius II	August 579	26 November 579	7 February 590
Gregory I	**January 590**	**3 September 590**	**12 March 604**
Sabinian		13 September 604	22 February 606
Boniface III	19 February 607		12 November 607
Boniface IV	25 August 608		8 May 615
Adeodatus I	19 October 615		8 November 618
Boniface V	23 December 619		25 October 625
Honorius I		**27 October 625**	**12 October 638**
Severinus	28 May 640		2 August 640
John IV	24 December 640		22 October 642
Theodore I		24 November 642	14 May 649
Martin I		**5 August 649**	**17 June 653***
Eugenius I	10 August 654		2 June 657
Vitalian		30 July 657	27 January 672
Adeodatus II	11 April 672		17 June 676
Donus		2 November 676	11 April 678
Agatho	27 June 678		10 January 681
Leo II		17 August 682	3 July 683
Benedict II		26 June 684	8 May 685
John V	23 July 685		2 August 686
Conon		21 October 686	21 September 687
Sergius I	15 December 687		9 September 701
John VI	30 October 701		11 January 705
John VII	1 March 705		18 October 707
Sisinnius		15 January 708	4 February 708
Constantine[ii]		25 March 708	9 April 715
Gregory II		19 May 715	11 February 731
Gregory III	11 February 731	13 March 731	10 December 741
Zacharias	**3 December 741**	**10 December 741**	**22/23 March 752**
Stephen II[iii]	March 752		March 752
Stephen II (III)	**25 March 752**		**26 April 757**
Paul I	29 May 757		28 June 767
Stephen III (IV)	1 August 768	7 August 768	24 January 772
Hadrian I	1 February 772	9 February 772	26 December 795
Leo III	**26 December 795**	**27 December 795**	**12 June 816**

Name	Election	Installation	Death or Abdication
Stephen IV (V)	22 June 816	22 June 816	23 January 817
Paschal I	24 January 817		17 May 824
Eugenius II	May or June 824		August 827
Valentine	August 827		September 827
Gregory IV	late 827		25 January 844
Sergius II	January 844		27 January 847
Leo IV	**January 847**	**10 April 847**	**17 July 855**
Benedict III	July 855	29 September 855	7 April 858
Nicholas I	**24 April 858**		**13 November 867**
Hadrian II		14 December 867	14 December 872
John VIII	December 872		15 December 882
Marinus I	December 882		c. May 884
Hadrian III	17 May 884		September 885
Stephen V (VI)	September 885	November 885	14 September 891
Formosus	**3 October 891**		**4 April 896**
Boniface VI	April 896		April 896
Stephen VI (VII)	May 896		August 897
Romanus	July/August 897		November 897*
Theodore II	December 897		December 897
John IX	January 898		January 900
Benedict IV	January 900	1 February 900	August 903
Leo V	August 903		August 903*
Sergius III	29 January 904		September 911
Anastasius III	September 911?		October 913
Lando	November 913		March 914
John X	April 914		May 928*
Leo VI	June 928		December 928
Stephen VII (VIII)	January 929		February 931
John XI	March 931		January 936
Leo VII	January 936		July 939
Stephen VIII (IX)	July 939		October 942
Marinus II	October 942		May 946
Agapitus II	10 May 946		early December 955
John XII	16 December 955		4 December 963*
Leo VIII	4 December 963	6 December 963	February 964*
		23 June 964	March 965
Benedict V	22 May 964		23 June 964*
John XIII	1 October 965	1 October 965	6 September 972
Benedict VI	Sept' or Dec' 972	19 January 973	July 974
Benedict VII	October 974	October 974	10 July 983
John XIV	September 983		20 August 984
John XV	August 985		March 996
Gregory V	**3 May 996**		**18 February 999**
Sylvester II	**2 April 999**	**9 April 999**	**12 May 1003**
John XVII[iv]	16 May 1003		6 November 1003
John XVIII	25 December 1003		June 1009
Sergius IV	31 July 1009		12 May 1012
Benedict VIII	17 May 1012	21 May 1012	9 April 1024
John XIX	19 April 1024		20 October 1032
Benedict IX	21 October 1032		September 1044*
		10 March 1045	1 May 1045*
		8 November 1047	16 July 1048*ᵛ

Name	Election	Installation	Death or Abdication
Sylvester III	20 January 1045		December 1046*
Gregory VI[vi]	1 May 1045		24 December 1046*
Clement II	24 December 1046	25 December 1046	9 October 1047
Damasus II	5 December 1047	17 July 1048	9 August 1048
Leo IX	**2 February 1049**[vii]	**12 February 1049**	**19 April 1054**
Victor II	September 1054	13 April 1055	28 July 1057
Stephen IX (X)	2 August 1057	3 August 1057	29 March 1058
Nicholas II	6 December 1058	24 January 1059	27 July 1061
Alexander II	30 September 1061	1 October 1061	21 April 1073
Gregory VII	**22 April 1073**	**30 June 1073**	**25 May 1085**
Victor III	24 May 1086	9 May 1087	16 September 1087
Urban II	**12 March 1088**	**12 March 1088**	**29 July 1099**
Paschal II	**13 August 1099**	**14 August 1099**	**21 January 1118**
Gelasius II	24 January 1118	10 March 1118	28 January 1119
Callistus II	**2 February 1119**	**9 February 1119**	**13 December 1124**
Honorius II[viii]	16 December 1124	21 December 1124	13 February 1130
Innocent II	14 February 1130	23 February 1130	24 September 1143
Celestine II[ix]	26 September 1143	3 October 1143	8 March 1144
Lucius II	12 March 1144		15 February 1145
Eugenius III	**15 February 1145**	**18 February 1145**	**8 July 1153**
Anastasius IV	8 July 1153	12 July 1153	3 December 1154
Hadrian IV	**4 December 1154**	**5 December 1154**	**7 September 1159**
Alexander III	7 September 1159	20 September 1159	30 August 1181
Lucius III	1 September 1181	6 September 1181	25 November 1185
Urban III	25 November 1185	1 December 1185	20 October 1187
Gregory VIII[x]	21 October 1187	25 October 1187	17 December 1187
Clement III[xi]	19 December 1187	20 December 1187	March 1191
Celestine III	March/April 1191	14 April 1191	8 January 1198
Innocent III[xii]	**8 January 1198**	**22 February 1198**	**16 July 1216**
Honorius III	18 July 1216	24 July 1216	18 March 1227
Gregory IX	**19 March 1227**	**21 March 1227**	**22 August 1241**
Celestine IV	25 October 1241	[xiii]	10 November 1241
Innocent IV	25 June 1243	28 June 1243	7 December 1254
Alexander IV	16 December 1254	20 December 1254	25 May 1261
Urban IV	29 August 1261	4 September 1261	2 October 1264
Clement IV	5 February 1265	15 February 1265	29 November 1268
Gregory X	**1 September 1271**	**27 March 1272**	**10 January 1276**
Innocent V	21 January 1276	22 February 1276	22 June 1276
Hadrian V	11 July 1276	[xiv]	18 August 1276
John XXI[xv]	8 September 1276	20 September 1276	20 May 1277
Nicholas III	25 November 1277	26 December 1277	22 August 1280
Martin IV[xvi]	22 February 1281	23 March 1281	28 March 1285
Honorius IV	2 April 1285	20 May 1285	3 April 1287
Nicholas IV	15 February 1288[xvii]	22 February 1288	4 April 1292
Celestine V	**5 July 1294**	**29 August 1294**	**13 December 1294**✳
Boniface VIII[xviii]	**24 December 1294**	**23 January 1295**	**11 October 1303**
Benedict XI[xix]	22 October 1303	27 October 1303	7 July 1304
Clement V	**5 June 1305**	**14 November 1305**	**20 April 1314**
John XXII	7 August 1316	5 September 1316	4 December 1334
Benedict XII	20 December 1334	8 January 1335	25 April 1342
Clement VI	7 May 1342	19 May 1342	6 December 1352
Innocent VI	18 December 1352	30 December 1352	12 September 1362

Name	Election	Installation	Death or Abdication
Urban V	28 September 1362	6 November 1362	19 December 1370
Gregory XI	**30 December 1370**	**5 January 1371**	**27 March 1378**
Urban VI	**8 April 1378**	**18 April 1378**	**15 October 1389**
Boniface IX	2 November 1389	9 November 1389	1 October 1404
Innocent VII	17 October 1404	11 November 1404	6 November 1406
Gregory XII	30 November 1406	19 December 1406	4 July 1415*xx
Martin V	**11 November 1417**	**21 November 1417**	**20 February 1431**
Eugenius IV	**3 March 1431**	**11 March 1431**	**23 February 1447**
Nicholas Vxxi	6 March 1447	19 March 1447	24 March 1455
Callistus IIIxxii	8 April 1455	20 April 1455	6 August 1458
Pius II	**19 August 1458**	**3 September 1458**	**14 August 1464**
Paul II	30 August 1464	16 September 1464	26 July 1471
Sixtus IV	9 August 1471	25 August 1471	12 August 1484
Innocent VIII	29 August 1484	12 September 1484	25 July 1492
Alexander VIxxiii	**11 August 1492**	**26 August 1492**	**18 August 1503**
Pius III	22 September 1503	8 October 1503	18 October 1503
Julius II	**1 November 1503**	**18 November 1503**	**21 February 1513**
Leo X	11 March 1513	19 March 1513	1 December 1521
Hadrian VI	9 January 1522	31 August 1522	14 September 1523
Clement VIIxxiv	19 November 1523	26 November 1523	25 September 1534
Paul III	13 October 1534	3 November 1534	10 November 1549
Julius III	8 February 1550	22 February 1550	23 March 1555
Marcellus II	9 April 1555	10 April 1555	1 May 1555
Paul IV	23 May 1555	26 May 1555	18 August 1559
Pius IV	**25 December 1559**	**6 January 1560**	**9 December 1565**
Pius V	**7 January 1566**	**17 January 1566**	**1 May 1572**
Gregory XIII	14 May 1572	25 May 1572	10 April 1585
Sixtus V	**24 April 1585**	**1 May 1585**	**27 August 1590**
Urban VII	15 September 1590	xxv	27 September 1590
Gregory XIV	5 December 1590	8 December 1590	16 October 1591
Innocent IX	29 October 1591	3 November 1591	30 December 1591
Clement VIII	30 January 1592	9 February 1592	5 March 1605
Leo XI	1 April 1605	10 April 1605	27 April 1605
Paul V	16 May 1605	29 May 1605	28 January 1621
Gregory XV	9 February 1621	11 February 1621	8 July 1623
Urban VIII	**6 August 1623**	**29 September 1623**	**29 July 1644**
Innocent X	15 September 1644	4 October 1644	7 January 1655
Alexander VII	7 April 1655	18 April 1655	22 May 1667
Clement IX	20 June 1667	26 June 1667	9 December 1669
Clement X	29 April 1670	11 May 1670	22 July 1676
Innocent XI	21 September 1676	4 October 1676	12 August 1689
Alexander VIII	6 October 1689	16 October 1689	1 February 1691
Innocent XII	12 July 1691	15 July 1691	27 September 1700
Clement XI	23 November 1700	8 December 1700	19 March 1721
Innocent XIII	8 May 1721	18 May 1721	7 March 1724
Benedict XIIIxxvi	29 May 1724	4 June 1724	21 February 1730
Clement XII	12 July 1730	16 July 1730	6 February 1740
Benedict XIVxxvii	**17 August 1740**	**21 August 1740**	**3 May 1758**
Clement XIII	6 July 1758	16 July 1758	2 February 1769
Clement XIV	19 May 1769	4 June 1769	22 September 1774
Pius VI	15 January 1775	22 February 1775	29 August 1799
Pius VII	**14 March 1800**	**21 March 1800**	**20 August 1823**

Name	Election	Installation	Death or Abdication
Leo XII	28 September 1823	5 October 1823	10 February 1829
Pius VIII	31 March 1829	5 April 1829	30 November 1830
Gregory XVI	2 February 1831	6 February 1831	1 June 1846
Pius IX	**16 June 1846**	**21 June 1846**	**7 February 1878**
Leo XIII	**20 February 1878**	**3 March 1878**	**20 July 1903**
Pius X	4 August 1903	9 August 1903	20 August 1914
Benedict XV	3 September 1914	6 September 1914	22 January 1922
Pius XI	6 February 1922	12 February 1922	10 February 1939
Pius XII	**2 March 1939**	**12 March 1939**	**9 October 1958**
John XXIII[xxviii]	**28 October 1958**	**4 November 1958**	**3 June 1963**
Paul VI	21 June 1963	30 June 1963	6 August 1978
John Paul I	26 August 1978	3 September 1978	28 September 1978
John Paul II	**16 October 1978**	**22 October 1978**	**2 April 2005**
Benedict XVI	19 April 2005	24 April 2005	

NOTES

i Felix II, 356–65, was an antipope

ii There was an antipope of the same name 767–68

iii He died four days after his election and was, rather confusingly, replaced by another candidate of the same name who took the title Stephen II because his short-lived predecessor, not having been consecrated, was not counted in the list of popes. From the 16th century, however, it has been usual to recognise a pontificate from the election of the pope, not from his consecration, which would make this Stephen the second of his name, and his successor Stephen III. The numbering of Stephens is therefore given in two forms, as can be seen in the list

iv John XVI, 997–98, was an antipope

v Died between 18 September 1055 and 9 January 1056

vi There was an antipope of the same name 1012–13

vii The emperor had named him pope in December 1048, but he insisted on being formally elected at Rome

viii There was an antipope of the same name, 1061–64

ix There was another pope of the same name, properly elected on either 15 or 16 December 1124, but forced immediately to abdicate (16 December)

x There was an antipope of the same name 1118–21

xi There was an antipope of the same name, 1084–1100

xii There was an antipope of the same name, 1179–80

xiii Probably never consecrated, though one account suggests he was consecrated on 28 October

xiv Never crowned

xv There was never a Pope John XX

xvi Marinus I and II were mistakenly known as Martin II and III, hence Martin IV

xvii He at first refused to accept, and asked for a second vote, which also elected him, on 22 February

xviii Boniface VII was an antipope

xix Benedict X was an antipope

xx He abdicated of his own accord, to end the Western Schism; he died 18 October 1417

xxi There was an antipope of the same name, 1328–30

xxii There was an antipope of the same name, 1168–78

xxiii Alexander V was an antipope

xxiv There was an antipope of the same name, 1378–94

xxv He was never consecrated

xxvi There was an antipope of the same name, 1394–1422

xxvii There was an antipope of the same name, 1425 – date of death unknown

xxviii There was an antipope of the same name, 1410–15

INDEX